The *Next* Millionaire Next Door

ALSO BY THOMAS J. STANLEY

Marketing to the Affluent
Selling to the Affluent
Networking with the Affluent and Their Advisors
The Millionaire Next Door (with William D. Danko)
The Millionaire Mind
Millionaire Women Next Door
Stop Acting Rich

The *Next* Millionaire Next Door

Enduring Strategies
for Building Wealth

**THOMAS J. STANLEY, PhD, and
SARAH STANLEY FALLAW, PhD**

LYONS
PRESS

Guilford, Connecticut

In loving memory of my father, Thomas J. Stanley;
to my courageous mother, Janet G. Stanley; and
to Tim, Anna, Kate, and Julie

An imprint of The Rowman & Littlefield Publishing Group, Inc.
4501 Forbes Blvd., Ste. 200
Lanham, MD 20706
www.rowman.com

Distributed by NATIONAL BOOK NETWORK

British Library Cataloguing in Publication Information available

Library of Congress Cataloging-in-Publication Data available

ISBN 978-1-4930-5275-2 (paper : alk. paper)
ISBN 978-1-4930-3536-6 (electronic)

♾™ The paper used in this publication meets the minimum requirements of American National Standard for Information Sciences—Permanence of Paper for Printed Library Materials, ANSI/ NISO Z39.48-1992.

Contents

List of Tables and Figures

This publication is designed to provide accurate and authoritative information in regard to the subject matter covered. It is sold with the understanding that neither the author nor the publisher is engaged in rendering legal, investment, accounting, or other professional services. If legal advice or other expert assistance is required, the services of a competent professional person should be sought.

Most of the names in the case studies contained in this book are pseudonyms used to protect the privacy of the individuals involved.

Preface

For nearly 40 years, my father, Thomas J. Stanley, studied the affluent in America to discover and highlight paths to financial independence and economic success that did not depend on inheritances or other large monetary gifts. He found in his work some universal components, but also saw that there were many paths to wealth involving many unique career, consumer, and business choices.

Despite the evidence-based financial planning principles embodied in his book *The Millionaire Next Door* and the tried-and-true paths to wealth accumulation that have been documented quite clearly, many people continue to ask, "How come I am not wealthy?" Whether you're a small business owner, teacher, attorney, or sales professional, a disciplined, methodical approach to building wealth has been proven to work. As my father wrote in *The Millionaire Next Door*, "They [the millionaires profiled in the book] did it slowly, steadily, without signing a multimillion dollar contract with the Yankees, without winning the lottery, without becoming the next Mick Jagger."[1]

This slow and steady approach applies to many of life's challenges, such as learning a new skill, getting or staying in good physical shape, raising children, or starting a new business. Achieving any major goal—including financial independence—requires disciplined action over time, an awareness of one's own abilities, and the effective allocation of resources.

But a desire for a certain type of lifestyle—one with a requisite level of consumption and displayed status—still makes the journey difficult for most of us. A lifestyle that is dictated by what others do, drive, and wear cannot be sustained by most without a steady fire hose of incoming cash flow. Many of us simply accept our current habits, or refuse to do the hard work to change them, all the while complaining and often giving in to a life of dependency and worry.

Despite the protestations of some critics of his work, my father was not naïve and stated very clearly that the odds of becoming extraordinarily wealthy while starting with nothing were not very high. But his research demonstrated time and again that behaviors can change one's circumstances, and his life was just such a story. He had meticulously and consistently changed the way he behaved in order to become financially independent and overcome his incredibly humble beginnings.

My father never wanted to create a second edition of *The Millionaire Next Door*, a book that has become a classic since its publication in 1996, partly because he preferred to create new works for his readers that offered different (or fresh) viewpoints on the topic of affluence and building wealth in America. His follow-up works included *The Millionaire Mind*, *Millionaire Women Next Door*, and *Stop Acting Rich*. The research and development for this book began in 2012 in anticipation of the 20th anniversary of the publication of *The Millionaire Next Door* in 2016. The original aim was to examine trends over time related to some new topics, as well as to include comparisons to the data collected for my father's prior works.

Together, we decided to take another look at millionaires in the United States to examine what (if any) changes could be seen 20 years after the original publication of *The Millionaire Next Door*, as well as years after his other works. Our objective was to re-examine the key behavioral traits of millionaires next door while also considering what building wealth looks like today. My father, the original founder of the Affluent Market Institute and author of the original title, brought his baby-boomer point of view and marketing research expertise to the project, while I, a Gen-Xer and industrial psychologist by training, worked alongside him.

There was another plan in store for us, one that significantly altered the book you are reading. My father was killed by a drunk driver in 2015, on the eve of when the first wave of research invitations were to be sent out. After his death, I took on the task of compiling his notes along with the research findings from our latest study, weaving the notes, blogs, and ideas he wanted to have included in a new book into chapters along with interpretation of new data and data he had advised me on collecting in the years prior. This bittersweet task took me more than three years. While I had access to many of his notes and writing, I couldn't replace my father's unique perspective on the new data and the headlines of today. For that, I would be required to humbly submit my own interpretations.

There were several reasons why I felt this project, despite the absence of my father, needed to be completed. They are the same reasons why research within the fields of consumer science, financial planning, behavioral finance, and social psychology dedicated to helping individuals become financially successful must continue as well. In short, we need an ongoing scientific study of how individuals can build wealth on their own to confirm or refute myths about wealth, anecdotes, and feel-good stories. We need to use scientific rigor to separate what *sounds good* from what *actually works*.

Myths about wealth still abound in this country. Income continues to be confused with wealth by the media, the government, and in the minds of Americans. Anyone who has amassed a fortune on his or her own is often viewed with suspicion, as if the only pathway to financial success requires either high levels of "economic outpatient care" (financial gifts from family members), winning the lottery, or dishonesty. Shiny, glittering images fill our social media feeds and continue to confuse us about the reality of becoming financially successful.

Many of us are also woefully unprepared and, in some cases, unable to manage our own financial affairs. Nearly half of all Americans could not cover a $400 expense without selling something or borrowing money.[2] We continue as a nation to be worried about our finances. The American Psychological Association found that nearly 64% of Americans feel money is a "somewhat or very significant" source of stress within their lives.[3] This ebbs and flows with the economy, but money tends to be the top stress factor for Americans ahead of work, health concerns, and family issues.

Finally, it's important to note that some critics of *The Millionaire Next Door* suggested that the stock-market boom fueled by the developing Internet economy in the mid-1990s was the reason for the success of the individuals included in the book, or alternatively that survivorship bias (asserting that the data only looked at those who had succeeded in becoming wealthy and not whether the same traits were exhibited by those who failed) was the explanation for the results. The critics ignored that there were clear comparisons (and often significant differences) in his work between the *prodigious accumulators of wealth* who were effective at transforming their income into wealth and the *under accumulators of wealth*, those who, with the same level of income, had very little to show for it in their accounts. The same behaviors and habits examined in *The Millionaire Next Door* have also been applied to populations of mass market and mass affluent individuals—i.e., those who haven't "survived" to be wealthy yet—and the data from these nonmillionaire populations is consistent in revealing the positive correlation between accelerated wealth-building and factors such as making prudent financial decisions, ignoring societal pressures to spend, and being focused on goals.[4]

This book not only includes descriptions and interpretations of the data collected just before and after my father's death but also passages he wrote on his own, typically in the form of blogs that he had marked to include in the book. For the most part, the data highlighted in this book was collected during 2015 and 2016, but I also included survey results from other ancillary studies conducted between 2012 and 2018, along with data and research collected by my data research firm, DataPoints, at various points in time.

In terms of narrative voice, I decided to use the pronoun *we* throughout this book. In some cases, however, the reader will also see sidebars that highlight my father's individual work including notes, blogs, chapter ideas, and data reviews. I felt these were critical to the book and that the reader should know that these were his own words. In other cases, I have included a few sections in my own voice, noting that it is my own experience and research to which I am referring.

His untimely death in 2015 has left a void not only in the lives of his immediate family but, based on the numerous communications we received through his website and other sources during the time after his death, also in the lives of the readers of his books and blog who were seeking assistance or encouragement on their journeys to financial independence.

With all of these moving parts as a backdrop, I offer this book as a continuation of my father's research and work. In the days after the tragedy that took his life, some in the media used the opportunity to make the assertion that the millionaire-next-door concept is dead. That's not what our data says. I hope this book will demonstrate that the millionaire next door is still very much alive and well and that financial success continues to be attainable for almost anyone who is willing to work for it.

Sarah Stanley Fallaw
Atlanta, Georgia
June 2018

Chapter 1

The Millionaire Next Door
Is Alive and Well

Believe it can be done. When you believe something can be done, really believe, your mind will find the ways to do it. Believing a solution paves the way to solution.

—Dave Schwartz, *The Magic of Thinking Big*

DR. THOMAS J. STANLEY SPENT THE MAJORITY OF HIS PROFESSIONAL CAREER examining how Americans achieved financial success on their own. He studied business owners, executives, teachers, engineers, and a whole host of individuals with average to above-average incomes to answer the question: Why are some individuals better able to *transform* income into wealth? The works published from this lifetime of research answering that question have sold more than five million books.

Why did this work have such a significant impact? Perhaps it was because the research revealed that wealth could be achieved via our own behaviors; there were no preconditions such as privileged birthright or ethnicity. Despite sensational headlines to the contrary, it is still possible today to build wealth without a lump-sum inheritance or a lucky lottery ticket. So long as the freedoms that we enjoy exist in the United States, there will be individuals who will build wealth, not because of luck or the color of their skin or their parents' success, but because of the goals they set, the behaviors they employ to reach their goals, and their ability to ignore distractions and naysayers along the way.

The hallmarks of what made *a millionaire next door* 20 years ago continue to hold true. Living below your means is just another way of expressing a mathematical equation: an equation that works regardless of changing political landscapes, economic environments, and fads. The math always works, but the distractions of the day, whether the "trading up" mentality of the 1990s or early 2000s or the ever-present social media of today, pull many people away from the simple power of saving more than they spend. The increased costs of health care and education also require us to think differently about the way in which we live our lives: The traditional lifestyle or career path that our parents and grandparents followed may not be conducive to building wealth today.

Still some critics have argued that the very concept of the millionaire next door is dead, that the Internet-fueled stock boom of the 1990s led to the success stories my father covered in *The Millionaire Next Door*, and that survivorship bias was at work in our data set (i.e., the idea that we analyzed only the "winners" and that the economic "losers" may have shared the very same traits). But fortunately for those who are seeking financial independence, our most recent study and resulting data indicate that the behaviors, habits, and lifestyles that are conducive to building wealth haven't changed in the last 20 years, and they are not dependent on the economic, societal, or technological concerns of the time. We've seen that even in nonaffluent populations, the same characteristics separate those who are more successful at transforming income into wealth from those who are less successful.

Identifying Millionaires Next Door

There is a science to finding millionaires, but because they are such a small subset of the American population, obtaining large numbers of them for any survey research effort can be challenging. There are massive data sets and addresses tied to zip codes that allow researchers to sample within presumed high-income and high-net-worth neighborhoods, even though within those neighborhoods not all the residents are millionaires. Traditional survey research and target-market procedures are not necessarily foolproof methods to find millionaires next door, because millionaires often build wealth by not spending a fortune on their primary residence, thus making them less likely to live in affluent neighborhoods. Even though they can be seen in crowdsourcing efforts and financial independence blogs, they typically keep the reality of their financial success to themselves. After all, a willingness to not *look* rich helped them get there in the first place.

But today there continues to be a group of individuals who build wealth on their own and certainly on their own terms. Many of the millionaires next door featured in this book and in prior works wrote to us to share their stories. While this group doesn't take pride in broadcasting their success to the world, they do tend to relish in sharing their experiences (often anonymously) with others who are interested in following their lead. Through our research with crowdsourced samples, we also encountered people who are properly labeled as *emerging* millionaires next door. These are individuals who are not yet millionaires but most certainly on their way.

Identifying those who are adept at transforming income into wealth takes more than an isolated consumer purchase or job title. True, the millionaires next door that my father studied and interviewed in 1996 often worked in what some people might think of as dull or mundane industries, like accounting or scrap metal. Today, just as was the case in 1996, professionals such as engineers and teachers often have the characteristics, personalities, and abilities that allow them to prodigiously transform their incomes into wealth. But it has never been the case that *all* small-business owners, scrap metal or otherwise, are successful at transforming income into wealth. It's also never been the case that *all* owners of older model cars, inexpensive watches, and modest homes have the necessary knowledge, skills, abilities, and competencies to build wealth on their own. These are markers, as my father showed, but not necessarily *predictors*. No, instead we have to consider a broader pattern of behaviors and experiences versus a single financial decision or lifestyle choice.

Someone Forgot to Tell the Financial Independence Community

Since the publication of *The Millionaire Next Door* in 1996, an entire community has evolved that focuses its lifestyle and efforts on the ability to retire (or have the option to leave salaried work) at a stage of life that today is mostly unheard of. Thirtysomethings saving up enough to retire? Some of the best evidence that millionaires next door are alive and well is the vibrant online community commonly referred to as "FI/RE" (financial independence/retire early). In 2011, a blogger with the pen name Mr. Money Moustache began documenting his saving and spending habits, his investing practices, and his philosophy on consumer behavior (using colorful language like "Your current middle-class life is an Exploding Volcano of Wastefulness," which is one of my favorites).[1] While he wasn't the first to talk about frugality and frugal living online, he was one of the first to be widely read and cited. Mr. Moustache left salaried employment at age 30 with roughly $900,000 in total assets. Through his writings and those similar to his, a cultural movement was born.

Today, more than 1,700 blogs related to FI/RE can be found ranked on Rockstar Finance (a sort of directory for the FI/RE community).[2] Most involve some variation of a similar theme: a focus on saving money and being able to do what you want with your life as soon as possible. Many bloggers in the community reference *The Millionaire Next Door* as a transformative work in their journeys. The case studies and personal journeys of these bloggers are more voluminous than could be covered in one book and include a multitude of different approaches, from doctors and attorneys earning high six figures to other professionals with lower salaries. Some writers have multimillions accumulated but have not yet jumped ship from their careers, while some with less than $1 million in net worth have already retired. They preach being purposeful and disciplined in designing a lifestyle that allows you to stop being beholden to a company or organization so you can decide on your own what you want to do with your days. Again, these people are not in their 60s or 70s, but in their 20s, 30s, and 40s.

Take 30 minutes and peruse through some of these blogs and get to know these individuals. Note the lifestyles they describe and the details of how they got there. You may not *like* how they live their lives, but it would be hard to argue that their behaviors and choices don't *work* for them. It will become clear that the millionaire next door is alive and well in this particular community.

Respect for Money: A Prerequisite for Wealth

Allison Lamar, who grew up in a remote part of the United States, had an alcoholic mother and a father who struggled to make ends meet while taking care of his wife. In the end, it was Allison's grandparents who served as mentors to help her take control of her financial life. When I interviewed Allison, she shared her unique perspective with these words of advice related to respecting money: "Take care of money responsibly, and it will take care of you later. When people say they don't care about money, I believe that is an excuse not to deal with it."

Allison is now 54 years old, the mother of two college-aged children, and a homeowner. She's happily engaged to be married and has lived in the same town for 20 years. She told me it was her early experiences and corresponding behaviors that allowed her to build wealth and become a millionaire twice over:

I was the oldest, and I was going to help figure out how [Mom] was going to live. There were things I wanted as a 13-year-old, and it wasn't a pity party that I couldn't have them. . . . I got a paper route, even when it was –40 degrees, I was there. I'm naturally a doer and worker and a problem solver. . . . There was no extra fluff in our life. . . . I spent a lot of time with my grandparents. My grandfather worked hard all his life and built wealth. I saw how disappointed he was in some of my cousins who felt entitled to his wealth. Now you see this instantly on Facebook—you see all of these people with what look like incredible lives but in reality, it's not that way. . . . My dad constantly told me to save 10%, and so did my grandparents. Even when I was in college, making $6.50 an hour, I saved 10%. My friends would laugh and say, "Why don't you wait until you have a real job?" It was the habit—I started this habit and never stopped. . . . It wasn't a sacrifice to me— it was just a habit. I also felt like I was honoring my grandparents in saving to become a millionaire. I was content with the process of becoming a millionaire: hit one goal, then I wanted another one. I always knew I would be a millionaire—it wasn't a big deal. I just worked for it. . . . Working hard—it's ok to work a fourteen-hour day sometimes. Those sacrifices are worth it. And, you look back and they are sweet in a way – driving a car without air conditioning, for example—they're sweet. . . . First became a millionaire when I was about 35 and now have about $2 million in net worth. I'm 54. My friends would never suspect that this is the case as I act pretty "average." Money is itself "nice" but I am more concerned about what money can do than the actual accumulation of money.

Allison shared her thoughts on why so many people are challenged when it comes to building wealth:

- They're playing the game of comparisons by using social cues to decide what's important and how they compete with others. "Parents especially can be so competitive," she says.

- "People need to face the reality of where they are." In other words, gaining an awareness and appreciation of your financial situation can lead to realistic decisions about how to move forward.

- They think small decisions do not have consequences. Allison learned to appreciate the compounding power of small decisions as she worked in the below-freezing chill of the Midwest to earn money.

Allison's early influences and experiences helped to shape her financial journey. At many points along the way, she could have given up, or made easier short-term decisions. But by respecting money and taking a long-term view, resulting in part through the influence of her grandparents, her journey is now giving her great freedom:

> You have to be able to face your situation where you are and not be fearful, but be aware—facing the reality of your balance sheet. . . . It really played out when I got divorced. I knew I had options. Some women stay in relationships because they don't understand money or are afraid. I knew I had options. . . . I work in a fire department—I work because I want to work. I make more money now with my investments than working, and people have no clue. I like it that way.

Allison shared her story not for fame or fortune, not for an Instagram post, but rather to demonstrate to others that regardless of your circumstances, achieving economic success depends not on what has happened in the past but instead on the behaviors you employ today and tomorrow, behaviors that were described in 1996 and still hold true today.

More Millionaires Next Door: Hate the Methods, Love the Outcomes?

No one would argue with the reach and influence of Dave Ramsey in the world of personal finance. According to the Ramsey Group website, 13 million people tune in each week to Mr. Ramsey's nationally syndicated radio show and more than 4.5 million people have attended his Financial Peace University 12-week classes.

Some aspects of his message have drawn criticism from other purported "experts." We will leave the discussion of specific financial advice for others to wrestle with and argue over. We'll focus instead on the the behavioral side of his methodology and its associated outcomes. Mr. Ramsey instructs individuals to pay off their smallest debts first, thereby providing a psychological incentive to continue to pay off debt, ultimately leading to larger debts (e.g., student loans, mortgages) being paid off and placing the household in a position to save and invest. And in his group consensus peer pressure, it appears, can serve as a positive influence in personal finance. The training courses (often multiple weeks of group meetings), associated materials, books, and technologies all provide ample reinforcement for positive financial behaviors.

Many of my father's readers and fans have referenced Mr. Ramsey and his organization as the means by which they were able to correct their financial behaviors and achieve economic success, many either approaching or having just accomplished the goal of reaching millionaire status when they described their journey. Like the FI/RE community, these individuals are often demonstrating the outcomes associated with behaviors that are conducive to wealth, and becoming millionaires in the process.

Meet the (Very Much Alive) Jacobsons

The Jacobsons are not front-page news, not by any means. They didn't win the lottery or start a tech firm that was bought by Amazon or Google. Their fortune came from a steady, simple lifestyle and decades of choices that were conducive to building wealth. Their 1,900-square-foot home is more than likely not in any zip code data set that includes America's top wealth holders. They followed what could be described as a typical millionaire-next-door path. After amassing that wealth, they continue to spend in a way that ensures that their wealth will be sustained and grow, as Mrs. Jacobson described in a letter she sent to my father, which he referenced in the updated preface to *The Millionaire Next Door* in 2010:[3]

> *I married the right spouse and have a simple lifestyle. We've been married 22 years, 3 children, 3 dogs, 2 horses. We have lived in the same, modest 1,900 square foot [1975 era home] for 20 years. I have an MS in chemical engineering; my husband has a Ph.D. in chemical engineering and is now a VP at a chemical company.*
>
> *I made all As in high school; 1170 SAT. I was the first person in my family to go to college. I was born in the backwoods of Arkansas. After college, my husband and I both got good jobs; we lived on one income and saved the other. Anytime we got raises we just saved more. I am now a stay at home mom.*

We are already millionaires. However, we still have 3 kids to put through college so we don't feel rich. Sometimes my kids ask me if we are poor because I make them order from the $1 value menu!

It's worth mentioning here that the average single-family home in America is approximately 2,400 square feet (about 500 square feet larger than the Jacobsons' house). But even though this family is below average in terms of home size, they are in the top 10% in terms of net worth. Statistically speaking, the larger the home, the less the owner has to transform into wealth. Approximately 92% of homeowners are not millionaires, but a whole lot of them live in homes larger than 1,900 square feet.

The Jacobsons don't have to worry about the $400 trillion shortfall that is expected to hit retirement savings in the next 30 years.[4] Because Americans now live longer and fewer pension options are available, the burden to ensure financial independence and comfort in retirement is likely to be mostly the responsibility of the individual, and the Jacobsons aren't taking any chances. Regardless of headlines to the contrary, they are millionaires next door, and they are very much alive and well.

But It's Not for Me!

Some cannot imagine the early career experiences of Allison Lamar. And the Jacobsons' lifestyle isn't for everyone. Some people may not want to order from the value menu. Some people may want a bigger house for any number of reasons. And retiring at 35 but "having" to live a frugal lifestyle isn't attractive to everyone. It is understandable that not everyone can or wants to live this way.

But consuming today in anticipation of higher levels of future income and trying to keep up with the arms race of gadgets, cars, and accessories are universal problems that derail people from the economic success path and certainly the millionaire-next-door path. Individuals adopting this strategy are easily targeted by marketers, making it even tougher for them to stay focused on a goal of financial independence. The consumer arms race, and the reality that large populations are engaging in such battles, are often neglected in politically charged commentary on the state of wealth accumulation. But, as we've seen time and again, behaviors drive wealth.

Consider how many people you know who may live:

- In a house they cannot afford without their current level of income,
- In a neighborhood filled with conspicuous signs of wealth,
- With friends or family who do not want to take responsibility for their financial future,
- With little saved for either retirement or other life events (e.g., college), and
- With constant worry and concern that their lifestyle is in jeopardy.

People who are stuck in these kinds of scenarios don't have the freedom to do something outside of the norm, like start a new business, or weather an economic disaster. You may not want the frugal lifestyle described by our millionaires next door above. But if not, you will need a high income to fuel consumption *and* be prepared for what may come your way in the future.

Income Is Not Wealth

There is great freedom in the United States to choose the kind of life we want to lead and the way we build or maintain wealth. Whatever path we choose, generating income for our household will be of paramount concern at some point in the process. But income isn't the same as *wealth*. Income is what you bring home *today*. *Wealth* is what you have *tomorrow*. And the next day. And the next day.

Wealth is not income; income is not wealth.

Wealth is how much you accumulate. Net worth is your balance sheet—the net of your assets less your liabilities. Income is what you bring in over a period of time, and you report it on your annual income tax return. Periodic income certainly affects your net worth (balance sheet), but doesn't define true wealth. Consider an individual who makes $1 million in wages in a year and spends $1.2 million in consumption during that same year. The wealth (balance sheet) impact would be *negative* $200,000.

The media often portray wealth as *income* instead of *net worth*, creating the erroneous perception that simply receiving a big paycheck necessarily leads to wealth. One similarity between the high-income and high-net-worth crowds is that most of these people are economically productive as a result of their own efforts.

And personal wealth in the United States is rising over time. In 2017, there were approximately 11,500,000 millionaire households,[5] roughly 9% of the of all US households.[6] By comparison, in 1996, there were 3,500,000 millionaire households, representing 3.5% of all American households at that time. Personal wealth in the United States was $22 trillion in 1996, but nearly one-half of this wealth was owned by 3.5% of households. The distribution is similarly disproportionate today: With personal wealth at approximately $84.9 trillion in 2016, nearly 76% is held by 10% of households.[7]

We are by any definition a very affluent country. But most people in America today are far from wealthy. Don't be confused when you learn that the *average* (mean) net worth of an American household is $692,100.[8] You may think that even if a typical American worker loses his job he will be able to live off his wealth for five, maybe even six years. But there is a problem with this figure. It is very misleading. The presence of high-net-worth households (think billionaires such as Warren Buffett or Bill Gates) skews the average disproportionately.

The *median* measure of household net worth paints a much more accurate picture of the character of wealth in America. The median is that of the typical household, the midpoint range of the more than 124 million households ranked from bottom to top along the net worth scale. With few exceptions and where noted, we use the *median* figure when we discuss dollars in this book. For example, the median income in the United States (as of 2013) was $59,039, while the *mean* or average, was $83,143.[9] The estimated median net worth of Americans in 2016 was $97,300[10]—far from the frothy $692,100 (average) figure—and is just shy of the cost of a one-year stay in a nursing home.[11] This means that less than one-half of all households in the United States have enough to pay for such a service even if they sold everything they owned.

Most American households are nowhere near being financially independent, which we define as being able to live for some period of time without a paycheck from an employer or other earned income. Nor will most be able to retire in comfort. And there is more bad news. What if the equity in homes is factored out of the median-net-worth figure? Then the median figure drops to roughly $25,116, or about half of the annual median income generated by a typical American household. Who will care for these people when they are no longer able to support themselves? Don't bet on the government. In the not so distant future, it is likely that you will only be able to rely on yourself and your loved ones. Survival, like charity, begins at home.

Figure: Ratio of Mean to Median Net Worth for Years Available[12]

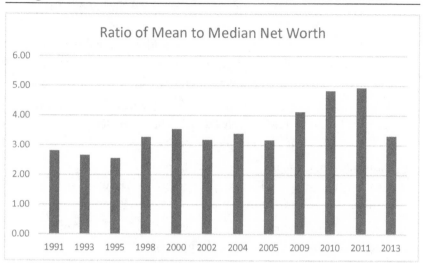

Let's look at net worth as the indicator of wealth status. We often hear, both directly as well as in the media, the following: "One million dollars? That's nothing anymore." So while $1 million is certainly worth less today than 20 years ago ($1.5 million today would equal approximately $1 million in 1996)[13], it's still more than 10 times the median net worth in America.

As was the case in 1996, most households are far from millionaire status. And even more so today, millionaire status in retirement may not be enough to perpetuate a lifestyle that includes heavy consumption. If this is your lifestyle, then securing high levels of recurring income is paramount. But earned income can be fleeting. Those who want to be truly financially independent rely instead on savings and passive income that invested capital can generate.

A Portrait of Today's Millionaire

So who are the millionaires of today? We wanted to determine if there were differences over time in the lifestyles, behaviors, and attitudes of millionaires, the "subject matter experts" of wealth accumulation. Were there key behaviors that would transcend time and lead to building wealth? What does this group of individuals who have amassed a median net worth of $3.5 million (the median net worth in our most recent survey sample) look like today? Below is a portrait of these millionaires:

- We're mostly 61-year-old men (87%) who are either married (69%) or remarried (25%). More than 80% of us believe our spouses are critical factors in our economic success.

- Our median income in the previous year was $250,000, and our median net worth is $3.5 million. Compared to the average American, we earn four times as much, while our net worth is just about 36 times the average.

- Education has been critical to our success. More than 93% of us have at least a college degree, and nearly 60% of us have a graduate degree. A little more than half of us attended a public college.

- Nearly 20% of us are retired. For the 80% of us who are not yet retired, we work approximately 45 hours per week as business owners, attorneys, engineers, leaders, managers, physicians, and consultants.

- We live off what we've made, as more than 86% of us had 0% of our income from trusts and estates in the previous year, and only 10% received any gifts of cash, securities, properties, or vehicles from relatives.

- Nearly 90% of us are satisfied with life, and nearly 80% of us say we're in general or consistently good shape physically, and we get 7.65 hours of sleep per night on average.

- We are frugal and we budget. A full 70% of us know how much we spend on food, clothing, and shelter each year, and 59% of us have always been frugal. More than 60% of us consider frugality as a critical factor in our success.

- The most we've ever spent on jeans is $50, on a pair of sunglasses is $150, and on a watch is $300.

- But we don't shop sales in person. Roughly 77% of us haven't stepped foot inside a store for Black Friday in the past five years.

- Luxury cars? We tend to drive Toyotas, Hondas, or Fords that are at least three years old. On average, our most recent car purchase was $35,000. The most we've ever spent on a car? $40,000.

- Approximately 70% of us said our parents were very frugal. Most of our parents were married and remained so until we were at least 18 (86.3%). Nearly 75% of our parents encouraged us to excel, but only 42% of us

believe that having attentive parents accounted for our success. Less than
one-third of us said our parents were better off than others while growing
up.

- We are confident investors: 70% of us say we know more than most
  people about investing, and only approximately one-third of us say we
  rely heavily on an investment advisor. More than 70% of us have at least
  one account at a full-service investment firm.

- But we have made mistakes along the way. More than 60% of us have
  sold a great stock too early, more than 73% of us sold a bad stock too late,
  and nearly 40% of us have tried to time the market.

- When it comes to investing, taking risks helped us early on. While 56%
  of us would call our current investment strategy "balanced," when we first
  started working, more than half of us called our investing strategy risky or
  very risky.

- When we do want professional advice on investing, we don't pay a lot for
  it: 56% of us paid 1% of our income from the previous year on fees, while
  33% of us paid zero.

- Do we practice economic outpatient care? Yes, a little less than two-thirds
  of us give gifts to our children and grandchildren. Roughly 34% of us
  give 1% of our income, and 23% of us give 5% of our income as gifts to
  relatives.

This portrait of what a millionaire looks like in America today is just a starting point. The real value in studying the wealthy is to understand what they did
along the way to achieving financial success, that is, the patterns of behaviors
that led to success. It is also critical to highlight case studies shared with us over
the past few years of other millionaires who provided detailed accounts of their
attitudes, lifestyles, and behaviors.

The Research

Most of the data in this book comes from the survey we conducted of affluent
Americans between 2015 and 2016 (see Appendix A). This allowed us to make
comparisons across time of the behaviors and habits of millionaires. We also used
data collected at various times by the Affluent Market Institute and DataPoints.

Much of this information is featured in the tables that appear throughout the book.

In many cases, we describe the findings for *millionaires* in our latest sample, that is, individuals with a household net worth of $1 million or more. In other cases, and specifically to help guide the review of economic success, we divide the sample into two groups using the expected net worth formula first described in *The Millionaire Next Door*. We calculate expected net worth by multiplying age by income, and dividing that product by 10, or:

Expected net worth = Age x Income x 0.10

The primary purpose of this approach is to empirically (and numerically) demonstrate how well an individual or group has been able to transform income into wealth.

Some commentators have questioned whether the findings in *The Millionaire Next Door* and prior works are unduly influenced by *survivorship bias*: in other words, that the research sample focused on those who have "made it" in terms of their net worth or incomes or careers, and therefore the conclusions about the behaviors that self-made individuals engaged in could have also been present in the remainder of the less-successful population. To this objection we have two counterpoints.

First, in addition to simply reporting averages and percentages related to the characteristics of millionaires, prior works have examined the different habits, behaviors, and attitudes of what we call "prodigious accumulators of wealth" *and* "under accumulators of wealth." To examine potential differences in the behaviors and attitudes of these groups in our current study, we divided the affluent sample into quartiles based on the difference between their *actual net worth* and *expected net worth*. This difference provides a measure of financial success: those individuals at the bottom quartile are considered to be *under accumulators of wealth* (UAWs): They tend to have less wealth than they are expected to have given their age and income. Likewise, those in the top quartile were considered to be *prodigious accumulators of wealth* (PAWs) and tend to have a net worth much higher than expected given their current income level and age. The division into these groups is *normative*; in other words, it is sample specific based on age, income, and net worth. This allows us to compare groups based on a consistent metric of success looking at *both* the successful and not-so-successful segments. This same methodology can be used regardless of the population in question.

Second, we have been able to demonstrate the power of patterns of financial behaviors in the prediction of net worth, regardless of someone's age or income. In other words, there are key behaviors that relate to your net worth whether or not you are young or old, or just starting to work, or are making six figures. During the past several years, I joined my father in his field of research, transitioning from studying how employees would be successful in specific jobs to studying how individuals are successful at building wealth. Using the science of predicting performance on the job for leaders or employees, we see the same habits, behaviors, and attitudes that distinguish those who are adept at transforming income into wealth from those who are not in samples of mass affluent Americans as well—that is, a sample where a significant portion of the participants have not yet "made it." In other words, the same factors for building wealth relate to net worth across the entire range of the affluence scale (including those who are not affluent). And we also know that many of the same financial-related tasks that are conducted in high-net-worth households are conducted in mass affluent households:[14] The tasks are similar, and the competencies required to conduct those tasks are similar. We note in Chapter 5 that *patterns of behaviors*, regardless of group membership, relate to wealth accumulation.

In a way, the research and writings over the past 20 years have served as a *job analysis*,[15] or scientific examination of what it takes to build wealth. Job analysis is used in the world of human resources to study the key tasks and characteristics of individuals who are proficient in their jobs or professions. Those competencies are then put to the test to see if they are valid (or accurate) predictors of future success on that job. This discipline is used to assist employers in selecting applicants who are most likely to succeed in a job or function.

In the job of managing finances we measure success by the difference in actual versus expected net worth. Past behavior and experiences are among the best predictors of future performance when an employer hires a new employee. For those attempting to build wealth—which we argue is one of the critical jobs of anyone running a household—there are clear tasks that comprise the job[16] and clear sets of behaviors that *predict* how well we will perform at this job.[17]

Of course we know that net worth is strongly influenced by income and age: Higher income gives individuals greater potential to build wealth. The older an individual is, the longer he or she has had to build wealth. And a large inheritance helps as well. Despite these factors, behaviors and experiences matter when it comes to building wealth, regardless of whether we're studying the affluent, as is the case in this book, or studying those in the mass market or mass affluent segments. Patterns of behaviors and experiences matter when building wealth, and the same behavioral patterns—including discipline in spending, saving, and financial management behaviors—differentiate under accumulators of wealth from prodigious accumulators of wealth regardless of age, income, or percentage of inherited wealth.

What conclusions were reinforced by our research? The overarching lessons of financial success are universal and clear. They do not change because of elections, technology, or cultural norms. Nor do they change because of a boom or bust economy. The same skills, abilities, and competencies that are required to become financially independent and successful on your own are timeless. Regardless of your status, age, and income level, you can find your path to wealth and financial independence.

Table 1-1. Percentage of Income Received through Trusts, Estates, and Inheritance in Previous Year by Percentage of Millionaires (1996 & 2016)

Year	0%	1%–5%	10%–30%	50%	75% or More
1996	80	7.8	9.7	1.2	0.9
2016	86	6.5	5.9	0.7	0.7

We have a choice in our lifestyles and whether or not we pursue economic independence. We can either play the part of mimicking those around us (and be easy targets for marketers and salespeople), or we can pursue our economic freedom quietly.

What does being financially independent—not being beholden to debt repayments, an employer, or a paycheck—allow you to do? It grants you freedom. You are free to solve problems the way you see fit; free to volunteer or spend time with family; free to take a job that perhaps pays less but gives you more satisfaction; free to create your own economic opportunities. And add to this list: free to leave behind the cubicle and regular paycheck at age 35 or 40, as many in the FI/RE community discuss in their stories of economic freedom.

Still the Land of the Free

My father often reminded us that we have great freedoms in our country to, put bluntly, do what we want. He often talked about his grandmother, who immigrated to America from Hungary with little more than a sack in the early 1900s. He wrote this piece in 2013, focusing on the nature of freedom and finance:

In the Declaration of Independence, Thomas Jefferson succinctly specifies the rights of individuals: "We hold these truths to be self-evident, that all men are created equal, that they are endowed by their Creator with unalienable Rights, that among these are Life, Liberty and the pursuit of Happiness."

We as Americans have been given the opportunity to grow, to achieve, to prosper, and to build financial independence. Given this blueprint, it is no wonder that so many people in countries all over the world have lined up to immigrate to America throughout her history.

Professor Denise Spellberg's research about Jefferson was highlighted in *The Chronicle of Higher Education*.[18] Jefferson was a strong advocate for religious liberty having been strongly influenced by John Locke. In 1689, Locke wrote "A Letter Concerning Toleration." Professor Spellberg quotes Locke: "neither Pagan, nor Mahometan, nor Jew ought to be excluded from the Civil Rights of the Commonwealth, because of his Religion." But that is not all that Jefferson read in preparation for writing the *Declaration of Independence*. He read the Qur'an which is still in his library today.

Jefferson's blueprint for freedom provided a base for the development of our great nation. For it is the many opportunities to achieve that result in our society's millions of success stories. Some countries may call themselves democracies, but a real democracy is evidenced by its peoples' behaviors and outcomes. It's interesting that countless immigrants and their children have prospered in our country while they barely eked out a living in their homelands.

Economic freedom, like the freedom we experience in the United States, has a cost: the discipline and work it takes to get there and then to maintain it. Not everyone is willing to pay this price.

Opportunities to Prosper

Financial success in this country is not commonly the result of being handed money, despite the increasing number of large-scale wealth transfers from the baby-boomer generation to their offspring, lottery winners, and celebrities who capture the public imagination. And there will always be stories of people who have squandered their riches. In fact, the likelihood that even self-made millionaires' children will have the same level of economic success is low.

As our research has shown, the path to becoming economically successful requires thinking differently about life and money, as illustrated for example by those in the FI/RE community. It requires discipline and hard work. It requires knowing one's own strengths and weaknesses, environment, and markets. It takes great skill in allocating resources—financial, emotional, cognitive, and time, to name a few.

For many this means being frugal while building wealth, not being susceptible to fads, and not buying into myths about how to "act rich." In other cases, it's managing a high income now in a way that allows for freedom later. In other words, not buying a house that requires a continued six- or seven-figure salary and generally living in a manner that allows above-average saving and investing. For others, it is spending one's emotional and cognitive resources to create a working life that allows for financial independence and freedom. All of these paths require courage and perseverance.

Sadly, because only 28% of Americans feel "extremely or very prepared" for retirement[19], and only 54% of Americans could manage a $400 emergency expense[20], the experiences of Allison Lamar or families like the Jacobsons seem extremely out of the ordinary. Despite the proliferation of self-help books, personal finance blogs, and so-called experts who typically have something to sell, Americans are still behind the 8-ball in terms of their financial well-being. Maybe this is because adopting a simple lifestyle and building wealth over time are too simplistic to sell advertising and apparently too difficult for most Americans to do. The expense side of the ledger is typically the challenge, particularly for those with higher-than-average incomes.

Paths to Wealth

Despite this somewhat dreary national outlook, there are many roads to economic success. What paths to wealth are available in America? Consider the latest survey we conducted, targeting some of the wealthy zip codes in the United States. As we discussed earlier, the ability of simple geocoding to find millionaires next door is limited. The moonlighter or the millionaire who is living in the original house he purchased when he first started working is not represented here. Though in this sample of high- and ultra-high-net-worth Americans we are able to discern distinct paths to economic success, the truth of the matter is:

There isn't an exclusive path to financial independence.

If there were, the cottage industry of personal finance blogs, books, publications, podcasts, and financial planning in general surely would not exist. This industry, founded in part on the idea that wealth was something that could be *created* versus inherited or gifted—essentially the key premise of *The Millionaire Next Door*—now has its own conferences, critics, and informal leaders.

But even *The Millionaire Next Door* described only a few paths to wealth in detail, typically defined by disciplined spending, focused savings, and a diligence in money management. In reality, achieving economic success is an *individual* endeavor, but commonalities have emerged from the more than 16,000 case studies, interviews, and surveys we have conducted and letters we've received. In this book we highlight those commonalities while also demonstrating how, in more than 20 years since the first publication of *The Millionaire Next Door*, many of the same behaviors and success factors that led to independence and wealth endure today.

Here we look at how specific decisions and behaviors relating to consumption, budgeting, careers, investing, and financial management in general can affect wealth-building. We focus on how the areas of technology, media, and consumerism have changed between the 1990s and 2000s when we conducted research for the previous books and today. For example, we were interested in how the very same technologies that give freedom to those wanting to manage their own finances, create their own businesses, and educate themselves can also serve as a distraction from financial (and other) goals. We wanted to understand how rising costs, such as in education and health care, would impact individuals who were frugal in nature. How would the behavioral-finance biases in investing, which have captured the attention of many in the financial services industry, impact prodigious accumulators of wealth? Would they make the same mistakes?

Table 1-2. Career-Lifestyle Groups of Affluent Sample

Path	Mean Age	Median Annual Income	Average Difference in Actual vs. Expected Net Worth	Sample Job Titles
Above-Average Earners	57.4	$250,000	$1,360,000	IT Director, Engineer, Director, Manager, Professor
High-Income Earners	58.2	$400,000	$1,160,000	Attorney, Physician, Vice President, Head of Private Equity Firm, Investment Manager
Small Business Owners/ Entrepreneurs	59.8	$400,000	$2,510,000	Accounting, Engineering, IT, Real Estate

Note: The median net worth for each group was $3.5 million. The larger the difference in actual versus expected net worth, the higher the likelihood of being a prodigious accumulator of wealth.

Above-Average Earners

While *The Millionaire Next Door* included other examples of self-made, economically successful Americans, the prototypical millionaire next door in this book is an individual in a somewhat "boring" occupation with an above-average income, who is frugal and unaffected by trends and social norms. But this is a path that may ultimately not suit everyone. The strategy is good defense, and the lifestyle is typically simple and unassuming. Seventy percent of millionaires state they have always been frugal. This behavior transcends job types and income levels.

High-Income Producers

The often-prone-to-being-Income-Statement-Affluent group (or "IA" group, referring to those with big incomes but low net worth) typically includes the executive leadership of larger organizations as well as professionals such as investment managers, doctors, dentists, and the like. If surrounded by exuberant consumption, this group is often tempted to look the part of their cohorts by buying big houses, luxury automobiles, and other expensive consumer goods. To build wealth with a high income takes considerable discipline in the consumption arena. To have economically self-sufficient children, this group must apply and teach a steady dose of frugality.

Small Business Owners

Assuming they have creativity, courage, and determination, along with a clear ability to target market opportunities, small business owners tend to have a higher net worth than those who work for others. For the small business owner, his source of revenue is derived from a business he created which funds all of his other investments. But self-employment does not automatically translate into big income and wealth. Consider that of the more than 25 million Americans who were self-employed sole proprietors in 2015, their average annual net income was only $13,154.[21]

Moonlighters, Gig Workers, and the FI/RE Community

Nearly one-third of all working Americans are moonlighters, which means they generate revenue in addition to and outside of their regular full- or part-time employment. Looking for multiple sources of revenue is a prototypical millionaire-next-door kind of behavior. It is much easier to have multiple sources of income than it was a decade ago. With technological resources at your fingertips, you can create multiple businesses in a matter of minutes. Typically, the most successful moonlighters have experience or access to potential customers to identify their needs and test the market.

Many of these moonlighters and gig workers are what we might call the "stealth wealthy"—in other words, they cannot be "found" in a sampling of affluent neighborhoods or through traditional means. But in our surveys we were able to find several emerging and actual millionaire-next-door types who use crowdsourcing[22] as a means to supplement their incomes. They represent developers, administrative staff members, teachers, professors, lawyers, marketing professionals, retail sales clerks, nurses—the full range of job types, interests, and levels. This group often values their family's economic success and financial freedom over the consumption of goods.

Favorite Chapters from
The Millionaire Next Door

Millionaires often reached out to my father to share their experiences and feedback about The Millionaire Next Door *and his other books. He would invariably ask them what they liked about the book, and their collective feedback was captured in this piece he wrote in 2014:*

I like to ask millionaires who have read *The Millionaire Next Door* what their favorite chapter is. You may be surprised to learn that it is not Chapter 2 ("Frugal, Frugal, Frugal"). This chapter details the frugal lifestyle of millionaires in terms of the modest prices paid for clothing, shoes, watches, motor vehicles, etc. This is merely a review for millionaires, affirming who they are. However, this chapter (which ranks third) is the one they most often tell their children to read!

Chapter 5 ("Economic Outpatient Care") ranks second. Often after a millionaire reaches the financially independent threshold, a new set of issues develop. The typical millionaire next door has three children and around six to eight grandchildren. How millionaires interface with these offspring in financial terms can be the cause of much worry and unpleasantness. Of course, not all children of millionaires are underachievers. But as mentioned in *The Millionaire Next Door*, "in eight of the ten occupational categories, gift receivers [those who receive economic outpatient care] have smaller levels of net worth (wealth) than those who do not receive gifts." These occupations include accountant, attorney, marketing professional, entrepreneur, senior manager, engineer, physician, and middle manager. Of course, these data do not account for economic "inpatient care." Keep in mind that one in four sons (ages 25–34) of high-income parents live with them.

Chapter 6 ("Affirmative Action Family Style") ranks first in popularity. The subtitle of this chapter, "Their Adult Children are Economically Self Sufficient," succinctly summarizes the chapter. Yet parents often distribute their wealth in ways that instigate friction among their adult children. Those children who are the least productive in economic terms often receive the lion's share of their parents' capital. The results of this inequity of distribution are predictable. It further weakens the weakest child and strengthens the strongest child. Or as a millionaire told me, "The [children] who achieve do so by conquering obstacles . . . [they] were never denied their right to face some adversity. Others were in reality cheated . . . sheltered . . . [and] never really inoculated from fear, worry, and the feeling of dependency."

Another Visit with Ken

Those who are economically successful often have a guide, a North Star, and a plan to build wealth over time. They make decisions that are conducive to their financial goals, versus what might seem easier paths. Pursuing economic independence can begin at any time, but the earlier the better, as in the case of Ken, whom my father first interviewed and profiled more than a decade ago in *The Millionaire Next Door*. To be sure, Ken's father was an economic success story, but Ken and the rest of his family didn't know this until after his death. So with no knowledge of or benefit from his family's wealth, Ken started on his financial path. We present Ken's experience as a good template of wise yet tough decision making related to lifestyle and wealth. Consider his case as you contemplate how you and your household are planning for economic success.

Values Learned at Home

Ken was raised in a frugal environment, though his father was a high-income-producing surgeon. Although achievement was emphasized, conspicuous consumption was frowned upon. Ken was also encouraged to stay physically fit by playing golf and running. When Ken's dad passed away he left his mother an estate worth more than $10 million. How does Ken explain his family's success in accumulating wealth?

> *My Dad was frugal. We never knew he was wealthy until we received an accounting statement for his estate. We were shocked. He used to buy a new car, a Buick, about every eight years. That's when the wheels would likely fall off! I get a tremendous amount of satisfaction from saving and investing . . . that's what Dad did. Like father, like son. I am frugal; my wife is even more frugal. I buy my cars used from small size leasing companies, often undercapitalized, that take back vehicles from lessees who can't make the payments. I recently bought a car for $22,000 . . . a year and a half old. It listed for $35,000. The leasing company had four of the same model. I just call the leasing companies listed in the Yellow Pages.*

Now in his early 60s, Ken is on track to exceed the considerable wealth accumulated by his father. Ken's dad often told him, "I am not impressed with what people own. I am impressed with what they achieve . . . always strive to be the best in your field . . . don't chase money. If you are the best in your field, money will find you." (In Chapter 3, we'll talk about the influences on how we build wealth, including early experiences.)

Strategic Location

Initially Ken and his wife lived in a nice part of Manhattan within walking distance of his job. But when the couple began putting together a 30-year financial plan (yes, a 30-year plan!), they quickly realized that it would be difficult to accumulate wealth in one of the most expensive cities in the world. Ken then proposed to his boss that he be allowed to work out of a southern city. When his boss agreed, Ken and his wife purchased a house in suburban Atlanta for about $300,000, which they still live in 30 years later. A similar home would have cost them $1 million in the suburbs of New York City. (In Chapters 3 and 4, we discuss homes and other consumption factors in building wealth.)

Capitalizing on Strengths, and Early Work Experiences

Ken used his skills in working with others to network at the state university where he got his MBA. He sought out a faculty member to sponsor a field project related to his chosen field of interest, which was sports broadcasting. After graduate school, Ken landed a job in sports television broadcasting primarily because he had the experience of a field project. His starting salary was around $100,000. In this job, he was responsible for one of four regions in the country. The three other managers were all Ivy League grads. So why was Ken hired at the same level? Ultimately it was because he had experience through his field project in his MBA program. (In Chapter 5, we'll talk about the factors that play into the success of millionaires and highlight how the same factors are related to success in other facets of work life. We then talk about early career experiences in Chapter 6.)

Allocating Resources

For transportation, Ken and his wife bought several new minivans that they kept for 8 to 10 years each. (In Chapter 4, we'll cover consumption and frugality, the continued hallmarks of self-made, economically successful Americans. In Chapter 7, we'll discuss how affluent Americans approach the allocation of their resources, including how they invest.)

Ken ignored the myth that to succeed he needed to spend lavishly on his education. He attended public schools and universities. So did his kids. Ken and his wife deliberately selected their neighborhood in part because it had the top-rated public schools in the state. Today the total cost of private school tuition in Ken's area for grades 1 through 12 is between $110,000 and $264,000 per student for 12 years of education. Imagine how many pretax dollars one would have to earn to pay this tuition. Not surprisingly, 72% of the millionaires we surveyed report that when purchasing a home, they sought a neighborhood that had excellent public schools. Ken and his wife saved more than $300,000 this way. This one decision alone earned Ken and his family a small fortune when considering that this avoided annual expense was able to grow in the form of invested monies over the decades. (We'll talk more about the myths of wealth, and the myths surrounding education, in Chapters 2 and 5.)

The outcome?

Ken retired at age 55 as a decamillionaire.

Requirements for Self-Made Economic Success

What about those with average to better-than-average incomes seeking financial independence today? If you were to simply explain how an individual can build wealth over time, and you believed it was still possible, how would you do it? You might explain that the way to do it is to spend less than you earn, and then save and invest the remaining money in a way that allows it to grow on its own. It's simple, but not easy. The real difficulty lies in the external pressures that are telling us not to take these simple steps.

In conjunction with the most recent survey research, this book attempts to focus on the key habits, traits, and behaviors of self-made Americans based on data spanning 40 years to see if these patterns have changed over the decades. What we see is that they have been constant regardless of a dot-com boom or a housing bubble crash. The behavioral components of economic success have even been consistent regardless of who's in the White House. Whether it's the Jacobsons' value meal perspective or Ken's 30-year financial plan, there are key factors that separate those who are able to transform income into wealth from those who are not.

Do Environmental Changes Impact Wealth-Building?

Much has changed since *The Millionaire Next Door* was first published in 1996. Undoubtedly the biggest change is the proliferation of personal technology. These advancements gave us social media, which allows us to easily establish or keep relationships with an almost infinite number of family members or friends. On the positive side, social media provides a way to stay connected with others virtually. On the negative side, it is also a way for marketers to constantly remind us of the consumer goods we "need" and consumer-related experiences that our friends and family members are having: purchases, parties, events, entertainment, and even high-priced educations. Even if you can somehow avoid the marketing side of social media, you may find it hard to avoid being influenced by the behaviors of your friends and family, as nearly 70% of Americans are on social media.[23] This steady inundation of what other people are doing, driving, and buying has made it increasingly more important to be disciplined in deflecting the influence of the proverbial Joneses.

Next, an individual investor's ability to make his own securities trades was in its infancy in the 1990s, but today the tools are available to anyone. This has pushed down the costs of hiring financial advisors, and it's changing the nature of investing and financial planning, both for average Americans and for those with a significant amount of wealth. We'll discuss this more in Chapter 7 as our focus shifts to investing.

Finally, the boom economy of the 1990s had some critics and people in the academic world assuming there were more chances for increasing wealth on one's own than there are today. Living expenses in general have increased since 1996, of course, but nowhere more so than in health care and education. The cost of higher education, in particular, has been rising well above inflation, and recent articles and books question what value a four- or five- or six-year degree has today.[24] Do these costs mean that building wealth by following the behaviors and habits of self-made individuals is out of reach for most? We cannot argue that these rising costs have no impact on your ability to become wealthy on your own. Instead, based on our research, we simply see that the very characteristics that made the original millionaires next door that way in the 1980s and 1990s can be applied to the changes: frugality, discipline, and thinking differently continue to allow those with the desire and drive to build wealth to do so.

The Wealth Discipline

Throughout the course of our study of the affluent, there is a common theme that is celebrated by some and reviled by others: discipline. Our millionaire sample rates this as the top success factor. In 2000, 95% of millionaires agreed it was critical to their success, and in 2016, 91% of millionaires rated *being disciplined* as an important success factor.

Specifically, discipline is required to take *income* and transform it into *wealth*. This discipline includes knowing (a) how much you bring in, (b) how much you spend, and (c) creating a budget, or spending plan, to ensure the difference is in the positive camp. The mathematical equation involves basic addition and subtraction. *Discipline* is the component of building wealth that allows for the math to work.

The more you save, presumably, the more opportunity there is to invest. Then we can apply another mathematical equation: compound interest. Here, too, discipline comes into play. The "magic" of this math cannot be seen in frequent trading, market timing, or exotic investments, unless you are in the vanishingly small population of investors who can reliably and consistently "beat the market."

Discipline is the factor that riles those who are looking for excuses why they cannot amass wealth, particularly among the hyper-consuming, high-income crowds. These people perhaps live in expensive urban areas and have amassed high college debt because they thought they had to.

Does the "d" word trip some of us up because it requires us to make choices and not have everything we desire? Discipline often requires going against the tide, including the tide of your social influences, and perhaps even how you were raised or your long-held beliefs about what you are entitled to *today*.

Discipline and Awareness

The millionaires in our latest study, similar to those we've studied previously, tend to be attuned to their financial health. They are keenly aware of the small, perhaps mundane aspects of their financial lives even though they have both income and net worth levels much higher than the average American. In our latest study, 70% of millionaires know how much they spend on food, clothing, and shelter each year. More than 65% of them, despite their high net worth, continue to operate their households on a budget. They engage in activities that align with building and sustaining wealth such as studying investments, reading trade magazines, and working.

Most economically successful Americans have or gain an awareness of their own abilities, skills, and competencies and how those can be transformed into careers, jobs, and businesses. They have the ability and foresight to examine trends in the environment, the market, and their communities and target future or growing needs with their services or products. Typically, this awareness is gained through parental guidance, early career experiences, and trial and error.

Awareness is required to make choices that are congruent with your own strengths, interests, family goals, and what is happening within your chosen playing field, including your neighborhood, social circles, job market, or industry.

Allocation of Resources

Critical to all goals, financial or otherwise, is the allocation of time, energy, and money in an intentional, disciplined manner. As discussed in Chapter 3 of *The Millionaire Next Door* and Chapter 9 of *The Millionaire Mind*, those who are or who become economically successful have the ability to allocate their resources effectively to meet their goals and do not become distracted from reaching them. Prodigious accumulators of wealth spend more time planning for future investments than under accumulators of wealth. The same is true today. Millionaires next door still spend time on activities that are conducive to building wealth or to "building wealth" in the areas of health and wellness. (As we'll see in Chapter 5, millionaires spend about half the time as the average American playing video games yet twice as much time exercising and reading for pleasure.)

Economic independence belongs to those with the willingness to allocate time, money, energy, and cognitive resources to achieve financial goals.

Bucking Trends

Assume for a moment that everything you've read in the popular or social media press with regard to wealth accumulation in the United States is true: that with the rise in costs related to health care and education, the lack of pensions and retirement funds from employers, and the increased mechanisms by which companies can influence your consumer behavior, few people can build wealth on their own. What if you buy into the idea that only the top 1% or 10% (or some percent) will continue to stay there?

And, what if you decide you want to buck the trend, to try on your own to do what some are saying is essentially impossible today? My hope is that you will read the following chapters with some glimmer of hope in a world where many say doing anything on your own isn't possible without the help of government, handouts, or incredible good luck. What might it take for you? It will certainly take some self-reflection and, more importantly, some critical changes in attitude and behavior related to wealth such as:

- You have to understand and dispel many of the myths related to what wealth is and how it is accumulated. You will have to stop blaming those who have achieved economic success and instead examine how you can succeed based on your own unique background and talents.

- You will need to examine how everyone around you today, and those who were around you while growing up, faced financial matters. You will need to recognize that the errors of your parents and caregivers don't have to be yours. Perhaps more importantly, you will need to recognize the level of influence those around you are having on your financial behaviors and make conscious decisions as to whether or not you will allow those influences to persist.

- You will need to consider your consumer behavior, starting with major purchases including your home and car, as well as smaller purchases. Where you "plant" yourself or your household will have considerable influence on other major financial decisions. You will have to determine if those purchase decisions are conducive to your overall financial goals, or if they are being made to emulate those who are either glittering rich or, as is more often the case, those who pretend to have great wealth.

- Part of your self-reflection must include a self-assessment of your strengths and weaknesses when it comes to all things financial. Where do your unique characteristics help you in creating and meeting financial goals? You will have to add to your list of self-improvement goals those related to financial matters: becoming more focused, more confident in financial decisions, and more frugal.

- It will take generating revenue on your own and thus must include a reflection on what work means to you, where and how and for how long you want to spend 40+ hours a week toiling for some entity, or if you can create a business on your own, with its requisite ups and downs, to generate income. Perhaps, instead, you make the decision to pursue early retirement on your own terms, saving money aggressively during your early working years, and leaving the 30-plus years of 9 to 5 (or now 8 to 6) to others.

- Finally, that revenue must be invested to grow, and you will have to decide, after reflection, how to invest it and where to get financial advice. You will have to make intentional decisions about how to spend cognitive resources as well. These resources, our attention and time, are non-renewable and either increase our opportunities for economic freedom or keep us enslaved to the income-spend-income-spend cycle.

Chapter 2

Ignoring the Myths

One man pretends to be rich, yet has nothing; another pretends to be poor, yet has great wealth.

—Proverbs 13:7

DESPITE SIGNIFICANT CHANGES IN GOVERNMENT, SOCIAL ENVIRONMENT, AND economic markets in the United States, the advice over the last 20 years to those in early adulthood can be summed up by this statement: To build and maintain wealth over time, it will be necessary for you to approach all financial management—spending, saving, generating revenue, investing—in a different, more disciplined approach than anyone else around you. That requires action on your part, as opposed to mere belief, attitude, or personality. While the latter three can impact your behavior, ultimately your ability to build and grow wealth over time will be shaped by what *you do*, not what is in your head.

What does it mean for the current millionaire next door, and those of the future, that there have been significant increases in health care costs, or that college costs have increased 153% between 1984 and 2016?[1] It means that current and future generations that desire to build wealth on their own and on their own terms will have to shift their mindset in relation to these expenses. They will have to change their way of doing things, even where (or if) they go to college or how they chart a path for a career. We cannot control costs or governmental policies or the financial markets. We can control what we spend, how we invest, the opportunities we seek, and other aspects of our financial lives, for better or worse.

What Does It Take?

What does it really take to build wealth? Can you still build wealth in America today? My father wrote the following summary of economic success in 2014, outlining what it (still) takes to become financially independent:

Contrary to what is often touted in the media, there are greater affluent opportunities in our economy today than ever in our nation's history. But in order to take advantage of these, it is important to appreciate the eight key elements of the economic success equation as given in my book, *The Millionaire Mind*:

1. Understand the key success factors our economy continues and will continue to reward: hard work, integrity, and focus.

2. Never allow a lackluster academic record to stand in the way of becoming economically productive.

3. Have the courage to take some financial risk. And learn how to overcome defeat.

4. Select a vocation that is not only unique and profitable; pick one you love.

5. Be careful in selecting a spouse. Those who are economically productive married husbands or wives who had the characteristics that are compatible with success.

6. Operate an economically productive household. Many millionaires prefer to repair or refinish rather than buy new.

7. Follow the lead of millionaires when selecting a home. Study, search, and negotiate aggressively.

8. Adopt a balanced lifestyle. Many millionaires are "cheap dates." It does not take a lot of money to enjoy the company of your family and friends.

These are basic truisms founded on incontrovertible principles. But the fact remains that many people continue to buy into the *myths* of wealth, thus decreasing the likelihood of taking on the responsibility of building wealth on their own.

Myth 1: You Are Your Group.

Believing that you have the same likelihood of success as others around you with similar demographic characteristics ignores the unique characteristics and drive that actually allow you to succeed on your own. If we look back at the not too distant past, there were *laws* in place that held back certain groups based not on their abilities or knowledge or skills, but rather on the color of their skin or gender. This wasn't 500 years ago; this was just a few *decades* in the rearview mirror.

Even today, some of us in different generations (again, a group by year of birth) laugh about millennials with their lattes and avocado toast, or perhaps more positively, say that the baby-boomer generation was one that will never be seen again. In many ways these general conclusions about groups of people, while convenient and perhaps useful at a marketing and policy level, are less helpful when we want to discover what it takes to build wealth.

The obvious outcome of such thinking? It gives all of us an out. Blame the fact that I'm in this or that group for why I cannot get ahead or why I act the way I do. "I see you're a Gen-Xer female, white, with three children, married, and you live in this zip code. I'll put you *here*."

A wise professor once reminded her graduate students in psychology that "there is more variation *within* a group than *between* groups." In other words, there is more variation in our psychology and behaviors within a group (e.g., variation in our interests, personalities, and abilities) than between two demographic categories. Instead, as we will see in Chapter 5, our *behaviors*, not the color of our skin or when we were born, can significantly impact our ability to build and maintain wealth over time.

Ethnicity and Drive?

One of the areas of focus in *The Millionaire Next Door* related to ancestry, or where your parents and grandparents came from. When I joined my father in his research endeavors several years ago, I started to guide the focus more toward characteristics that could *change* over time and behaviors that could be altered.

Group membership, while interesting and easy to report in articles and survey results, does little to help us change and grow and succeed.

In that same vein, though, it is difficult to imagine that the experience of immigrating to the United States, spurred on by a desire to improve your family's life, does not have an effect on the ability of first-generation Americans to build wealth on their own. That desire and drive to reach our shores or borders may explain more about success within immigrant populations than their ethnicity.

Consider the following example of a millionaire next door who came to America and his *behaviors* and choices that allowed him economic success despite the challenges of starting over in a new country:

> *I'm a first-generation immigrant who moved to the US when I was seven years old. For the most part, our family was poor but not destitute. The high school I attended had no advanced placement classes and about half of the freshman class did not graduate. Fortunately, I recognized the value of education and was able to get into the University of California.*
>
> *I choose to study Computer Science partly because of career prospects. My first job out of school in 1996 paid $38,000 per year. The economy picked up quickly and so did my pay. Housing was relatively cheaper and I put down 10% on a $192,000 condo in San Francisco. In 2000, I had a good career opportunity in New York City for a large investment bank. I would eventually work twelve years in New York. My pay was fairly good but nothing insane (average total comp was maybe $200,000).*
>
> *I invested wisely and last year decided to "retire" and move to . . . Oregon. . . . I generate about $3,000 per month in rental income and another $3,000–$4,000 per month in dividends. I have IRAs that generate another $1,500 per month in dividends. At 41, I can no longer work if I choose to do so.*
>
> *Other notes: I don't own a car now and the most expensive car I've ever purchased was for $2,200. I have never owned a watch. I have never spent over $200 on a pair of shoes.*

It is hard to imagine that this individual's history did not significantly impact his work ethic and spending behaviors, and ultimately his financial success.

Immigrating to the United States?
Just the First Step

It's not enough, of course, to get to America. Not all of those who arrive, just like not all of us who live here, realize that the freedom we have in the United States gives us the opportunity to work hard, create business-es, and live our lives the way we want to. No, our streets are not paved in gold, as my father reminded us in this essay from a few years ago:

It took Natasha 30 minutes of nonstop talking to answer the following question: "How do you like living in America?" Natasha, aka Natasha "Complainski," is not happy living in the USA. She, a hairdresser and sole proprietor who rents her chair, and her husband, who installs and repairs hardwood floors, moved here from Russia in 2004. Both thought they would be rich by now. But they are not even close. The couple apparently read only the headlines about the vast amount of personal wealth in the US, about $65 trillion in total. And don't forget all those billionaires featured in the *Forbes* 400; even the Russian press highlighted the multimillions paid to pro athletes, senior corpo-rate executives, and even college presidents.

Natasha may have been even more impressed with the Federal Reserve's estimates of the average household net worth in Amer-ica, roughly $575,000. Even before they immigrated, it was over $400,000. She and her husband believed that they would quickly prove that they were better in generating wealth once they settled here. Attention Mrs. Complainski: buried in the details is the fact that the median net worth of an American household is less than $85,000 or about 15% of the $575,000 average. And the median income is nowhere near $1 million; it's about $52,000, slightly more than what the Complainskis earn. It's not easy to become a millionaire on $50,000 a year.[2]

Natasha also is despondent about the market value of her home. They bought it with a small down payment just before the real estate meltdown and assumed that the market value would appreciate rapidly. But today it's actually worth 70% of its purchase price. In reality, even in good times, the real net appreciation of a home is much less than most people estimate.

The Complainskis made the mistake of thinking that wealth would just happen to them in America, without any hard work, discipline, or sacrifice. For all but the luckiest of immigrants, that's a myth too.

Myth 2: Income Equals Wealth.

While we just highlighted the converse in Chapter 1, it is critical to remember that the two concepts of income and wealth are often misused. It continues to be the assumption of those who increase consumption as their income increases that they are the same. And believing this myth gives the false perception that those who *appear* to be rich (neighbors driving luxury cars or friends in $200-plus jeans) are wealthy when in fact it only means they spent more than real millionaires on these purchases.

"Along with many parents, students, and teachers, many writers, reporters, and politicians need to go back to school. Income continues to be confused with wealth," my father once wrote. Many people believe that income equals wealth. In fact even the Tax Foundation talks about "millionaires" in terms of their income tax returns, versus their net worth.[3]

When we use the term *wealth*, we are referring to the net worth of a household, i.e., all of its assets less all of its liabilities. We define household income in a simple way: It is income (realized) that is or should be reported on one's personal income tax return. The confusion about these two terms leads to erroneous conclusions about a multitude of economic and societal topics. The practical effect of this confusion is that it distorts the metrics or numbers we pay attention to while trying to achieve financial and economic independence.

A Millionaire's Income Is Only 8.2% of His Wealth

Several years ago, Brit, age 36, and his wife were upside down on their heavily mortgaged home, had a negative net worth, and owed more than $60,000 on their credit cards alone. Today the couple has a positive net worth of about $20,000. Brit explains that paying off their debts was extremely difficult and took much sacrifice. The couple is genuinely proud of this accomplishment. But, in spite of this, Brit reports that he is depressed, "bummed out . . . I can't see how we are ever going to become wealthy even with us both working our tails off."

People who believe that they will never become wealthy generally fulfill this prophecy. My father explained to Brit, who was once a member of the ultimate income-statement affluent club, that he had an excellent chance of becoming a millionaire-next-door type and that the typical millionaire next door was 57 years old (at that time). The will and discipline that this couple demonstrated in paying off their considerable debt is telling. The same determination can be used in setting aside *at least* 15% of their income for savings and investing.

What should you anticipate as a typical member of the millionaire-next-door fraternity?

1. Looking at the wealth equation from Chapter 1, actual net worth exceeds its expected value by a factor of two or more.

2. The market value of a home is less than 20% of net worth.

3. Debt equals the equivalent of less than 5% of net worth.

4. Annual income tax is the equivalent of about 2% of net worth.

5. Total annual realized income is approximately 8.2% of net worth (median), or the equivalent of $8.20 of income for every $100 of wealth.

This $8.20 figure from my father's research is fairly consistent with the findings of other researchers. For example, three scholars employed by the Treasury Department compared the wealth characteristics of millionaires via 36,352 federal estate returns for decedents who passed away in 2007 with the incomes of these individuals when they were living. Those millionaires, who were married and under the age of 70 (like the large majority of the millionaire-next-door types my father surveyed), realized the equivalent of $8.45 for every $100 of their net worth. This figure is within approximately 3% of the dollar figure ($8.20) that was determined from his surveys.[4]

Income and net worth of course are related factors, but they are not equivalent. Each should be used in different ways to assess overall financial health and progress.

Myth 3: You Can Judge a Person's Wealth by What He Drives, Buys, and Wears.

Everyone has an opinion about "the rich," perpetuated in part by narratives from the media and different political factions used for their own purposes. Dispelling myths about wealth, both what it takes to create it and what the wealthy do with their money, was of critical concern throughout my father's lifetime of research. He often demonstrated the myths through the case studies he related about those who demonstrated a clear adherence to those myths. Take, for example, Ranger

X. Rich, a pseudonym for an individual my father met in 2010 in a national park near Atlanta. His observations about Mr. Rich provide an illustration on the perils of holding on to myths regarding wealth, and how false assumptions about money and those who do or don't have it can impact satisfaction as well as diligence in pursuing one's own financial independence:

> *We first noticed the ranger as we hiked out of the large parking lot adjacent to the wilderness area. He was just opening his ticket book when my wife said to me, "Did you put your parking pass on the dashboard?" I had not; I had left it on the console. With that, I said to the ranger, "I better run back and put my pass on the dashboard; otherwise you are going to give me a ticket." He smiled, pointed to the parking lot and asked me what kind of car I drove. I reported to him "a Toyota 4-Runner."*
>
> *He then said something that shocked us: "I'll probably never get around to the Toyotas. Most people who drive Toyotas . . . Fords . . . Chevrolets pay the $3 to use the park. It's the people with Mercedes, BMWs, Jaguars, the worst, and Range Rovers who usually don't pay. I've been doing this a long time. It's the working man who pays in this country. Rich people don't pay taxes. They don't pay to park."*

Our empirical research does not cover the parking habits of the rich. So we cannot say whether Ranger X. Rich was correct in his assumption that people who drive status makes of motor vehicles are more likely to scoff at the notion of paying parking fees. It is interesting to note that Ranger X. Rich asserted that those people who drive these status cars are by definition "rich." But as my father pointed out in *Stop Acting Rich*, 86% of those who drive status motor vehicles are not millionaires. So, it may be that many people who drive expensive cars don't have enough money left to pay the parking fee, or tip the waiter at a restaurant, the caddy, etc.

Drive Rich or Be Rich

Ranger X. Rich believed in the "rich-first system" when distributing tickets. He sought out prestige makes of motor vehicles to ticket first because he thought that rich people don't pay taxes, and they don't pay to park. And Ranger X. Rich believed that rich people drive prestige makes of cars. But as pointed out in my father's blog and in *Stop Acting Rich*, "The median price paid by millionaires for their most recent acquisition was only $31,367. The typical price paid by decamillionaires was $41,997. . . . Many millionaires drive so-called common, nonprestige makes of cars. . . ." In our current study, the median price paid by millionaires for their most recent automobile purchase was $35,000.

But Ranger X. Rich is like many people who define *rich* in terms of income instead of net worth. Certainly, many drivers feel the need to display their socioeconomic achievements by acquiring prestige makes of motor vehicles. They may think that those who are successful in generating high incomes drive luxury brands. And correspondingly, drivers of more common makes have average income credentials. But the hard data suggest that the level of prestige of a car and the income of its driver are not anywhere near being perfect correlates. In fact, many drivers of luxury cars have neither the levels of income nor net worth which would qualify them as high economic achievers.

Along these lines, Joann Muller, writing for Forbes.com[5], wrote a piece titled "What the Rich People Really Drive." She defines rich people in terms of income, not net worth: "the richest people were the most likely to buy luxury brands [39% for people with household income above $250,000 vs. 8% for those people who earn less than $100,000 a year]. . . . 61% of people who earn $250,000 or more aren't buying luxury brands at all."

Her analysis indicates that those households with high incomes are more likely to drive luxury cars. But just because someone is driving a luxury brand does not necessarily mean the driver has a high income—or a high net worth, for that matter.

But as my father wrote in 2012: "[I] estimate that there are 2.5 million households or nearly 2.2% of the total that have annual realized incomes of $250,000 or more. Using Ms. Muller's estimates that 39% of 'the rich' buy luxury brands, one can estimate the number who do so to be approximately 975,000. Ah, but this population is much smaller than those households who drive prestige makes but have annual incomes under $100,000. About 30 million households have annual incomes in the $50,000 to under $100,000 bracket alone. Translation: 8% of 30 million = 2.4 million who are buying luxury cars but are not in the so-called rich category. This population is nearly 2.5 times the size of the high income/ luxury vehicle buyer population."[6]

Could it be that it is the pseudo-affluent, the aspirationals, who are keeping the manufacturers of prestige makes of motor vehicles in business?

Not in My Club!

Perhaps the most timeless takeaway from The Millionaire Next Door *is the idea that a millionaire doesn't "act rich." My father wrote this piece in 2011, high-lighting, once again, the concept that millionaires often don't dress the part:*

Targeting affluent, millionaire-next-door types continues to be an objective of those in the professional advisory services today. But not everyone who sets out to market and serve that population will succeed. Who are among the best at serving the needs of the millionaire-next-door types? Often, they are those who have had experiences with these types of people during their formative years.

Tony Schuman, a successful investment manager, was sensitized early in his life to the significant differences between the low-profile millionaire next door and the pseudo-affluent. Tony had a newspaper route when he was 10 years old. He reports that "the blue-collar people always paid on time and tipped. [In contrast for example] one woman, an attorney, would run around her house for 20 minutes or more before she would think of giving me 55 cents for the paper. Both she and her husband worked but would never tip."

Later Tony became a caddy, as I did. His early impressions were similar to mine regarding the characters who can be found at golf clubs. I mentioned in *Stop Acting Rich* that the blue-collar, self-made millionaires for whom I caddied at a public course were significantly better tippers than most of the aspirationals for whom I caddied at a private country club. But those who did tip offered a very generous gratuity. Tony shared the following observations:

> I look back now and realize that I learned more about business work-
> ing there than all my time in business school. The self-made men
> all tipped well and continued to encourage me while I was working
> my way through college. One member mentor, Mr. R, owned a large
> general contracting business and had bankrolled more than half of
> the club's construction. Because of the cold Connecticut winters, he
> had to double his work time during the summer months. He couldn't
> play golf on Saturdays with the rest of the members because he
> was working. Mr. R would come to the club Saturday afternoon for
> a beer on the patio . . . wearing his "millionaire next door" uniform
> of work khakis and steel-toed boots. One day a new member's wife
> who had designated herself the club's doyenne saw Mr. R drinking
> his beer and smoking a cigar on the patio. . . . She scream[ed] at
> him . . . that he, as a mere workman had no right to sit on the patio
> to drink and smoke. Her final bombshell . . . "Who do you think you
> are; do you think you own this place?" Mr. R calmly answered back,
> "Almost, lady, almost." Naturally she ran screaming [to the manager]
> who proceeded to inform her that Mr. R actually owned about 75%
> of the club equity and if she had any more questions, she should talk
> directly to him.

Both from our current study, as well as research from 2007 in a survey of 1,594 high-income/high-net-worth households, we see that *annual realized household income* is a superior predictor of the price paid for motor vehicles than net worth (wealth). In the 2007 study, 48.5% of respondents with incomes of $200,000 or more paid less than $32,000 for the vehicle they most recently acquired. More than one in three, or 35.9% of those in the $500,000 and over bracket paid less than $32,000. More than one-half, or 54%, of those in the $200,000 to under $500,000 bracket paid under $32,000.

Myth 4: The "Rich" Don't Pay Their Fair Share.

Ranger X. Rich disliked "the rich" for other job-related reasons. He believed that the rich don't pay their fair share of the taxes in America, and that they were responsible for the decline in tax revenue collected by the state that employed him, which in turn necessitated cutbacks and a change of his job description.

The myth regarding income and wealth is helpful here in understanding why Mr. Rich would believe that the "rich" don't pay their share of taxes. First, Mr. Rich was confused by luxury cars and *wealth*—he instead might have talked about *income*—and in that vein, he was wrong again.

Ranger X. Rich would have been wise to consider the taxes paid by those high-income, glittering rich, those who can purchase the luxury automobiles with an amount that serves as just a drop in their coffers or yearly salary.

Income Taxes: The Other Big-Ticket Item

Chairman and CEO of Berkshire Hathaway Warren Buffett is the best of the best at transforming income into wealth. How did he do it? Wise investing, you might say, combined with his reputation for having enormous integrity and his well-publicized frugal lifestyle. When it comes to consumption, he seems to possess traditional midwestern values. Despite his substantial wealth he lives in a relatively modest home and drives American makes of cars. Ah, but there is something else. As my father stated in *The Millionaire Next Door*, "Millionaires know that the more they spend, the more income they must realize. The more they realize, the more they must allocate for income taxes. So . . . adhere to an important rule: To build wealth, minimize your realized (taxable) income and maximize your unrealized income (wealth/capital appreciation without a cash flow)."

The Benefits of Continued Supercar Consumption

In Stop Acting Rich, *my father profiled a man he called Mr. "Multi-plinski," who had scrawled the following notes in the margins of one of my father's research surveys: "I don't own a Ferrari, I own three! . . . Rolex? I have three plus . . . Breitling, Cartier, Movado, Omega, Tag Heuer . . . [wine collection] 2,000 bottles." My father explained why Mr. Multiplinski, a member of the "glittering rich" club, wasn't shy about communicating his financial achievement: he "has a very strong need . . . to separate himself from his dirt poor working class family background. . . . those who travel the longest distance along the wealth scale in one generation [tend to] hyper spend on status symbols." He also had this to say:*

Mr. M's first full-time job was in sales. He was an instant success. He paid 100% of his college expenses via "commissions . . . solely on commissions." He purchased his first home at the age of 21 and crossed the $1 million net worth threshold when he was 32. He was not yet 30 when he was offered an equity position by his employer.

Mr. M is 100% self-made, but he's also a big spender. To spend big, one must earn big. And if you earn big you pay big bucks to the tax man. As an example, consider Mr. M's cash purchase of a $330,000 Ferrari. Given what he allocates to federal, state, and local income taxes, how much earned income did he have to generate to make this purchase? He had to make $600,000 just to pay (cash in this case) for this Ferrari. ($600,000 times his share 55% = $330,000.) The balance of $270,000 goes to Uncle Sam and his state relatives. The glittering rich are, as I wrote in *The Millionaire Next Door*:

Real patriots...big incomes (huge tax bills) mint a new medal for this type of patriotism.[7]

Too many people in this country don't understand the important role played by the members of the glittering-rich population. Some think that the Mr. Ms of our nation don't pay their fair share of taxes. Some even believe that none of the glittering rich got that way on their own. Rather it was via hook, crook, or inheritance. It is this belief that can be ammunition for some ambitious politicians.

For a moment, consider the following scenario. Imagine that a glittering-rich couple decides one day to spend a long weekend at a plush mountain retreat. It is a great drive in their top-of-the-line Ferrari. As reported by Justin Berkowitz in 2013 for *Car and Driver* magazine, just as the couple approaches the resort, their car and several other "High-end cars were pulled over, and their drivers were asked to sit tight while the home office checked tax records[!] One in six—42 vehicles in total—were being driven by someone who had reported a meager annual income insufficient for supercar ownership. . . . Emboldened, tax cops set up checkpoints . . . and even dropped in on a Ferrari owners club get-together. . . . [Now] the government is initiating an automated check of tax records for anyone making large purchases."[8]

This actually happened in 2013 in Italy. Class envy was leveraged politically as Berkowitz's title indicates, "Checkpoint Carlo: How Tax Cops Killed Italy's Super Car Market." What if this system were adopted in America? Not only will we lose markets for "super brands," but tired of being hounded, the Mr. Ms may stop buying multiple $330,000 sports cars. As a result, they may not feel the need to continue generating high levels of taxable incomes to pay for these symbols of success.

Let's salute the glittering rich rather than hate them. Many pay the equivalent of 50% of their earned income in various federal and state taxes. Interestingly about 50% of American households pay 0% of their income to the tax man. But what about those 6 out of 42 drivers found by the Italian police to have too little income to pay for their supercars? Could it be that most or all are just living off their considerable capital?

The typical millionaire next door has a realized income that is equivalent to only 8.2% of his wealth (median). But Mr. Buffett is much better at minimizing his income as a function of net worth. According to the 2012 *Forbes* 400 list, Mr. Buffett had a net worth of $46 billion. *CNN Money* reported that "his taxable income was $39,814,784" in 2010.[9] That is the equivalent of only 0.087% of his net worth! Translated, the typical millionaire next door's percentage of realized income to his net worth (8.2%) is nearly 95 times higher than Mr. Buffett's (8.2%/0.087%).

Also consider something else in this equation: income tax as a function of net worth. The typical millionaire next door pays the equivalent of approximately 2% (median) of his net worth in income tax annually. But here again Mr. Buffett is far, far better at minimizing his income tax. According to Reuters, he "paid only $6.9 million in federal income taxes in 2010."[10]

In a nominal sense, $6.9 million in income tax might appear to be a significant amount of money. But look at Mr. Buffett's tax bill as a function of his net worth—that is, $6.9 million as a percentage of his $46 billion in wealth. At this rate he is paying the equivalent of only 0.015% of his net worth. Compare this with the 2% paid by the median millionaire next door. This rate is more than 133 times greater than Mr. Buffett's. In fact, if Mr. Buffett were taxed at the same rate (2%) he would owe the Treasury Department $920,000,000 or nearly $1 billion. You might say that it is un-American not to pay your fair share. But Mr. Buffett gets special dispensation regarding this topic. Why? He has pledged to leave the vast majority of his estate to noble causes. And according to *Forbes*, he has already demonstrated considerable generosity: "He gave $1.5 billion to the Gates Foundation in July [2012], bringing his total giving to $17.5 billion . . . in August he pledged $3 billion of stock to his children's foundations."[11]

And it certainly helps his cause that most if not all of his taxable income comes in the form of long-term capital gains—realized upon disposition of capital assets held for long periods of time—that carry preferentially low federal income tax rates.

Who is more likely to do an efficient job distributing money from your estate, the government or enlightened charitable organizations? You know the answer, and apparently so does Mr. Buffett.

Myth 5: If I Can't Make It, I Can Blame the Rich.

Many of the letters and e-mails that we've received are authored by people who blame others for their lack of economic success with comments such as these:

> *I would really be wealthy if I hadn't paid 3% of the value of my portfolio all these years to an investment manager. He made money every year; I didn't.*

> *My 28-year-old brother, a high school dropout who still lives at home, just received 90% of my grandmother's estate. It didn't help that I had an MBA!*

> *If I had only majored in business, not fine arts (as Mom and Dad insisted). . . .*

Most economically successful people know how to leverage adversity. They have learned how to capitalize upon disadvantages, reversals, biases, nepotism, "bad calls," and lousy luck. They do not dwell on an unfortunate situation; they direct their emotional energy into succeeding rather than resenting. Many a millionaire has told us that their very success was a direct function of experiencing "bad calls" from relatives, teachers, employers, pricey financial advisors, the press, and a myriad of other so-called unbiased referees. Or, as one disinherited multimillionaire recently said, "from proving that my parents bet on the wrong horses."

We know that learned helplessness, the belief that no matter what behavior you engage in you cannot impact your success, can be a great deterrent to building wealth. We've seen this concept of *who is responsible* in our work related to building and maintaining wealth long term. Across multiple samples, the characteristic of behaving and believing that our own actions impact our ultimate financial standing is related to net worth, regardless of one's income or age.[12] Those who believe there is little that can be done on their own to impact their financial success tend to engage in less advantageous financial-related behaviors.[13] Indeed, it appears that believing in myths can be very detrimental to long-term economic success.

But many of the so-called "solutions" to the economic conditions in the United States have governmental regulation and control at their core. When we hear from the media, talking heads, and others, their solutions often have control in mind. Whether on the right or the left of the political spectrum, there seems to be an assumption that we can regulate an individual's way into becoming wealthy. Instead, we would argue that achieving goals begins at home and in our minds, shifting attitudes first and then subsequent behaviors (although the latter could change first): challenging the way things may have always been for you or your family, ignoring what others are doing by way of consumer-driven frenzies, and focusing time and energy on achieving goals, both financial and otherwise.

More with Ranger X. Rich

Back to our parking attendant: Ranger X. Rich had always been an outdoor type. This is one of the major reasons he took a job as a natural resources ranger for the state. Before the last recession, he was assigned to patrolling wilderness parks and forests. He loved his job. Pride and enhanced self-esteem were products of the tasks involved in protecting the state's natural resources. But shortly after the recession hit in 2008, things changed for Ranger X. Rich. Cutbacks and a hiring freeze necessitated that he adopt a different job description. Today he no longer does any patrolling in the wilderness areas and no more rounding up violators of game laws. Today he is relegated to being a monitor, patrolling parking lots and giving out tickets to those who don't pay to park. Other times he mans parking lot booths, collecting parking fees.

Today Ranger X. Rich dislikes his job. But he realizes that if he wants to continue working for the state he has to accept this parking-related assignment. In his mind, it's not the recession that's the root cause of his low job satisfaction. The recession, according to Ranger X. Rich, was caused by "the rich." Note that he did not elaborate nor detail a definition of "the rich" and how they caused the recession. He just was certain that the rich were ultimately responsible for the change of job description. It was their fault that he's no longer a "protector of natural resources." He's become essentially a parking lot attendant and "ticketer." Color him unhappy with his job and angry with the rich.

Ranger X. Rich never even tried to improve his job skills by taking continuing education courses. He could have made himself more marketable. If he loves the woods, forests, and trees so much, he could have taken night courses in timber management, forest farming, and so on. Several colleges in his area offer such courses and many more related ones. Often, by going back to school, students have a chance to interact with classmates whose employers are looking to fill job openings in these areas.

From the time they both started working, Ranger X. Rich and his wife had a good chance of becoming part of the blue-collar-affluent segment. But instead this blue-collar couple chose to travel down the income-statement affluent highway. This working-class, two-income household, given their lower-middle-class occupational status, education, and related socioeconomic characteristics, was not "socially required" to live in an expensive house in a tony neighborhood. Nor were they socially required to wear pricey clothes to work. Nor did they feel obligated to dress up for social occasions. Given their low overhead, their family could have easily saved or invested 20% of their realized annual income each year they were working. But they went in a different direction: no budget, no financial plan, and no contributions to the "pay yourself first fund."

Myth 6: I Cannot Get Ahead on My Own.

For the most part, America is still a country where you can create a business and succeed without regard to your religion, the color of your skin, or whether your family arrived here yesterday or 250 years ago. If you can produce something or a service of value, either in an employment setting or in self-employment, you have the opportunity to prosper in America. This freedom continues to attract people of all nations to our shores: approximately 13% of our 311 million citizens are first-generation Americans.[14]

Regardless of how long your family has been in the United States, or what country you originated from, the critical wealth-related questions you must answer are these:

- Can you create something (a product or service) of value that generates revenue, and then, can you keep and invest that money to make it grow?

- Can you use your skills and experience to create a career working for others that allows you to save consistently and leads to satisfaction?

- Can you be disciplined enough to save money and aware enough to understand how markets (employment, financial) are changing and how your skills need to change over time?

- Can you ignore the distractions of consumerism and media?

Anyone, regardless of ethnicity, race, religion, or gender, can use their knowledge, skills, abilities, and other characteristics to add value through working or by starting their own business. But hard work and discipline are required—even more so if the cards you are dealt are disadvantageous.

The topic of income inequality is a popular one. It is true that the bottom one-fifth of income-producing households in America progressively accounts for a smaller and smaller percentage of total income, while the top one-fifth continues to account for an increasing proportion of the income pie.

So is it true, as the media purports, that "the rich are getting richer while the poor are getting poorer?" Note that today, as in 1996, most people, including the press, confuse income with wealth. America is supposed to be the land of economic opportunity. Our data suggests that this is still the case. The variations between the top and bottom categories of income are real. But not all those who were in the bottom group 20 years ago are still there today. Nor do all of those who were at the top remain in that position. There is a tremendous amount of socioeconomic mobility in our country. Even within one generation people tend to encounter this mobility by moving up or moving down. It is even more pronounced within the context of multiple generations. As many parents find out too late, most of the children of self-made millionaires do not repeat their parents' success.

But still, many continue to argue that this wealth must certainly be inherited, and that those who are getting wealthier are simply the recipients of gifts or transfers. Contrary to that assertion, 86% of millionaires report having 0% of their prior year's income derived from gifts, inheritances, or trust funds, and north of 86% report having received no more than 10% of their net worth from these transfer sources.[15] Indeed, as in 1996, our data indicates that most millionaires build wealth on their own.

Self-Made in America?
Self-made wealth is not a new trend in America. According to economist Stanley Lebergott, an 1892 study of millionaires found that 84% were first-generation affluent. Our research findings are also congruent with those of Professor Steven G. Horwitz. He takes issue with those economists who tell us that "the U.S. is suffering from a widening gap between the rich and poor." One's lot as either rich or poor is not cast in cement like it is in many nondemocratic nations. As Horowitz states, "According to U.S. Treasury data, an astounding 86% of households that constituted the bottom fifth in 1979 had climbed out of poverty by 1988." The bottom fifth he refers to is composed of "newly formed households . . . recent high school graduates, new immigrants . . . taking their first steps up the income ladder."[16]

America: Where Millionaires Are Still Self-Made

One of the most surprising aspects of The Millionaire Next Door *was the finding that 80% of millionaires were self-made. We continue to see this trend today, despite some who insist that the era of becoming wealthy without heavy economic outpatient care or incredible luck is long past. My father discussed this in a blog in 2014:*

In my decades of surveying and studying millionaires, I have consistently found that 80 to 86% are self-made. That also applies to decamillionaires. In 1982, according to *Forbes*, about 38% of America's wealthiest people were self-made. In 2012, the percentage jumped to 70%.[17]

In what many consider to be the most exhaustive study of socioeconomic mobility in America, Professors Chetty of Harvard and Saez of California-Berkeley studied about 50 million federal income tax returns of parents and their adult children.[18] Part of this study as mentioned in the *Wall Street Journal* stated that "The odds of a child moving up the economic ladder have remained the same for about the past three decades . . . that contradicts the narrative in Washington that economic mobility has declined in recent years."

Economic opportunities continue to abound in this country. Yet most Americans are not wealthy. It is easy to blame the so-called "inequities" in our economy. But it is more about the fact that Americans spend all or most of their income on things that have little or no lasting value! They lack the discipline required to accumulate wealth. Most households are on a treadmill of working and consuming. The typical American household has a median annual realized income within the $50,000 to under $75,000 bracket. Only 6.3% of these people have any realized capital gains income.

Even so, a similar *New York Times* headline from 2014 concurs with the findings of Chetty and Saez with this headline: "Upward Mobility Has Not Declined, Study Says."[19] Articles such as these should be shared with friends and especially with children. When the economic winners of today look back on their attitudes and beliefs during their early years, what do they tell us? Much of their success can be attributed to their belief that they could succeed and that economic opportunities abound in America. Their belief and reality are congruent. It is unfortunate that an increasing number of media reports claim that the tide of economic opportunity is increasingly against upward economic mobility.

Keep in mind that the study mentioned above deals only with intergenerational contrasts in terms of income. Income is a correlate of wealth, aka net worth. But given the choice of a measure of economic success, it's wise to select net worth over one's income. Only a minority of the variation in wealth is explained by income and, of course, vice versa. Studies dating from the late 1800s up to today indicate that 80% or more of those in the high-net-worth category are self-made affluent. And it matters little whether "affluent" is defined in terms of millionaires, decamillionaires, top 5%, top 2%, top 1%, of wealth holders and so on.

In terms of actual wealth (not using income as a surrogate), we have consistently found that at least 80% of America's millionaires are self-made. In *Stop Acting Rich*, with data collected in 2005 and 2006, about one in four millionaires (24%) reported that their fathers were blue-collar workers (the largest occupational category to produce millionaires). Nineteen percent were owners of small businesses; 4% were farmers. Conversely only 9% were senior corporate executives while 3% were physicians. Only 47% of their fathers and 40% of their mothers attended college. About one in three millionaires paid for their own college expenses. About 42% of the millionaires had a net worth of zero or less when they began working full-time. Most (88%) reported receiving zero dollars from trusts, estates, gifts, etc. from relatives in the year prior to being surveyed. Today only one-third of millionaires indicated that their parents were better off than their high school classmates, and essentially the same percentage (approximately 63–65%) indicated that their parents were very frugal.

Myth 7: The Rich Are Evil.

There is a growing concern among wealthy people that members of the press and politicians are portraying them as "evil." No doubt that among a population of an estimated 5 to 10 million millionaire households in America there are some no-goodniks among them. But the vast majority of people who are wealthy did it the old-fashioned way—they earned it legitimately. In spite of all of the research that we and others have published about the traditional values of most wealthy people, that is not what gets the headlines.

My father received the following e-mail from Mr. D.P. of Texas who suggested a countermeasure to enlighten our youth about the true nature of the rich:

> *Have you considered creating/marketing a curriculum based on your work with* The Millionaire Mind *to the public schools? After all, in most public schools we currently teach our children to despise and make enemies of the "rich"; maybe if we taught them to emulate them instead we could actually get on top of the situation before they entered the work force, and make more wealth for everyone. I am contemplating a run for school board here in my home town, and would love to see something like this for the children of Texas and the United States.*

It is indeed flattering to receive comments like this. There was even a wealthy man from a "one–high school" town in Oklahoma who purchased a copy of *The Millionaire Next Door* for every graduating senior. These are just a few of the people who have given their time and energy to teach our children how to become financially independent and to appreciate such a goal.

Honesty and Getting Along

There's much ado about honesty and integrity related to wealth. The concept of the evil Mr. Scrooge seems to be omnipresent through time. Certainly Ranger X. Rich believed in this persona. But the research on the personality factor of conscientiousness, and its cousin, integrity, demonstrates their importance in the pursuit of financial goals, as we'll discuss in Chapter 5. And take for example Dr. Lawrence in the Pacific Northwest, an optometrist millionaire worth more than $5 million today, and the creation of a business that ultimately used both his interests and expertise, but was founded based upon ensuring his customers came first. He shared this with us:

> *[I] enjoyed a career enhancing and preserving the human vision system. Optometry is a healthcare career which still allows one to be independent and entrepreneurial. I developed a strong practice by always placing the needs and desires of the patient first and foremost. With a combination of "word of mouth" referrals and advancing technology, I gradually developed a thriving practice. Although my practice was never "For Sale," a young doctor approached me for the purpose of taking over the practice. At the age of 61, I sold the practice to him and now work 2 days per week for him. My original intention was never to acquire wealth. However, I learned that if one practices with good and honorable intentions, that may happen. Always be sincere, honest, forward thinking and future focused. With the exception of our home, all purchases were paid with money which had already been saved. This eliminates those spur of the moment and emotional purchases which are frequently regretted at a later date.*

The Motives of Millionaires . . . and Billionaires

The perception of the "evil rich" is occasionally demystified by the very organizations that often perpetuate the myths in the first place. Take these examples from my father about the benevolence of the affluent:

In a 2011 article in *The New York Times*, Andrew Ross Sorkin explored Steve Jobs's motivation for success and wrote, "Mr. Jobs has clearly never craved money for money's sake and has never been ostentatious with his wealth. He took a $1 a year salary from Apple before stepping down as CEO. . . ."[20]

Mr. Jobs, who was a billionaire at the time of his death, had much in common with the typical millionaire next door who achieves a great deal but not for the sake of a hyper-consumption lifestyle. For example, Mr. Allan, who was profiled in *The Millionaire Next Door*, stated succinctly, "If your motive is to make money to spend money on the good life. . . you're never going to make it. Money should never change one's values . . . making money is only a report card. It's a way to tell how you're doing."

Mr. Jobs is quoted in Sorkin's article as saying, "You know, my main reaction to this money thing is that it's humorous, all the attention to it, because it's hardly the most insightful or valuable thing that's happened to me."

The motives of the millionaires next door are misunderstood by most people. Building wealth is much more about becoming financially independent than living in a mansion surrounded by expensive artifacts. In a 2011 article published by *The American Thinker*, Chris Corrado provides an excellent counter to those who advocate increasing the taxes of the so-called "rich."[21] He briefly discusses the characteristics of the millionaires profiled in *The Millionaire Next Door*:

"Thomas J. Stanley's insightful book tells us that the majority of wealthy people live quite frugally, and about 80% of them are first generation rich, receiving little to none of their wealth from inheritance. . . . It's hard [for advocates of taxing the rich] to talk about the greedy rich guy when he drives a 2004 pick-up truck and gets his clothes from Ross.

Instead, the conventional picture of wealth is a morally questionable man in an Italian suit, driving a Ferrari onto his yacht before enjoying a cruise on the Mediterranean while smoking fine cigars lit with $100 bills— and don't forget about the corporate jet. This is the picture of wealth from the perspective of the left, and it is very politically advantageous. If anyone deserves to be resented and hated for his excesses, it's certainly this oppressive character, no matter how fictitious he may be."

The Family with the Most Millionaires

The head of private banking for a large financial institution in New York once shared an interesting case study with my father. An attorney from small-town America referred a very wealthy client couple to this banker. The couple wanted to establish a banking relationship with an out-of-state institution. Like many wealthy people who live in small towns, they did not want the local establishment to know about the "considerable" wealth they had accumulated. This was especially important because they were anticipating cashing in many of their chips from a variety of businesses that they owned. They also planned to donate anonymously a significant portion of their wealth to a variety of charities.

Shortly after the couple arrived at the private bank in New York City, the banker began telling them about all of the ancillary services that clients could access including hard-to-get theater tickets, endorsements to join upscale clubs, A-list co-ops or townhouses for sale, art and antique purchases, and so on. After about 10 minutes of this, the wife pulled out a copy of a book from her large handbag. She placed it on the banker's desk and pointed to it. Then she said, "This is who we are, the millionaire next door. You ought to read this if you haven't already."

After the banker's red face returned to normal, they all laughed, which cut the tension in the room. The couple had made it abundantly clear that they wanted only the traditional financial services provided by a private banking operation, including anonymity. They weren't interested in hiring a consigliere, nor did they need their egos enhanced by gaining access to the New York social scene. Further they had no intention of buying a townhouse or any other residence in New York City.

Empathy for the needs of others is the key to success when marketing to millionaires. The banker in this case should have asked the couple, "How did you go from ground zero to where you are today?" In other words, the banker should have allowed the couple to tell their story. In most cases, no one ever asks the millionaire next door about his history and achievements.

This couple is part of an American "family" that has the highest number of millionaires. Yes, they are part of an anonymous family. My father was on a mailing list for a variety of annual reports from foundations, universities, and other organizations of the noble or charitable variety. It seems that no matter where he looked, Mr. and Mrs. Anonymous were listed in the reports, often under the five-, six-, seven-figure or more dollar categories.

Beyond the Myths

Why is it that some people can build wealth? Why are others, often with a higher than average income, a good education, and little in the way of hardships, unable to build wealth on their own? Perhaps they subscribe to Ranger X. Rich's myths. Without really knowing it, they buy in to the constant barrage of news, opinions, and self-fulfilling prophesies of the myths of wealth.

The economically successful in this country will continue to ignore myths, including some of those adopted by so-called experts and those with political agendas. Ranger X. Rich's disdain for the rich is emotional energy not well spent. He is caught up in negative emotion while at the same time ignoring his own serious lack of financial discipline. His social media feed includes a steady diet of biased news and one-sided commentary. Think about this issue in another way. Ranger X. Rich does not have enough money or net worth to afford spending time and energy hating the rich. Purposely selecting specific targets for his parking ticket campaign will never make him financially independent.

We have found that hate in general terms is a significant substitute for—not a complement to—wealth-building. What if Ranger X. Rich were to reallocate the time and energy resources that are required for him to maintain his habit of hate to a more productive goal such as becoming financially independent? If he did so, he would have much less time to hate the rich and his current job. It's ironic that many people who have low job satisfaction share something in common. They don't take intentional steps to ensure they don't have to be dependent on the jobs they dislike.

Often, we write about upper-middle-class people with good to great incomes. Given their social status, many of them feel required to spend, spend, spend, on luxury homes, prestige motor vehicles, expensive clothing, luxury vacations at exotic resorts, and so forth. But Ranger X. Rich and his family don't have this type of burden, so why is it that they are not close to being financially secure? It's because the Ranger X. Rich team is in the hyper-consumption category.

Ranger X. Rich, and those who buy into the myths of wealth, can learn a great deal from America's millionaires. Most don't hold grudges or hate on their way up the financial ladder. Yes, they have been ripped off at one time or another. But they move on, focusing on the positive. Hate does not build a career or a balance sheet. Better financial behaviors go hand in hand with increased financial satisfaction. Nearly 93% of PAWs, those who are astute at

Why Are Some People Poor and Others Rich?

What can we say to help Mr. Rich see past these myths and begin his own path toward economic success? Maybe very little if those beliefs are held closely, but we will try nonetheless. Maybe we can start with this, a blog my father wrote in 2014 which examined the reasons people believed some are rich and others poor:

The answer to this question was the focus of a national survey of 1,504 adults conducted earlier by the Pew Research Center.[22] Only about 4 in 10 (38%) of the respondents indicated that the rich are rich "because he or she worked harder than others."

But how do millionaires, the people who are actually wealthy, explain their own economic success? Nearly 9 in 10 (88%) rate "hard work" as a very important/important factor.[23]

In the same Pew study, 51% of the respondents were of the opinion that the rich are rich "because he or she had more advantages than others," while 50% indicated that the poor are poorer because of "circumstances beyond his or her control." Contrast these results with the fact that 80% of millionaires in this country are self-made. Also note that 95% of millionaires rated "being well disciplined" as a very important/important component in explaining their economic success.

The wide contrast in the beliefs of the general population as opposed to those of millionaires has many implications especially within the political arena.

Assuming that the Pew study was representative of the adult population in America only about 4–8% of the respondents were millionaires, if that many. How valid therefore are the opinions of those surveyed in this study in explaining the variations in wealth accumulation in this country? The typical American household has a net worth of just over $90,000 and an annual income of approximately $52,000 (2014 figures). What do these people really know about how to become rich?

If your objective is to become financially independent, you may find it more productive to follow the ways, means, and lifestyles of America's self-made millionaires as opposed to those of the population in general.

transforming income into wealth, report being extremely satisfied with life, more so than under accumulators of wealth (84%). Whereas 56% of under accumulators spend time worrying about not achieving financial independence, only just over one in four prodigious accumulators spend any time worrying about that concern. And nearly four out of five under accumulators spend time worrying about retiring in comfort, whereas just two out of five prodigious accumulators worry about the same.

Discounting Myths to Build Wealth

What's left if we ignore the myths of how wealth is built in America? The answer is: our own behaviors, choices, and lifestyle.

Our income, while related statistically to wealth, is not wealth. When we understand this, we start seeing the criticality of our *savings rate*, something driven not by what we make but instead by what we do (how we consume and save). It is up to us to save more than we spend and live below our means. This is a mathematical truth in building wealth.

Once we understand that a lifestyle of consumption, one that is more interested in appearing wealthy, is driving most Americans into a lifetime of dependency, work, and little economic freedom, we can begin to create an alternative plan for our lives and lifestyle. It may look very different than our parents or grandparents, and unless you are lucky, it will look very different than those around you or on your social media feeds.

Once we understand that few outside agencies or benefactors exist that will move the needle on our financial independence, it becomes obvious we can only rely on ourselves. Our financial future is up to us, not to our employer, government, or even family members. When we begin to understand that little outside of our own capabilities will allow us to build wealth, we begin to make decisions about how we spend our time, energy, and money. Taking responsibility for our financial future is a critical component of building wealth, as we'll see in Chapter 5.

If we can appreciate that those who have built wealth on their own aren't universally evil, or good for that matter, we can start examining the behaviors that allowed them to be economically successful instead of blaming them for their success and lamenting our own failures.

If we can move past the myths of wealth in America, perhaps then we can focus on the behaviors and choices that are conducive to building wealth. It is those behaviors and decisions that will ultimately allow us, regardless of our membership in a particular group, the opportunity in a free country to build our own wealth.

Only then can we begin to emulate the behaviors of those who have achieved real economic success. Maybe Mr. Rich will join us.

Chapter 3

Influences on Wealth

You have to do your own growing no matter how tall your grandfather was.
—Irish proverb, attributed to Abraham Lincoln

AS SCIENCE HAS SHOWN IN ALMOST ALL ASPECTS OF OUR LIVES, WHY WE DO
what we do is a combination of nature (our unique characteristics) and nurture
(how we were raised and other outside influences). When we think about behaviors, our nature puts the boundaries around what we will or can do, and nurture
decides, within those boundaries, how we will perform, what we will decide to
do, and so on.

In any discussion of economic success it is critical to focus some amount of
time on the *nurture* side of the equation, examining how our upbringing, choice
of spouse and friends, and social culture can influence how and if we're able to
transform income into wealth. We've found, for example, that harmony within
the family is a strong factor in building the character and prosperity of self-made
millionaires. Over the past three decades, nearly 70% of millionaires in national
surveys reported being raised in an atmosphere of love and harmony, and nearly
three-quarters of them said their parents encouraged them to achieve and excel.

But warmth and affection within households are not a universal condition.
And we cannot choose where we come from, who our parents are, or what kind
of early education we received. We may want to blame our upbringing for our
situation today—and some of that blame may be warranted. But as adults living
in a society that doesn't dictate our choices, we have the freedom to choose with
whom and how we spend our time. Those choices can influence our financial outcomes. Those who are financially independent focus on their own choices, taking
responsibility for their money-related actions and behaviors.

More Than a Class

Some experts have proposed an educational approach to correcting financial illiteracy and poor financial behaviors. But changing financial behaviors is more complex than providing workshops or six-week courses. There's no one class, special manual, or app that will lead to a lifetime of economic achievement. Instead, it requires a consistent pattern of financial behaviors. If this starts early, the likelihood of ongoing success is greater. For example, consider how the early experiences of a millionaire next door, John C., paved the way to behaviors that would become the foundation of his success and for the patterns of behaviors exhibited by his children:

> *I was raised by frugal parents. They didn't have a credit card until they were almost 50 years old—and only then because they started to travel and they couldn't get hotel or car rental reservations without a credit card. My dad spent an hour telling all six of us why they obtained the card and that you never use one unless you have the money to pay it in full by the first due date.*
>
> *I am the fourth of six children and when I was in fourth grade my dad sat us all in the living room and explained how we all were going to college. He would not be able to pay a dime in tuition for us, and we had to pay for it ourselves. We could not buy a car until we graduated college, but he would have used cars for us to get to part-time jobs that he expected us to obtain once we were 15.*
>
> *All six graduated college on our own dime. We six have earned three associate's degrees, four bachelor's degrees, two master's degrees, and two MBAs.*
>
> *My parents only had one debt—ever. A mortgage that was paid in 20 years. Never a car loan, never an equity loan, never a balance on a credit card that wasn't paid in the first month.*
>
> *Me? I hold a bachelor's degree in Finance and an MBA in Marketing and Finance. I have never had a credit card balance that was not paid off in the first month. I have had three car loans in my 28 years of owning cars. All with rates so low, I was able to make more money investing the amount of the loan than I paid in interest.*
>
> *I have a mortgage and one of the three car loans currently but no other debt. According to my 401(k) plan right now, I have more in outside investments than that 401(k) and pension.*

My wife has been a stay at home mom for 20 years raising our two boys. The oldest started college two weeks ago. He earned a scholarship for academics and I have enough saved to pay his tuition and room for all four years. He is paying for his books.

My college son's only paying job has been in my side business. In fourth grade he created designs for our side business that were purchased by customers. I told him that any money his designs earned, I would deduct the cost of producing the pieces, I also would deduct the taxes I would have to pay on the income since the sale occurred through my business. He could keep the rest, but 80% had to be put into savings for college. Ten percent also had to be put into savings because in life you have unexpected expenses and you need to have money ready to replace a washing machine, fix the car, or pay a medical bill. The final 10% he could spend, but his mother and I had to approve the purchase.

The first sale in fourth grade resulted in him earning $3,000 after paying me for production and taxes. He had $300 to spend on whatever he wanted. He saved the entire amount. And only several months later decided to purchase an iPod for far less than $300.

When he turned 15 he started to do the shipping paperwork for the side business. He did the unloading and inspecting of the product, he did the bookkeeping. He earned minimum wage. He sold a few more designs for good paydays. He invested in CDs in grade school. He volunteered at a local hospital.

He left for college with $15,000 in the bank, which was three times what I had when I went away to college. He started a side business of his own while in school.

My other 16-year-old son is following in his brother's footsteps. His grades are high honor roll too, and although he doesn't have the bank account up there yet, he has two years to get another $5,000 to match his brother.

Neither owns a car, neither has a credit card, both have paid for their own electronics. In grade school when they wanted the latest Game Boy, we told them they had to sell the current version they owned and could use the money to help pay for it. They learned how to keep things clean and in their original boxes because they could sell them for more money on eBay that way.

After a while they realized they could buy electronics used for much less than brand new, and they often sold their old version for nearly what they paid when they bought them used.

Are they going to turn out affluent? Time will tell. But they have a great start.

Obtaining outcomes like those in John's family is a combination of nature and nurture as we discussed earlier. But, the nurture side is the one we can control today. How willing are parents today to do the following in order to have a chance at achieving the outcomes John and his siblings, as well as John's children, had?

- Encouraging your child to save his or her own money.
- Encouraging or requiring your children to work.
- Having your children pay for their own electronics (latest smartphones included).
- Teaching responsibility with consumer goods and respect for the toys they have.
- Saving for your child's college education (both parent and child).

John's disciplined approach to raising his children, which included teaching them to respect money, requires a pattern of tough choices, choices that may not be conducive to a consumer-driven, social-media-sharing life.

Training for Economic Success

Let's consider how our experiences growing up can impact the financial decisions we make today. Few other factors help shape how we save and spend money like our upbringing and our family's influence. We can't say for sure that this nurture component is necessarily the *cause* of wealth, but there is certainly a correlation.

Financially successful people share many similar characteristics, as we'll discuss more in-depth in Chapter 5. But they also have similar early experiences: They often come from stable family backgrounds, they are well disciplined, and they are goal oriented. Even without stable childhood and adolescent experiences, they also have a propensity to overcome large obstacles by dissecting them into small pieces. In most cases, a seven-figure net worth begins with the first dollar saved, and then another and another—a pattern of consistent behaviors over time, versus a fleeting season of financial prudence.

Of course, you can be raised in a lovingly harmonious house and have little to no exposure to or experience with financial management. In other words, your blissful childhood could be completely devoid of any financial education or modeling.

We know, for example, that in this country alone, financial literacy is embarrassingly low. The TIAA Institute-GFLEC Personal Finance Index measures financial knowledge across several different areas of personal finance. In one of their studies, they found that only 16% of Americans had what they called a "high level of personal finance knowledge and understanding," which they determined by the respondents answering more than 75% of the survey questions correctly. On the other end of the spectrum, one in five had a lower level of knowledge.[1]

Research on adolescent and childhood life experiences demonstrates how our early years can have a dramatic and predictive effect on our careers, incomes, and personalities as adults. Research started in the psychology department at the University of Georgia back in the 1960s by a professor named William Owens demonstrated the effects of environment and adolescent life experiences on a number of adult-related outcomes. Dr. Owens and his students began surveying college freshman in the late 1960s and 1970s, and later when they were adults in the 1990s. The researchers found that college freshmen who had similar life experiences, including everything from the number of magazines and newspapers in their homes to the affection shown by their parents, tend to have similar career choices, personalities, and income levels later in life as adults.[2] Of course, some of these experiences are more likely in households with higher socioeconomic status.

In one of our studies with mass affluent and high-net-worth Americans from 2012 to 2013, we asked about patterns of adolescent experiences and behaviors on building wealth. We found that parental frugality and willingness to teach their children money management impact their children's ability to transform income into wealth. Our research conducted with both middle-income as well as affluent individuals found that *parental frugality* was positively related to children's net worth. In other words, if your parents' overall behavior was conducive to building wealth, there's a greater chance yours will be, too. Adult children who reported that their parents were frugal, discussed money-related matters, and demonstrated good money management skills were more likely to be prodigious accumulators of wealth compared to those who did not experience this same type of upbringing.

One study from the University of Minnesota provides rich insights on the influence of family lifestyle and parental influence on children in the realm of finances.[3] Researchers found that parents provide three themes of financial management to children including saving, how money is managed, and how financial matters are discussed. The vast majority of children in these studies learned about a family's propensity for saving and financial management through direct observation versus through conversations regarding these behaviors. In other words, parental behaviors tend to stick with children more so than discussions of what ought to be done related to money.

Despite these results, when it comes to what contributed to their success, our millionaires tend to rate parental influence as less important than other factors such as resiliency and hard work (see Chapter 5, Table 5.5). Fully 42% of millionaires indicated that having engaged or involved parents contributed to their success, and 59% stated that their success was due to having supportive parents.

Moving Past Early Experiences

What other types of early experiences can impact our financial outcomes? In addition to seeing good money management modeled by our parents and caregivers, financial stress can also have an impact on our financial trajectory. In fact, our millionaire respondents had some interesting observations from their childhoods during which they witnessed firsthand how finances can impact families and relationships. Many of these situations highlight the importance of moving past negative experiences:

I saw a lot of people my age whose parents threw money at them as if it was nothing, and these people turned out to be some very poor examples of humans, e.g., the daughter who received a new Mercedes for her birthday (as her first car), crashed it within a week, and then received another one.
—millionaire from New Jersey with a net worth of $1.2 million

[My] parents were a prime example of how not to manage money.
—millionaire from Miami, Florida, with a net worth of $1.9 million

I watched my father struggle with money management. Though he had a white-collar job, no matter how much money he made, he never had money. He spent it.
—business owner from Nashville, Tennessee, with a net worth of $1.1 million

[I] heard my parents fight about losing our home. Wish I would have learned about credit, savings, investments.
—managing director from Clearwater, Florida, with a net worth of $1.7 million

The stress of poor money management is not often lost on children, as this emerging millionaire next door (with a net worth of $825,000) from a small town in Georgia, recounted for us:

> *In high school I started to realize how financially stressed my parents were in spite of the fact that they worked very hard. In retrospect, I now realize that my dad was* horrible *with money. If he earned $50,000, he spent $60,000. All financial decisions were made with a sense of desperation. My mother has suffered greatly due to his financial immaturity/innumeracy. In spite of having millions of dollars pass through his businesses, my parents now live on Social Security. I blame that on my father. Almost all of my financial decisions now are made from the perspective of my father . . . I simply do the opposite of what he would do. . . . I wish I had learned about the importance of saving money, investing money, prudent credit usage, and net worth accumulation. I got* none *of this from my parents. However, my parents love my siblings and me greatly. They were great parents, but did not teach us about money. . . . At ages thirty-three and thirty-one my wife and I had a net worth of $−40,000; today at ages fifty and forty-eight we're worth $825,000. What changed? We started maxing out our retirement plans: 403(b) and IRAs. We also made sure to keep our debt load down. Luckily, we figured out how to manage our money, but we could have easily squandered our financial lives just like my parents did. . . . It is not fun writing about my parents' failings with money, but I hope my insights will help current and future parents realize the importance of teaching your children about money. We are drilling the importance of money management into our eight-year-old son. He will tell you very quickly that family and friends are much more important than money. At the same time, he will tell you that money is important because poor money management can ruin your life.*

Depending on the experiences you had while growing up, you could have had effective or ineffective practices engrained in your psyche, but it is your behaviors *now* that will make the difference in your economic success.

Respect for Money

Knowledge about finances is critical to building wealth, but *discipline* often plays an even greater role in savings and spending. The combination of the two, that is, financial knowledge *and* self-control in spending, can be a powerful mix for future financial success. Financial literacy and personal conscientiousness have been linked positively to holding assets (illiquid and liquid).[4] Researchers in one study concluded that linking financial literacy, discipline, and financial success provided "*support for early childhood, adolescent, and adult interventions aimed at improving self-control*."[5]

Wealth is attracted to people who respect money, and respect for money includes the *discipline* required to manage it effectively. Those who do not budget or account for annual consumption categories demonstrate a lack of respect for money. Children who are raised in such households tend to turn out like their parents and become "income-statement affluent." About 70% of millionaires in our latest study stated that their parents were very frugal.

My father shared that he had interviewed many millionaire-next-door types who never had a total realized household income in excess of $100,000, but they could tell you to the dollar amount how much they allocated to every consumption category in their budget. And they also constructed an annual budget based on their anticipated income, their consumption categories, and money set aside for investing, retirement, college funds, and so on. Imagine the impact on children who are socialized in an environment in which money is respected. As they watch their parents take account of their finances, they are exposed to the skills that will allow them to build wealth as adults.

Consider the experiences you had growing up related to financial management. If money was a taboo subject, or you never heard your parents or caregivers utter the phrase "that's not in the budget this month," the foundation of your financial behaviors may have a very different pattern from the early life experiences of a millionaire next door named Christy, whom my father first profiled in *Millionaire Women Next Door*. She attributes much of her success to her upbringing and particularly gives credit to her parents' diligence and openness in helping her develop a respect for money. Her father was a career army sergeant. Her mother was a full-time homemaker. Household budgeting and a frugal family lifestyle were part of her earliest socialization process. She explains, "We would all sit down the first Sunday afternoon of each month. We didn't have much money. . . . We would always look at Daddy's paycheck and then start doing our homework."

Her parents gave priority to charitable pledges, then outstanding bills, and then the upcoming expenses for the month were estimated. Christy recalled her parents smiling while they earmarked a good portion of their household income to their children's college funds: "I knew how hard it was for them to save for us to go to college. But each time Daddy wrote a check for the college fund he would smile and say . . . 'I love writing checks that will pay the tuition bills. You can do this for your kids someday.'"

One of the reasons for Christy's success today is the nurturing environment her parents provided. Christy and her siblings were respected as members of the family planning board. They learned early on about budgeting and planning. They had to justify their requests for a new notebook or new shoes. These experiences prepared Christy for her present vocation as a business leader.

Of course, extreme frugality can have a negative effect, especially if it feels like deprivation. In some cases, individuals who experience this during their childhoods may ultimately decide that any caution in saving or spending is not worth repeating in their own households. Time will tell if children in extremely frugal homes will view the frugal lifestyle of their upbringing positively. Some financially successful Americans who had this type of background have been able to take the best aspects of extreme frugality and use them to their financial advantage.

Table 3-1. Early Experiences of Millionaires

Statement	Percentage Strongly Agree/Agree		
	1996	2000	2016
Parents were frugal/lived below means?	66	61	70
Parents encouraged me to achieve & excel?	-	63	73
Raised in an atmosphere of love & harmony?	-	-	70
Parents were better off than high school classmates?	-	-	32

Young CPA Lives by the Principles Found in
The Millionaire Next Door

The early experiences and continued support of financial mentors can have a significant impact on financial success and can prepare those who receive any type of considerable financial gift from avoiding the trap of increased consumption based on the windfall. Consider the following case study of a millionaire next door who maintained effective financial behaviors despite a considerable gift from her parents. My father wrote this piece in 2014:

Many millionaire-next-door types and those on their way were raised in a nurturing environment filled with harmony, mutual respect, discipline, and frugality. As an example, here is a case study from one of my readers:

"While still in high school, my parents had both my brother and I read *The Millionaire Next Door*. The topic was something that interested us both, and we saw numerous similarities in the way our parents ran our family. My dad was a long-time state employee who worked 37.5 hours a week and was always present in our lives. My mom was a stay-at-home mom who loved shopping at garage sales. We ate out 4 times a year . . . My brother and I worked since we were very little because we enjoyed it! My parents gave us each an allowance so we could learn to manage money and not just ask for it whenever we needed it. My brother and I are now [in our late 20s] and the lessons we learned when we were young have paid off. . . . We lost my mom 3 years ago and due to her passing, our family has received a substantial amount of money. My father has kept a significant portion of it, but also passed down approximately $250K each to my brother and me. My dad has continued to live in the same house he had before and still drives his 2003 Toyota Avalon. My brother opted to buy a house in the same neighborhood, [and] still works and drives his 2005 Toyota Camry. I still work (at a very demanding job as a CPA) and choose to live in a house with four other girls, which is great for many reasons, including rent well below the average just outside of [Washington] DC. . . . I have left the inheritance in my investment account and continue to aggressively save 20% of my income for retirement. We are not misers, and we all enjoy some little luxuries. For me it's travel, for my brother it's good food, but it is all within our means. . . . I tell this story because I think my brother and I are anomalies in America today. When most 23 and 26 [year olds] (the ages we were when we received the inheritance) receive such a large amount (and often times, when they receive even smaller amounts) the kids quit their jobs, buy a fancy sports car, spend it all on shopping sprees & travel or numerous other activities. My brother and I kept our jobs, kept our same cars and have not changed our lifestyle one bit, simply because we know how to be content."

So, by preparing their children early in life to have a healthy view of money and equipping them with the tools to effectively manage it, these parents gave their kids (and themselves) the invaluable gift of liberation from economic outpatient care and a running start toward early financial independence.

The Experience of Hyper-Spending

The head of a wealth management firm who works primarily with high-income, high-net-worth individuals in the Southeast shared with us that his clients' wealth experiences were different than those featured in *The Millionaire Next Door*. Most of his clients are wealthy not because they are frugal but because their income is so high that, for the most part, it covers their expenses. Indeed, there are some people who may be able to amass great wealth without having to be frugal.

In a similar vein, in *Stop Acting Rich*, my father profiled people he called the "glittering rich." These are people whose incomes and net worth are so high that most of them do not have a household budget. They don't plan. They don't seem to need to. No matter what they spend their money on, it's just a fraction of their overall net worth. In other words, even the glittering rich spend below their means. If you are in this group, fantastic. You are in the top 1% of wealth holders in the United States.

Starting out with a high income, but without achieving that elite glittering-rich level, could lead one down a different path. Contrast an upbringing that is steeped in frugality and fiscal constraint with one of profligate spending and in displaying consumer behaviors that are in no way constrained. Yes, the glittering rich can do this with little consequence for generations beyond. But some of the income-statement affluent persuasion or under accumulator of wealth persuasion, likely model conspicuous consumption in what they drive, wear, or accessorize with, or in where they travel and how they entertain. In effect, this is *telling* their children and others around them that they spend money and what they value.

Let's imagine that children of high-income, self-made parents experience this type of childhood: riding in a luxury car on their way to a private school; having the latest in technology and fashion before their peers; taking trips to exotic, foreign lands; eating dinner in restaurants with names they can barely pronounce. Will these children be able to give up such luxuries once they are living on their own? Will they understand that Mom and Dad have a level of wealth that only a few will amass, and that this consumption was fueled by high incomes? These may be concepts that 10-year-olds cannot grasp. Indeed, economic outpatient care may be on the horizon.

In fact, one of the most frequently asked questions from readers of *The Millionaire Next Door* is, "Why are my adult children hyper-consumers?" The answer is simple and straightforward: Hyper-spending parents tend to raise hyper-spending children. These parents violated Rule 1 for raising productive adults from *The Millionaire Next Door*:

Never tell your children that you're wealthy.

Even worse, in many cases, parents *signal* wealth to their kids through hyper-consumption even though they don't have the wealth to back it up (just the income).

Despite high incomes and high net worth, even despite being in the glittering-rich category, some parents in this group decide to employ restraint in spending. Why? Perhaps they recognize two truisms about ensuring financial success: not sharing with children how wealthy you are, and frugality as an important, if not critical component in building wealth.

For those not fortunate enough to inherit large lump sums or to be the beneficiary of a trust fund, the only surefire way to amass wealth over time is by *spending less than you earn*. It's a function of discipline and math. As we'll discuss more in Chapter 4, frugality is a set of behaviors that predicts net worth independent of one's age, income, and percentage of wealth that has been received through gifts or inheritance. For those building wealth on their own, it is a requirement. As my father noted in *The Millionaire Next Door*:

Being frugal is the cornerstone of wealth-building.

If you're not glittering rich, while you and your children may be taken care of by the wealth you have accumulated, without prudence in saving and spending (that is, being frugal) on the part of your children, it's less likely that it will last to fund your grandchildren. Unless you are glittering rich, your grandchildren will not have the luxury of not planning, at least not without accumulating wealth on their own. And if your parents "acted rich" (something you may only learn later in life), you may have developed the sense that you can't "make it" like they did if your sense of making it requires a steady display of consumer goods and luxury items.

The Upside of Veering Off Course

Your parents and caregivers, your upbringing, and money-related lessons learned while growing up can all influence your spending, saving, and investing behaviors and ultimately impact your financial success. The promising news is that despite the path we're on because of our early experiences, it can be altered, albeit sometimes slowly, through an intentional change in behaviors.

It's worth noting that many of the millionaires studied over the past 20-plus years succeeded *despite* earlier experiences of adversity. Even when the odds were stacked against them, they found a way to survive and be successful. We have a choice of whether what we've endured in the past or the way our caregivers behaved will set the tone for our financial lives forevermore. Consider the stories of some of the millionaires next door who shared their early life experiences with us:

> *My parents were always big spenders, and never really saved. They appeared to be rich but [were] not. My father died at age 61 without much money to give my mom. . . . All of this pain has caused me to go the exact opposite direction.*
>
> —Business owner with a net worth of $2 to 2.5 million

> *I saw my father as a spendthrift, spending "rent money" (so to speak) on extravagant artwork and other status items that I couldn't understand because my mother would gripe that we never had "enough" money. I was the one who my dad would make answer the phone at home. At the time my mother was working second shift as a nurse. Several times a month it was Mastercharge or American Express trying to track him (my dad) down . . . They wanted to get paid and let's say it made an impression on a 14-year-old. They were divorced by the time I was 16 and I think it saved my mom's life. So the one thing: spending more than you make is a road to ruin.*
>
> —Marketing executive from Ohio with a net worth of $7 million

Many great men and women have been able to ignore the odds in order to beat them. In a way, they display a confident disregard for what is *probably* going to happen and instead focus on the hope for something better. Think about the failure rates for new businesses, the likelihood of becoming a leader within an organization, the chances of marital success, or the possibility of becoming financially independent. If we paid too much attention to the odds without considering our own behaviors and choices, we might not try in the first place. Consider this example from a soon-to-be millionaire next door, an engineer from Wisconsin:

> *I was twenty-three years old, newly divorced, with no job skills and struggling to support two kids on a minimum wage job. My grandparents were travelling in the area and dropped in unexpectedly. My phone was disconnected so they couldn't call ahead. My grandfather asked the most important question I've ever been asked: "Why do you want to live like this?" Of course, nobody wants to live like that, but he explained that we live in America and you don't have to be broke unless you choose to. Eventually he persuaded me to go to college and get a degree in engineering. Only in America!*

Or the case of this executive from Georgia, who now has a net worth of $1 to $1.5 million:

> *My mother (who was close to retirement) lost her job a few years ago. This event put extra pressure on my father who was four years older and working to pay for a new expensive house that they had just purchased with a 30-year mortgage. . . . Throughout my life growing up in my parents' home, it always seemed that my parents were financially strapped. Always paying for things with credit, financing new cars, etc. Looking back on [this] pattern of behavior, I vowed to not live the same way with my family and [have] done a decent job of staying out of debt, paying for vehicles with cash except for the big fancy home with a large mortgage that we owned. . . . This is an eye opener for me . . . [in my family] I was the only working spouse (my wife stayed home with the kids). I became resolute to pay off the mortgage as quickly as possible and have true financial freedom for my family.*

The cases above represent just a few of the stories and anecdotes collected over the past 20 years that demonstrate there are ways around an upbringing that is less than ideal for building wealth. These economically successful individuals, perhaps *because* of these early experiences, sought a life that was financially free, and set about achieving those goals. But, that change in trajectory came because they altered their attitudes toward financial goals and (most importantly) their behaviors, aligning them both to be conducive to building wealth.

The Real American Dream?

In our hyper-consuming, distracted society, we forget (or ignore) the great free-doms we are afforded in the United States, freedoms won by individuals who sacrificed much. Many of the millionaires who shared their stories with us have little or no recollection of their families' journey to this country. Many of us have no concept of our ancestors' journeys, the price they paid emotionally and psychologically and financially for the voyage to live and work in the United States. Instead of considering that journey and respecting the cost, we take for granted the opportunities afforded in our country. Learning from those who have recently joined us, those who have immigrated to the United States and begun a new life, paints a different type of picture. In the following paragraphs, another reader, Ms. H, provides a unique view of how her immigrant mother became a multimillionaire:

> I was raised by a single mom who immigrated to the US in the early 1980s
> . . . [She] did not speak or write English very well . . . [and was] perhaps the
> most frugal person I have ever known. She ran the family household like a
> miserly CEO, by cutting expenses . . . .

The money that her frugal mother saved was immediately plowed back into the family's business ventures, the first of which was a restaurant. Ms. H explained that she and her siblings worked enthusiastically in their family-run restau-rant beginning in grade school. Ms. H's mother also saved money by shopping for her kids' clothing, as well as her own, at a variety of thrift shops, Goodwill stores, and select flea markets. In spite of this, no one in the family ever thought that they were disadvantaged or financially poor. While building wealth, the family perceived itself as being in transition, between modest means and wealthy. Thus, they never felt degraded wearing the clothes purchased at thrift stores.

Later her mother bought the building that housed the restaurant. Then over time she bought more and more income-producing real estate, eventually acquir-ing several shopping centers and then retiring a multimillionaire. Presently Ms. H's mother is enjoying a life of leisure, as do most financially independent senior citizens.

Keep in mind that not all people who patronize Goodwill-type stores are at an economic ground zero. Some are entrepreneurial commandos and savvy consumers, as we'll see in the next chapter. They are intent on building a business and ultimately wealth by living a spartan existence. As we've noted, this type of lifestyle isn't attractive to everyone. But it doesn't mean that it isn't a reliable path toward wealth accumulation.

Ms. H's purpose in writing to us was not to criticize but rather to praise her mother as a loving and nurturing parent. Ms. H and her siblings recognized that their mother had the dream of financial independence for her family. Plus, her children recognized that no one worked harder, put in longer hours, or spent less on herself than their mother. Through her mother, Ms. H learned the following lesson:

> *She taught me the value of true character was not in how one "spent" money and allowed money to change them, but how one can do truly great things by accumulating money and treating others fairly. There is no task too undignified as long as it's an honest day's work.*

What can be learned from Ms. H's mother's method of building wealth? The outcomes associated with prudent spending and saving allow for economic opportunities that many can only dream of. Regardless of what others in the marketing or media industries try to dictate to us related to spending and saving and earning, regardless of how difficult it is to go against the grain of how even your adopted society tells you to spend, a life of financial independence requires a pattern of behaviors that is disciplined. Focus with clarity on the goal of becoming financially independent. Think about living a spartan lifestyle as a temporary step on the path of becoming a socioeconomic achiever in America.

Experiences Matter

Even though we are not child psychologists or parenting experts, the reason we discuss early life experiences is because of (a) the dearth of research demonstrating that patterns of life experiences predict future outcomes as adults, and (b) the numerous readers who have asked us for advice in this area. Our combined research on the lifestyles, habits, and psychology of those who accumulate wealth on their own has shown the following:

- There is evidence to suggest that parental frugality and money management habits lead to their children's increased economic success. This has been demonstrated empirically and anecdotally by the stories shared with us over the past 20-plus years.

- Regardless of what type of financial behaviors parents model to their children, ultimately the choices to continue those behaviors (or not) lies with each individual.

Yes, many millionaires start off with frugal parents, but only 32% of our millionaires said their parents were better off than those of their high school classmates. And as is still the case today, few millionaires derive income from the fruits of a wealthy relative. In fact, only 14% of our millionaires' income is derived from estates and trusts, and only 10% derive income from cash or related gifts from relatives.

Marriage and Building Wealth

As we spend, on average, 2.5 hours with our spouses each day,[6] it is easy to understand the influence of marriage on our financial and wealth-related behaviors and success. Millionaires in past surveys and in our latest research have consistently been married or remarried and have consistently cited their spouses as critical to their economic success. In our latest survey of millionaires, 93% are married or remarried, and more than 80% of them agreed that having a supportive spouse was one of the key factors in their economic success. The National Bureau of Economic Research found the median net worth of married couples between 65 and 69 was 2.5 times that of a single person in the same age range.[7] And, staying together in a loving, respectful relationship has economic benefits: an Ohio State study found that divorce decreases wealth by an average of 77%.[8]

Within the roles of a household, as we'll discuss in Chapter 5, someone has to take on the various tasks related to financial management. This is easier if both spouses are on the same page, even if they are dividing the tasks. Financially successful couples tend to work together on their finances and generally agree about goals and methods for reaching those goals.[9] There is even evidence that similar credit scores of spouses are predictors of future togetherness.[10] One retired millionaire shared with us his views on marriage and wealth:

I would say meeting my wife was my life-changing experience. She had 100% belief in me. She knew that I would be successful even when I doubted myself. We had similar life goals. We lived within our means and always saved with an eye on our future. We both worked for the first eight years of marriage. We purchased a home based on one salary knowing she wanted to be home (at

least until the kids were in school) to be with the kids. We knew the benefits.
Her continued support of me throughout my career allowed me to take some
business risks that paved a way for an independent financial life today.

If we consider a typical household as a business for a moment, we can see how the leaders of that household have different roles in managing resources. One wife of a millionaire-next-door type told us this:

My husband laughs that while I am the COO of our household, I'm also the
CPO, Chief Procurement Officer. In his role as CFO, we are often at odds on
how to allocate budget . . . well, and whether the budget should be examined,
used, stuck to, etc. When there's friction about money, everything else seems to
be falling apart. But, we work hard to make sure we're on the same page most
of the time, even if we have different views on money.

In some cases, one spouse has to take on the lion's share of financial management. Again, this is ideal especially if one of the spouses tends to be on the spendthrift side of the spectrum, which, according to the wife, is the case with this millionaire-next-door couple:

My husband became interested in our finances only a few years ago, as we
[move] into retirement. We've been married 32 years. If it wasn't for me, I
do not think we would have any savings to speak of. We had to separate our
personal spending early in our marriage to keep the peace. He needed a free
spending account, while I've handled the household expenses and savings.

In *The Millionaire Mind*, nearly all millionaire respondents reported that their spouses were honest (98%), responsible (95%), loving (95%,) capable (95%), and supportive (94%). Most of these millionaires knew that their future mates possessed these qualities before proposing to them. A decamillionaire and senior corporate executive told us about how his wife had played into his success. After two years of marriage, he had asked her what she wanted for her birthday. She replied that the best gift in the world would be for him to return to college and finish his degree. She offered to downsize into student housing and to work full-time to support them. This gift ultimately bore major fruit in terms of his career and their lifestyle.

We were reminded of this case study when we read an e-mail from a senior corporate sales executive named Owen. When he hit the 50-year-old mark, Owen began thinking that his best years were behind him. Whether real or imagined, he had begun to worry. Jobs were being eliminated. His wife would hear none of it! She fervently believed in her husband's career future and spent $5,000 of her own money to hire a top-level career placement professional to help Owen land job offers.

A Litmus Test for the Future Spouse?

Some forward-thinking readers would often ask my father about choice of spouse. Clearly they knew or had read that this could greatly impact their future financial success. Our research doesn't provide us with a crystal ball on this issue. All my father could tell them was that there seem to be certain qualities in a spouse that contribute to a millionaire's successful marriage. A large majority (86%) of male millionaires reported in *The Millionaire Mind* that "being unselfish" was a major contributor. Also, most of these millionaires told my father that their wives were raised in loving, stable, and nurturing environments. They didn't seem to be driven by the need to hyper-consume to overcompensate for their humble beginnings either.

As stated in the chapter "Choice of Spouse" from *The Millionaire Mind*:

> *The typical millionaire couple has been together for nearly thirty years and their bond tends to be permanent as well as economically productive. . . . Ask the husband or wife to explain their household's productivity. . . . Each gives substantial credit to the other.*
>
> *For every 100 millionaires who say that having a supportive spouse was not important in explaining their economic success, there are 1,317 who indicate their spouse was important. Of the 100 who did not give credit to their spouse, 22 were never married and 23 were either divorced or separated. That leaves only 55 in 1,317 [4.2%] who believed that their spouse did not play an important role in their economic success.*

Spouses . . . and the 1%

My father wrote this blog a few years ago to highlight the difference between blaming a certain group for one's situation and learning from that group:

In a *Fortune* editorial several years ago, Nina Easton wrote, "don't blame the rich: a defense of the 1%." Instead of constantly criticizing the one percenters, most people could learn a lot about accumulating wealth through understanding the habits of these wealthy people. She stated succinctly, "It's entertaining to wail about the fat cats and the greedy rich. But if we're serious about addressing widening inequality, we should figure out what the 1% is doing right—and apply some of those ideas to closing the gap.[11]

The original title of *The Millionaire Next Door* was "That's Why They're Wealthy." Stable and long-term marriages, while not a predictor of wealth necessarily, tend to run alongside millionaire status. And we know that divorce, moving, dividing assets, and demonstrating (financial) care for children of divorce are unfortunate and unbudgeted expenses related to the dissolution of a marriage. As stated in *The Millionaire Mind*, "consistent participation in marriage results in significantly higher wealth. Conversely those people who are not married continuously over time have a propensity to accumulate lower levels of wealth during their adult life cycle."

Millionaires and those who will probably attain the status have a unique ability to select mates with a certain set of qualities. Among the first things [millionaires] say [about their spouses] include "down to earth," "unselfish," "has traditional values," "my emotional backbone," "patient," "understanding". . . . "[12]

Among the nearly 670 millionaires surveyed nationwide in a prior study, 68% were married to the same spouse throughout their lifetime, while 25% were remarried. In the same survey, 86% of the millionaires indicated that their parents were never divorced or separated any time prior to their 18th birthday, slightly down from 90% reported in 2005 in *Stop Acting Rich*.

It is well documented that income is a high correlate of wealth. High-income households tend to be of the traditional husband/wife type. Approximately 85% of tax returns at the $200,000 and above income level are filed jointly. Only 18% of tax returns with incomes under $50,000 are joint returns.[13] More than ever before the high-income household is composed of a husband and wife who are both working full-time.

Honesty Is the Best Marriage Policy

What if you are contemplating marriage and you have outstanding debts? Honesty is the best policy here. You should advise your future spouse about your financial situation, and you'd be smart to discuss further your proposed way of eliminating the debt. We were reminded of this fact by a man named Doug who shared this life-changing moment:

> *For me it was meeting my [future] wife . . . she told me that "she would not marry anyone who had any debt." It took me 14 months to clean up the debt [$45,000]. . . . She introduced me to Dave Ramsey and* The Millionaire Next Door. *Both had a profound impact on me.*

Lack of honesty, particularly about financial obligations, can bring an abrupt halt to a flourishing courtship. As an example, consider the case of Henry and Sally. After dating for several years, they decided to get married. But not long before the wedding Henry received a letter from one of Sally's lenders. His name had been given as a credit reference on several of her loan applications. Later he discovered that she had violated her loan agreements. She had already defaulted on a $20,000 consumer loan and was about to do so on $15,000 more; these did not include her outstanding student loans.

When Henry confronted Sally about her credit situation, she had a proposed solution. It called for Henry, who was a high-income producer, to "help" pay her outstanding debts! She believed that her credit problems would not be a major concern to Henry once he said, "I do." She badly misjudged Henry. He broke off the engagement. And it was not just because of the credit issues and the betrayal of trust. Henry determined that Sally was totally irresponsible when it came to money.

The Company We Keep

Regardless of whether your home life was loving and provided some degree of education regarding financial management and your spouse or significant other shares your worldview on financial matters, there are two other important influences that we have some control over which can impact our ability to achieve financial goals.

The first is the game of comparisons: comparing what we own, what we can consume, and our successes with others around us. The field of *sociometrics* concerns how individuals fit into a group, and much of the focus within this field is how those rankings, that is, where we stand in relation to those around us, influence our behaviors and attitudes. Research has found that your subjective well-being (generally how you feel about yourself and your lot in life) is tied to your *sociometric* status, rather than your socioeconomic status. In other words, satisfaction with what you have is not necessarily related to where you stand in terms of the wealth or income of the national population, but instead is tied closely to your community.[14] Sociometric status is defined by how much others in your immediate peer group (usually people you interact with daily) respect and admire you.

The second is ignoring the consumption habits of those around us in the first place. Our research with millionaires as well as other populations has consistently found that the concept of ignoring what others are doing (one of the main themes in *The Millionaire Next Door*) is related to net worth regardless of age and income.

We know, for example, that shopping in groups can influence how we view spending and ultimately on how frequently we shop. These results are typically found related to in-person shopping (teenagers are a good example).[15] Even with frugal shoppers, frugality can wax and wane depending on who's around us, as self-perceived frugal shoppers tend to spend more when they're around high-spending friends.[16] We'll focus on consumption in the next chapter, but for now, let's consider a family we all tend to know: the Joneses.

Social Indifference: Who Cares About the Joneses?

The concept of ignoring what others are driving, buying, and wearing is what we refer to as *social indifference*. Those who demonstrate high levels of social indifference across all consumption categories have a better opportunity to build wealth. This indifference to what others are driving, wearing, and playing with (think the latest smartphone) is related to the ability to build wealth over time.[17] Specifically, social indifference can help inoculate us against the competition in life for conspicuous consumption.

When measured reliably, we find that an indifference to the trends around us is related to net worth, independent of one's age and income. Those who focus intently on what others buy and consistently want the latest and greatest in consumer goods (such as technology or accessories) are less likely to build wealth over time. Social indifference predicts net worth regardless of age, income, or how much wealth someone inherits or is given. Like the prodigious accumulators of wealth in *The Millionaire Next Door*, those who practice social indifference have a greater likelihood of building wealth.

Those who are successful at transforming income into wealth demonstrate a consistent pattern of behaviors related to what others have in their driveway or wear to work or post on social media, like this millionaire from Ohio:

> *The first 10 years of building my business we (my wife and I) did not / would not "keep up with the Joneses". . . My friends had season tickets to sporting events, concerts, nice cars, etc. I worked a lot and we chose not to join them in many of these activities. In retrospect, we didn't miss anything and we didn't truly "suffer." We've always been frugal, savers, but not cheap. Just that we didn't do much outside of growing our business and growing our immediate family—it's hard work—but we are now able to enjoy some of the blessings we've achieved.*

In the consumer arms race, you will never win. There will always be a trend, a style, a fad to replace the last. Those who are able to transform their income into wealth are able to ignore the spending habits, new gadgets, and shiny trendy accessories in their quest to build wealth. Take, for example, Mrs. C, whose friend is very much focused on one-upsmanship in the consumer game of life:

> *I didn't notice this pattern until other friends of mine mentioned it. I'd purchase a car; she'd get a bigger, more expensive one. My kids would do well in school; she'd respond with the awards, recognition of praise her kids received. I bought a house and kept my first house as a rental. She'd buy a bigger, more expensive one and rent her other home. This was happening at some level in everything—from child rearing, education, vacations, etc. and she always took time to point out how much these things cost as well as how much they were earning and how many "things" they had.*
>
> *If she was trying to get me to emulate her, she actually achieved the opposite. The more she spent—and bragged about it—the less I was willing to spend on things.*

When a little girl asked if Mrs. C's friend was rich, Mrs. C told her, "Having all those things only says how much [the neighbor] has spent not how much

Keeping Success to Ourselves

Have you ever wondered why so many millionaire-next-door types understate their considerable socioeconomic success? They don't have a strong need to display their economic productivity by buying luxury products and expensive homes. In a major way, their real achievements are the badges of their success. For example, financial success, especially economic independence, is its own reward. Conversely, those people who have an insatiable desire to publicize their considerable ability to spend predictably end up as members of the income-statement affluent crowd. Yes, it costs a lot of money to convince the faceless crowd that you are a big income producer. Typically, these people are living on a hyper-spending treadmill. Along with not playing the comparison game is the concept of status, demonstrating status to others through our consumption patterns. As we've seen in the study of millionaires, decamillionaires, as well as in our research with mass and emerging affluent, those who are indifferent to the Joneses, and do not have a need or drive to demonstrate status to others, are in a good position to achieve financial success. Consider, for example, successful members of the entertainment industry who are content with being behind the scenes versus in the spotlight. My father was struck particularly by an article in the Wall Street Journal *that demonstrated this principle:*[18]

Diane Warren has written more than 1,500 songs for everyone from Celine Dion to Rod Stewart. In fact, her client list reads like a "Who's Who in Popular Music." I have found that most of the people in the "singer" category are hyper-consuming income-statement affluent. They constantly need to be on stage in front of an audience, and not just to earn a living. In one way, these people are primitive life-forms. They personally have to hunt and gather income and fans relentlessly.

But Diane Warren is just the opposite. She's a member of the group that anthropologists refer to as "cultivators." Cultivators plant seeds, grow crops and trees, raise cattle and write songs. Songs, unlike live performances, can be inventoried and can pay royalties to the writer for more than a lifetime.

According to the article, "Ms. Warren doesn't care if the average listener doesn't know she wrote the song. 'I want them to believe the singer so much that they believe they wrote it. I just want my name on it and on the check!'"

The need to display success via consumption, whether that involves cars, homes, or experiences, is a major impediment to building wealth. Teach your children about the beauty of cultivating and the harsh reality of being a perennial hunter-gatherer.

she is worth." Mrs. C then thought to herself, "I am secure with my financial situation and I'm on track to have a comfortable retirement. According to my neighbor she is waiting for the payday to arrive that will fund her retirement."

In *Stop Acting Rich*, this question highlights the impact of consumerism and how one might combat its effects on children: "What happens when your children attend school and/or interact otherwise with kids who display an abundance of expensive consumer products? Your children are likely to ask you why you do not supply them with the same collection of products. Tell them . . . never judge the true quality, the caliber of a person, by what can be purchased. Often people who dress and drive as if they are rich are not."[19]

Feeling good about ourselves is tied to our standing in our immediate social groups. Some of us are more influenced by our social group than others. While spending time with friends can have a positive impact, it could be negative if we compare ourselves to others who are consistently spending beyond their (or our) means. You may find yourself unhappy. And broke.

The Trouble with the Status of Doctors

Physicians and surgeons earn more than four times as much as the average American each year ($210,170 compared to $49,630 . . . note these are averages and not the median). There are approximately 650,000 physicians and surgeons in the United States[20], and they have typically fallen into a (somewhat justified) stereotype of high-income earners who are challenged in building wealth. We see this in our trend research at DataPoints, where the majority of physicians fall into the 33rd percentile or below on our assessment of frugality and also tend to score low on financial acumen, a measure of knowledge and expertise in investing and financial management. My father addressed the timelessness of high-income-producing, low-accumulation-of-wealth individuals in the preface to the 2011 version of *The Millionaire Next Door*:

> *Are people with high realized incomes today better at accumulating wealth than those say twenty years ago? "Not really" is the clear answer. Most of what I wrote two decades ago still applies today. Yes, even today high income producing physicians, attorneys, and corporate middle managers are still below the norm when it comes to transforming income into wealth. And most high income producing couples in general are more of the income statement affluent types than the balance sheet affluent types.*[21]

I Can't Drive That.

As we've discussed, in many cases, and perhaps in your case, there is disdain for the financial decisions some people make, decisions that are typically reflected in consumer purchases. While they may be financially advantageous, they may be looked down upon, as my father discussed in 2014:

In *Stop Acting Rich* I profiled the glittering rich as people who generate extremely high incomes, have a vast amount of wealth at their disposal, and spend accordingly on high-prestige cars, mansions, etc. No matter what they spend their money on, though, it is just a fraction of their overall net worth. These people are highly concentrated in neighborhoods which my friend, Jon Robbin, refers to as "blue blood estates."

I spent over an hour at a reception in my favorite American history museum. While there I met Gillis, a highly compensated Fortune 100 senior executive, for the first time. After a brief conversation about the artifacts on display, we discovered a common interest in high-performance automobiles. Gillis told me that he has owned a stable of Porsches, BMWs, and V 12 Mercedes. Then he asked me, "What do you think of the new Corvette?" I responded that it was given the highest praise by *Car and Driver, Road and Track, Autoweek, Motor Trend*. Then Gillis told me that he really wanted to buy one, but he just couldn't do it. "If you live in the center of [blue blood estates] you can't drive a Corvette!" In fact, this topic had just been discussed among Gillis and his neighbors who didn't want a Corvette in the neighborhood.

I often explain why people like Gillis will not drive a Corvette. The glittering rich [Gillis is one] who drive Porsches do not want to be associated with what they perceive to be the "gold chain" crowd. That is why they will pay substantially more for a Porsche than buy a Corvette, which outperforms the Porsche. In earlier writings, I have asked which of the following three variables is the best predictor of consumption: income, net worth, or market value of home. The market value of a home is the best of the three. If you live in a pricey home situated in blue blood estates, there is enormous social pressure to forgo performance for prestige brands.

Often, physicians' median net worth is negative, due in most part to their student loans and age, but there is something else at play: the adherence to the stereotype of physician status.

What's especially challenging is when our neighbors, friends, friends of friends through social media, and coworkers are hyper-consumers. And it may be even harder when you're in a well-defined, professional occupation (i.e., physicians, lawyers, executives). There's a stereotype that many buy into about what doctors should be driving, or where they should be living. Consider this: The most ever spent by millionaires in our latest nationwide study on a watch was $300. Physicians in our study paid $700. In *The Millionaire Next Door* my father wrote, "Another reason very well-educated people tend to lag behind on the wealth scale has to do with the status ascribed to them by society. Doctors, as well as others with advanced degrees, are expected to play their part."[22]

To build wealth, even doctors must be contrarians: They must make choices that enable them to be financially successful versus playing a part dictated by what those around them, their fellow doctors, and what others think doctors should be doing. To build wealth, we need to mind our own business and focus on what it takes to transform that high salary into wealth. Ignoring what Dr. Jones is driving, where she is living, and that fancy watch she just bought is critical to building wealth.

The Financial Downside of the Connection Economy

Journalists and readers have continually asked us if it is more difficult today to become the millionaire next door than it was in the 1980s or 1990s. Maybe you have the same question. The answer is yes and no, or as many psychologists and social scientists would answer, it depends.

The price of health care and education makes it *seem* unlikely that you could save your way to millions. But the building blocks of economic independence and financial success have not changed, as demonstrated throughout the case studies, interviews, and survey research we conducted since the first publication of *The Millionaire Next Door*.

But this goal is made considerably more difficult because of the increased influence and proliferation of technology. Building upon the concepts related to sociometric status, technology now allows us greater connection to friends, family members, former colleagues, acquaintances, and celebrities. These connections, and the ubiquity of them, provide a constant way to check in on the myriad ways in which they spend both their time and money. As our relationships, careers, and the way in which we communicate increasingly include ongoing and persistent connections to others through technology, we would be remiss not to include its potential financial perils.

Today we carry the influence of others around with us in our pockets and pocketbooks and spend, on average, two hours on social media, and 50 minutes *per day* on Facebook alone.[23] Imagine if these two hours were spent developing a new skill, researching a new business idea, or engaging directly with friends, coworkers, or employees. By comparison, millionaires in our latest sample spend 2.5 hours *per week* on all social media sites combined. We know that social networks can impact the kinds of behaviors we believe are acceptable, and this is no different with shopping and consuming. What our friends are buying, wearing, and displaying can impact us psychologically through our desire to conform. The more time we spend on social media, the more the marketing of products, services, or experiences will affect our buying habits.[24]

As one millionaire in a recent interview told us, "Now you see this instantly on Facebook—you see all of these people with what look like incredible lives, but it's not that way."

Another millionaire was more critical: "If people spent even half the time they spend on curating their image on social media, we would all be a lot better. Certainly, they would be a lot better off. It's a time drain that leads to nothing— it's ephemeral—it's not a lasting product of any value. All that time is wasted and people neglect to spend time on serious things that matter."

Connectedness, it seems, comes with a cost: the cost of our cognitive and emotional attention, and when we consider our financial goals, our money. We have become accustomed to new, shiny, and now. More than in the 1990s, the proliferation of technology makes us like mice in the Skinner box, constantly touching our phones to get the next pellet of news, drivel, or consumer goods. Scientists have linked activity and satisfaction from screen time with dopamine and equated its use to other addictive habits.[25] Particularly if we are easily persuaded by either the consumption habits of others close to us (family, friends, neighbors) or others we see on social media (celebrities, politicians, professional athletes), that connectedness must be tempered with restraint to achieve economic success.

The New Marketing

Ignoring the trends around us from our virtual and face-to-face social networks is really only the start of a frugal lifestyle. There's another powerful source that our technology allows for today: social marketing. Up until the early 2000s, the reach of marketing into our lives was limited to nonsocial and untracked methods. In other words, you could turn the page of a magazine, change the channel on your TV or radio, or ignore the billboards you drove past. Marketers had to do research, create advertising campaigns, and then promote their brands through various, nonsocial channels. We didn't have to give them permission to interrupt our day. Now, with e-mail marketing, social media feeds, and website tracking, we often have the option of reserving our cognitive resources to things that matter. Consider for a moment the definition of permission marketing from the creator of the concept, Seth Godin, and his focus on the respectful way to use it, methods that many companies choose to ignore:

> *Permission marketing is the privilege (not the right) of delivering antici-pated, personal and relevant messages to people who actually want to get them.*
>
> *It recognizes the new power of the best consumers to ignore market-ing. It realizes that treating people with respect is the best way to earn their attention.*
>
> *Pay attention is a key phrase here, because permission marketers under-stand that when someone chooses to pay attention they are actually paying you with something precious. And there's no way they can get their attention back if they change their mind. Attention becomes an important asset, something to be valued, not wasted.*[26]

Today, your digital footprint leads marketers directly to you, tailoring the content, message, and frequency to your online behavioral patterns. Ingenious and effective, this new marketing strategy presents dangers to those prone to believe the tailored and persuasive images and messages. Inoculation against this marketing, that is, not giving away the precious resources of attention and focus, is critical to building wealth. The power we have in the marketplace is not spend-ing our resources, including our attention, with any entity that could influence us off the course of achieving financial goals.

The Consumer Science of Awesome Shampoo

Coming from a marketing research background, my father knew all too well the power and influence of consumer psychology on our behaviors. He wrote this piece in 2010 to demonstrate the absurdity of self-esteem tied to using a shampoo, the influence of marketing on our perceptions and potential well-being, and perhaps more importantly, the power of marketing and the requisite discipline we need to retain our cognitive attention if we are to build and maintain wealth:

I have noticed in the last week or so that I have felt more excited, proud, interested, and attentive. Conversely, I have felt less hostile, ashamed, nervous, jittery, and guilty. I thought this euphoria might have something to do with the upswings in the sales of my books or possibly the new 2010 Toyota 4-Runner brochure I received. But then I discovered what must be the real source of these heightened emotions—a change in my shampoo!

In the summer of 2010, I found a bottle of Pantene "Serious Care for Beautiful Hair" shampoo in our shower and started using it. I haven't had a bad hair day since. And then I read this insightful article in the *Wall Street Journal* which explained how Procter and Gamble went to extraordinary lengths to study how it can encourage more consumers to buy Pantene products.[27] Spending heavily on marketing research seems to be well worth the effort. According to the article, P&G's Pantene has $3 billion in sales. In P&G's latest study, it surveyed nearly 3,400 women and had them rank the intensity they experience regarding 20 emotions relative to their hair. Bad hair was found to be associated with the emotions of hostility, shame, and irritability. P&G went as far as to hire a Yale University professor of psychology to analyze the survey results. The professor, Dr. LaFrance, found "bad hair negatively influences self-esteem, brings out social insecurities, and causes people to concentrate on negative aspects of themselves."[28] Who knew?

Of course, I'm sure that P&G's promotional messages about Pantene will promise the end to "bad hair days." Consequently, it is implied that users will experience enhanced self-esteem. And I thought that one had to build wealth and become financially independent to do the same.

In *Stop Acting Rich*, I mentioned that my mentor, the distinguished professor of marketing, Dr. Bill Darden, often told his graduate students the following: "Get ready to compete in the marketplace with some real talent. The really brilliant ones in America don't work for the State Department. Not even in medical science labs. The great minds are working in marketing, designing ways of . . . convincing us that one brand of a hemorrhoid remedy is superior to another . . . that one wash detergent will produce whiter whites—thus assuring Mom will continue to be loved and admired by her husband and kids."

He was quite serious when saying this. If Bill were still with us today and we could ask him to evaluate the marketing efforts associated with the liquor [or hair care] industry, he would likely tell us that, clearly, some of the best of the very best minds in America are at work marketing shampoo.

Consider this quote from the leader of one of the largest marketing companies in the world, as he explains the "power" of the data we leave behind (i.e., "Big Data") and engagement in marketing:

> *As shopper behavior continues to change and shoppers' "engagement expectations" increase, advertisers must employ holistic strategies that deliver both mass-distributed offers for reach, as well as relevant, targeted content through both traditional and digital methods. Meeting these growing expectations while delivering value to consumers demands effective analysis of the Big Data created in the marketplace.*[29]

The power of data analytics and the footprints we leave online leave little doubt for marketers as to how to cater each product and service to us. The millionaires next door continue to ignore this hype and noise, as they did in the 1980s and 1990s. Those who are susceptible to the constant reinforcement of media and technology will find they need extraordinary discipline to ignore the hyper-targeted ads and pseudo-articles that appear side by side with posts of their friends' pictures.

Think about marketing today and how you might come to believe the hype about the Pantene shampoo discussed in the sidebar above:

- Content marketing would have led you to read an article in *Good Housekeeping* or *Redbook* that appeared to be written by an editor or staff writer, but in fact was written by P&G.

- Social media advertising would "follow" you around the web after you searched for shampoo on Google, so that every site you visited that had paid advertising would present shampoo.

- When you finally decide to purchase shampoo, the ratings provided on Amazon or elsewhere were bought and paid for by clever marketing companies that provided products in exchange for "honest" ratings of bought-and-paid-for raters.

P&G spent $7.1 billion on advertising in 2017 to influence us.[30] To build wealth today, we must become keenly aware of the kinds of information being presented to us, the source of that information, and the influence it could potentially have on our shopping behaviors . . . and self-esteem. I don't fault companies for using the most effective marketing methods and mining data: That's their business, and we must remember that we are the target. Those who focus on building and sustaining wealth will be wise to remember that nothing is really "free and always will be."

The Trend of Frugality

Some of the critics of *The Millionaire Next Door* seemed to display an air of superiority about the frugal shopping behaviors of those people profiled in the case studies. It's interesting that the economic downturn of 2008 to 2012 turned being frugal into a trend. Shopping at off-retailers, upcycling and recycling, and making things at home were in vogue.

The trendy frugal were more than happy to extol the virtues of living below their means occasionally, when it was convenient, and when they were still able to demonstrate their success via how frugal they were . . . particularly in buying name brands at off prices. For this group, and for many of us unknowingly, the fashion of frugality comes and goes with the changes in the economy and trends.

For example, like trends in other areas, the use of coupons by Americans is cyclical. Inmar is a global marketing research company that tracks both distribution (how many coupons companies are offering) and redemption (how many people are using the coupons). Their results provide a compelling look at frugality trends over time. In 2011, for instance, 3.5 billion coupons were redeemed. In 2015, only 2.5 billion were redeemed. Does coupon clipping make the millionaire? Not necessarily, and certainly not if the use of coupons is cyclical and the only method applied in the pursuit of financial independence. Those who are astute at building wealth demonstrate spending patterns that are more consistent and disciplined. So, the question of who can be frugal today is really instead: Who can be disciplined about spending regardless of the economy, trends, or where they are in life? *Consistency and discipline* are the frugal behaviors that are most important, versus simply following the trend with your temporarily pseudo-frugal neighbors. It's a consistent pattern of behaviors related to spending, not seasonal frugality. This idea is particularly relevant again today, at the time of writing this manuscript, as a robust economy, full employment, and a hot stock market have made frugality (once again) uncool.

To Be Happy, Stop Acting Rich

The pursuit of wealth in and of itself is a hollow one. The ability to spend with abandon and consume with little regard for what that consumption means for future freedom—freedom meaning not being a slave to work and perpetual revenue generation—is rife with shallowness. My father would frequently comment that money did not buy happiness, and that faith, relationships, helping noble causes, and creating meaning in one's life were the pursuits that led the millionaires he interviewed to greater satisfaction than their portfolio performance. In 2010, he wrote this regarding satisfaction and happiness in relationship to money:

What explains happiness in life? I don't have all the answers. But, as a review of both my books and blogs, happiness in life has little to do with the brand or price of the watch one wears, the stores one patronizes, the make of car one drives, or the brand of vodka one consumes. One's overall happiness in life has nothing to do with the overall price one pays for wine, the size or market value of a home, not even the price one pays for a haircut.

To shed more light on this issue, I examined the relationship between happiness in life and more than 200 characteristics, behaviors, and attitudes of 1,574 high-income, high-net-worth respondents from one of my national surveys. Note that correlations do not necessarily indicate cause and effect.

Beyond health, family, and job factors, why are some people more satisfied with life than others? In terms of statistical significance, the higher one's level of happiness the more likely he or she is to agree with the following statements (by rank order of variation explained):

1. I have more wealth than most people in my wealth or income group.
2. We are financially better off than our neighbors.
3. I donated 5% or more of my income last year to charity.
4. I live well below my means.
5. I was raised in an atmosphere filled with love and harmony.
6. My parents taught me how to invest and manage money.

7. Politically, I am more conservative than liberal.

8. I inherited less than 1% of my net worth.

9. My spouse is more frugal than I am.

10. I invested 10% or more of my income last year.

Also, note that both net worth and income are associated with happiness. Statistically, net worth is the more important of the two. But even more important than net worth is relative net worth (as suggested in Item 1 above). Relative net worth is all about how productive one is in transforming his or her income into net worth compared to others in one's income and age cohort as well as within the context of one's immediate neighborhood environment.

Those who can easily afford their consumption lifestyle tend to be significantly happier than those who struggle to make ends meet by acting rich. I have consistently found that those within the same income or age cohorts who were raised by loving and nurturing parents tend to spend less and save more of their incomes than those who are not raised in this type of atmosphere.

There are opportunities to succeed financially for those who make choices based on tried-and-true methods of building wealth. If you had positive experiences growing up related to all things financial, you may have developed a pattern of behaviors that will allow you to stay on the economic independence highway more easily than if you had the opposite experience. Taking responsibility for our financial decisions, regardless of our upbringing, relates to net worth. And the choices we make today and tomorrow about with whom we share our lives, choices that at least in this country we have the free will to make, will also impact our trajectory. Choose carefully.

Chapter 4

Freedom to Consume

I tell my family members often that my goal is to earn interest and not pay interest.

—millionaire from Georgia who retired at age 54

Economic success takes different paths. For those who make an average to above-average income in the United States, the path to economic success necessitates a certain amount of restraint in consumption. It requires an awareness of and inoculation from the consumerism and "affluenza" that plagues many households with significant income levels.

There are very few Americans who, with a modest to above-average income, can sustain high-consumption lifestyles and become millionaires in their lifetimes. We've seen that the majority of those who have become economically successful chose a path of moderation or simplicity in consumption while they were working toward economic success like the Jacobson family in Chapter 1. In many cases, they continue this practice even after they become millionaires.

Even if you have parents who modeled ideal financial management behavior and you managed to overcome obstacles to becoming wealthy, you may fall victim to heavy consumerism, fueled by whatever social groups or media may have an influence on you, or your own perceived needs that are fulfilled by the latest in consumer goods. Our freedom to consume, along with the freedom to choose how we spend our time, comes at a cost. If we choose to take full advantage of it, we must fund it somehow. The cycle of working to spend is difficult to avoid even if you've decided to live in a modest home in a modest neighborhood and surrounded yourself with others who have a similar lifestyle.

We are taught from an early age to consume, and America has much to offer professional consumers.

In the "Frugal, Frugal, Frugal" chapter of *The Millionaire Next Door*, my father wrote about the behaviors and habits of economically successful Americans in terms of consumption.[1] The frugal mindset, when applied to the consumption of consumer goods, can help a household live within its means and can lead to behaviors that encourage savings. For many, being a frugal consumer is a badge of honor, like on the TV show *Extreme Couponing*. But for others, frugality goes in and out of style depending on the economic conditions of the day.

For the purposes of this book, and for the study of wealth in general, we define frugal people as those who have a lifestyle that is simple and economical, and who consistently live below their means. Those who are frugal demonstrate a pattern of financial behaviors that are economical in nature and below one's means. As we have noted in the past:

Living a frugal lifestyle allows an individual to comfortably afford the level of consumption in their household.

Throughout the past 20 years, our research has demonstrated that millionaires report being frugal, and that when we split affluent samples into prodigious accumulators of wealth (PAWs, the top quartile) and under accumulators of wealth (UAWs, the bottom quartile), these groups differ in terms of their agreement with statements related to frugality. In samples of mass affluent and emerging affluent heads of households, there is a clear relationship between a consistent pattern of frugal behaviors and net worth, regardless of age or income.[2] This is true for those in the high-net-worth camp, as well as those in the median-income camp. Being frugal or at least having a simplistic consumption lifestyle requires equal doses of discipline and social indifference to trends. At its heart, a frugal lifestyle is highlighted by budgeting, planning, setting goals, simplicity, and discipline. Being frugal requires knowledge, ability, and personality, but most importantly, a certain set of behaviors that create a lifestyle that not everyone is willing to experience.

Regardless of whether you earn your revenue as an executive, a teacher, or scrap metal dealer, frugality doesn't go out of style for those who are committed to becoming economically successful and financially independent. Our studies have shown that 57% of PAWs indicate that they have always been frugal, while only 41% of UAWs agree with the same statement. This is consistent with our findings from 1996.

Home Is Where the Spending Starts

Where else do we find influences on our financial decision-making? We know that our choice of neighborhood influences attitudes toward work,[3] but it also influences our spending. We compare ourselves to those in our neighborhood and community (recall the concept of sociometric status). In *Stop Acting Rich*, my father wrote, "the greatest detriment to building wealth is our home/neighborhood environment. If you live in a pricey home and neighborhood, you will act and buy like your neighbors . . . the more affluent the neighborhood the more its residents spend on almost every conceivable product and service. We take our consumption cues from our neighbors . . . most self-made millionaires . . . were able to build wealth precisely because they never lived in a home or neighborhood environment where their domestic overhead made it difficult for them to build wealth."[4] As we discussed in the previous chapter, this is due in part to both the comparisons we make to those around us and the influence that others have on our consumption behaviors.[5] Does your neighborhood consist of high-income-producing, high-consuming, income-statement affluent types? If so, take a moment to consider your own patterns of consumption. Are they your own or based on someone who is more in line with an under accumulator of wealth?

More Than a House, It's a Lifestyle

In addition to the influence of our neighbors, our home's price relative to our income also has an impact on our ability to accumulate wealth over time. For most people in this country, owning a home is preferable to renting, but the key to building wealth is to live in a home that one can easily afford. Most millionaires next door whom we have studied report that they never purchased a home that was more than three times the amount of their annual income.

The median home value for millionaires in our latest study is approximately $850,000 (or 3.4 times their current income) and the median original purchase price was $465,000. Note that most millionaires in our study (66%) haven't changed locations in the past 10 years. Given that moving costs on average in the United States are more than $12,000,[6] staying put is economically advantageous.

What factors led to making a new home purchase? Of the millionaires surveyed in our latest study, none indicated that they changed homes because they received a cold call or letter asking them to sell, and only 3% of them said their realtor proposed they upgrade because of their financial success. Instead, a new home purchase for this group was typically driven by quality, appearance, public schools, and neighborhood (see Table 4-1). A little less than 60% of these millionaires were motivated by an increase in income. Both professional and societal marketing tactics related to homeownership had little influence on millionaires in our study.

Table 4-1. Most Important Reasons for Latest Home Purchase by Millionaires

Reason for Latest Home Purchase	Percent Indicating Important
Wanted better-quality home	81.2
Liked the appearance of latest home	80.2
Wanted high-quality public schools	71.6
Wanted to live in better neighborhood	69.0
Favorable interest rates	59.9
Income increased	59.1
Needed to relocate after career/occupational change	58.14
Built up significant equity in previous home	54.9

Table 4-2. Least Important Reasons for Latest Home Purchase by Millionaires

Reason for Latest Home Purchase	Percent Indicating Important
Received retirement plan distribution	6.9
Sold all or part of a business	6.1
Broker learned about financial success and proposed we upgrade	3.3
Sold rights to royalties/patents	1.6

Table 4-3. Purchase Price and Current Home Values for Millionaire Homeowners

Value	Percentage of Millionaires with Homes in Each Category	
	Purchase Price	Value Today
Under $400,000	41.4	4.7
$400,000–$599,999	19.9	19.6
$600,000–$799,999	15.2	21.4
$800,000–$999,999	7.0	19.0
$1,000,000+	16.4	35.2

Stretching for a Home

When we talk about social pressures of homeownership, we could mean the broad pressure from your peer groups or family to purchase a home in a specific location, community, or neighborhood. ("Springfield has the best schools. And the Hampton Heights neighborhood has a lot of young professionals.") We also refer to the pressure put on certain professionals, for example attorneys, who within the walls of high-paying law firms refer to an extra-large mortgage as an "associate retention policy." Again, we see the impact beyond the financial cost of living beyond one's means. In this case, stretching for a home would ensure the young associate would have to continue working to fuel his and his family's house payment and inevitable lifestyle creep. In addition, another cost of "stretching," as it's referred to, has to do with general wellness. Consider the following case study from a millionaire whose health and financial life needed revision:

It was July 2006. I was within a month of turning 40 and I was driving home from work. I was having chest pains . . . my doctor told me I was very close to serious heart disease and diabetes in my current condition. I started working on my health seriously . . . when I started fixing one area of my life I started noticing other areas that needed improvement. Financially we were fairly typical of a middle-aged six-figure income family. We had hundreds of thousands [of dollars] in mortgage debt, about eighty thousand [dollars] in consumer debt and [were] basically living check to check. We were saving for retirement, but our net worth, including personal property was just a little more than our income. We were told by several financial "experts" we were doing fine. We didn't feel fine. We woke up to our situation and started doing something about it. We set goals. We developed a plan and executed it. We paid off our consumer debt. We built an emergency fund. We paid off our home. Today we are debt free and over a million in net worth. We homeschool our children and live the life we want to. It has been a long, tough journey, and we still have several years to go before we're wealthy. (Wealthy meaning we don't need to earn an income and will never run out of money.) We have the goals and plans in place and we're working on them daily.

Lessons from Bubbles

The housing bubble and consequent economic meltdown in 2008 can provide some insight about the dangers of purchasing a home that requires more than three times your annual income and beyond. What can this teach us, and future balance-sheet affluent Americans, about home values, income, and wealth? In 2010, a man named Jerry shared his concerns about his real estate situation with my father. Jerry was a computer programmer, and his wife was a part-time dental technician. The couple's annual adjusted gross income was about $100,000. They had three children.

Just prior to the meltdown in the real estate market, the couple purchased a new home in a newly developed subdivision for $495,000. Between 2009 and 2010, three brand new homes similar to Jerry's in the same subdivision were sold for $300,000, each as foreclosures. "Ouch!" said Jerry. His dream of reselling his home "in a few years at a substantial profit" quickly vanished. But his mortgage balance of more than $300,000 did not. All my father could do was to tell Jerry not to panic. Fortunately, things did improve for Jerry, particularly because his home is located within a public school district that has a national reputation.

Other than the profit motive, why did Jerry and his wife trade up from a $280,000 home to one priced at $495,000? Here were his three reasons.

1. First, a mortgage broker told them they could afford to make the payments. As stated in *The Millionaire Next Door*, this is the equivalent of asking a fox to count the number of hens in your chicken coop, or like asking your barber if you need a haircut. Who is giving you so-called advice on what you can and cannot afford? How much is their advice tied to their compensation?

2. Second, the people in the neighborhood seemed to be similar to Jerry and his wife in terms of demographics and socioeconomic characteristics. In other words, their new neighbors had similar careers, interests, goals, and consumer desires. This could increase the likelihood that Jerry and his wife will want to join, buy, and do similar things as their neighbors to increase their perceived acceptance.

3. Third and most important, the couple's $100,000 income was more than they had ever earned in any year during their first 20 years of marriage. Now, at the six-figure level, they viewed themselves as "rich." And, according to Jerry's logic, rich people don't live in $280,000 homes or neighborhoods. Jerry's perception of what it meant to be wealthy got in the way of making a sound housing decision.

Attention, Jerry. Rich, wealthy, affluent—no matter. It is all about net worth. Income is not wealth, and wealth is not income. This couple's net worth was now less than $150,000. While Jerry was telling his story, my father looked over the numbers he had tabulated from the 2007 IRS estate tax data for those decedents with an estate valued at $3.5 million or more. The median market value of a decedent's home was $469,021. That is less than 10% of their median net worth. And on average these decedents had nearly two-and-a-half times more of their wealth invested in investment real estate than in their own personal homes. What if Jerry had known this beforehand? Would he still have bought a home priced higher than the value of the typical millionaire decedent? It would depend on whether Jerry wanted to *act* rich or actually *be* rich someday.

Affluent Neighborhoods as Requirements

Economically productive home buyers have a distinct advantage in their home search, primarily because they have fewer restraints related to the "show," or status, of where they live. They do not have Jerry's mindset of "my high income now requires that I live in a 'rich' neighborhood." But, there are more Jerrys, especially so many years after an economic decline. Deb, a soon-to-be millionaire next door, shared her thoughts about buying a home. She had just read *Stop Acting Rich*, and it reminded her of the following:

> My . . . husband and I . . . bought a house. . . . The housing market was down . . . and we were looking in a blue-collar area because he needed to move into [a specific] school district . . . There was a tiny development of new construction, and we got a new four-bedroom colonial. . . . later, a coworker of mine started to look for a house with her fiancé. She showed up for work in tears because they couldn't afford a nice house. "I want a house like yours," she said, but [she] was only looking in upper class neighborhoods. I told her that she could afford something better if she would buy in a blue-collar neighborhood like mine. She was so offended by this prospect that she refused to speak to me for a week!

Maybe Deb hit too close to home with her recommendation. Perhaps Deb's friend would have a more realistic perception of the so-called "upper-class" neighborhood if she had known that the rock star Bruce Springsteen once said in an interview that he had found some jerks in every neighborhood he had lived in from the bluest of the blue collar to those filled with expensive mansions. A top realtor of mansions in a major metropolitan area has found that these neighbors can be just as noisy, disrespectful of property lines, or neglectful of property as their blue-collar counterparts. Terrible neighbors, it seems, are normally distributed.

Deb's friend, though, was not alone in her reaction to economy in housing choices. As we've said before, frugality isn't for everyone. Consumption in moderation is not for everyone, either. One type of *The Millionaire Next Door* reader had quite a different reaction to the book than typical fans. Even going back to the late 90s, when the economy and stock market were booming, copies of *The Millionaire Next Door* were found shoved in the toilet of the airport bathroom in Atlanta, or given away. There could be several reasons for this behavior, but clearly the reader did not expect a lesson in consistency and discipline. Perhaps they were looking for a get-rich-quick plan, or maybe a pat on the back for achieving a $180,000/year income to pay for their home that stretched them *and* private schools *and* a luxury SUV in the garage . . . but little in the bank. They were sorely disappointed to learn that not only did the data not applaud this type of behavior, but in fact indicated that they were impairing their economic future.

Your Neighbors and Income from Estates

Just over 35% of millionaire homeowners in our most recent study live in homes currently valued at the million-dollar mark. When we look at how they generate revenue, we see some surprising (or not) statistics. First, when we examine the differences between millionaires with any amount of income coming from trusts and estates (approximately 14%) compared to those with no estate/trust income (86% of our sample), we see that there is a larger percentage of millionaires with income from trusts and estates living in million-dollar homes than the general millionaire population (that is, 55% of millionaires with income from trusts and estates live in homes worth at least $1 million).

The higher the market value of the typical home in a neighborhood, the higher the proportion of homeowners in that neighborhood who have inherited wealth. As an example, about one in four of those who live in America's toniest neighborhoods, where the current market value exceeds $1 million, had some amount of inherited wealth from estates or trusts. Contrast this with millionaires who live in neighborhoods where the typical home sells for less than $500,000. Only 8% of these homeowners received any income from estates or trusts.

If your explicit or implicit goal is to emulate and fit in with those around you, you may be playing a game that's difficult to win. Keeping up with the Joneses who earn enough to live in a $1 million home is difficult by itself. But it is more difficult if your competition next door was heavily subsidized by their wealthy relatives.

Table 4-4. Percentage of Millionaire Homeowners with and without Estate/Trust Income by Original Purchase Price of Home

Range of Original Purchase Price Values	Percentage of Millionaires Living in Homes in Range of Values	
	No Income from Estates & Trusts	Income from Estates & Trusts
Under $400,000	42.3	33.3
$400,000–$599,999	20.0	23.6
$600,000–$799,999	15.5	18.1
$800,000–$999,999	6.1	9.7
$1,000,000+	16.1	15.3

Table 4-5. Percentage of Millionaire Homeowners with and without Estate/Trust Income by Current Market Value of Home

Range of Current Market Values	Percentage of Millionaires Living in Homes in Range of Values	
	No Income from Estates & Trusts	Income from Estates & Trusts
Under $400,000	5.6	0.0
$400,000–$599,999	21.1	15.1
$600,000–$799,999	23.0	17.8
$800,000–$999,999	19.6	12.3
$1,000,000+	30.7	54.8

Homeownership Does Not Equal Millionaire Status

A couple once asked my father about the relationship between homeownership and net worth. They were contemplating buying their first home. "In your books, Tom, you mention that nearly all millionaires are homeowners . . . approximately 95%," they pointed out. But homeowners are not millionaires. And no one is going to hand you a check for seven figures when you close on your first home. However, there is some correlation between homeownership and net worth. According to government statistics, the median household net worth for renters has hovered around the $4,000 to $5,500 level during the last 20 years. For the same period, the median net worth for homeowners has been

30 to 45 times greater. The median net worth for homeowners in the United States in 2016 was approximately $230,000.[7] But don't count on the appreciation of your home to make you wealthy. In *Stop Acting Rich*, my father mentioned that if all costs are accounted for in real terms, homes appreciate very little, if at all. Again, one of the keys to building wealth is to live in a home that you can easily afford.

What is affordable? A few years ago, bankrate.com suggested that an affordable home is one where monthly housing costs (which include principal and interest on the mortgage, insurance, and taxes) would be less than 28% of a household's total income.[8] This is close to the three times recommendation from *The Millionaire Next Door*. Not only should you think about cost of living, but also how you measure your well-being within your new city, community, and neighborhood, specifically (see Table 4-6).

Table 4-6. Total Median Cost of Homeownership by Month and Satisfaction Indicators for Selected US Cities (2012)

City	Total Cost of Ownership[9]	Emotional Well-Being	Happiness Index[10]
San Francisco	$2,497.68	3	69.20
San Diego	$1,746.21	8	65.80
Washington, DC	$1,735.45	13	64.14
Seattle	$1,726.50	25	63.16
Minneapolis	$935.63	9	62.59
Los Angeles	$1,474.75	24	59.91
Denver	$1,160.94	53	59.25
Boston	$1,833.73	40	56.93
Portland, OR	$1,148.11	81	56.11
New York	$2,068.96	66	54.66
San Antonio	$938.13	79	54.55
Sacramento	$929.22	64	53.90
Atlanta	$606.92	51	52.97
Phoenix	$703.71	66	52.67
Dallas	$1,013.58	53	52.62
Chicago	$1,172.46	58	52.57

Pittsburgh	$756.60	109	50.67
Miami	$1,073.52	76	49.78
Houston	$1,033.51	70	49.77
Tampa	$840.12	121	46.65
Milwaukee	$1,068.35	105	46.44
Baltimore	$1,276.98	113	45.07
St. Louis	$728.92	132	43.06
Philadelphia	$1,183.43	142	42.77
Detroit	$509.88	150	27.78

We still argue that your more immediate community (your school district, neighborhood, and town) is more important when it comes to your personal happiness. When you're thinking of buying that 4,500-square-foot McMansion out in the suburbs to avoid a two-bedroom fixer-upper in the city, you're trading size of home for commute. What's more important to you?

Maybe a bit of wisdom from *The Millionaire Next Door* is in order:

Perhaps you aren't as wealthy as you should be because you traded much of your current and future income just for the privilege of living in a home in a high-status neighborhood. So even if you're earning $100,000 a year, you're not becoming wealthy. What you probably don't know is that your neighbor in the $300,000 house next to yours bought his house only after he became wealthy. You bought yours in anticipation of becoming wealthy. That day may never come.[11]

The concept of spending today in anticipation of future wealth continues to plague those who are unable or unwilling to understand the long-term financial impact of large-scale purchases. Remember Ken, who traded Manhattan for Atlanta? His peers viewed his choice with skepticism, but it ultimately paid off with 20-plus years of reduced living costs. In the current environment of rising real estate prices and stagnant wages, the idea of living below your means—not above them—especially when it comes to housing, is as important as ever.

Are Millionaires "Cheap Dates"?

Is your significant other dropping hints that indicate he is interested in certain levels of requisite gifts, entertainment, and activities that require spending beyond your (or his) means? You may be involved in a relationship with a consumer-focused partner, one who ultimately may find it difficult to adjust to a more frugal lifestyle which those who seek economic success adopt, as my father described in 2011:

When people ask me about the activities of millionaires, I have a short answer. As I wrote in *The Millionaire Mind*, the typical millionaire is, in three words, "a cheap date!" Yes, a cheap date even among a fraction of the top 1% of the wealth holders in America. Many of the favorite activities of millionaires are not at all costly. It matters not if you are rich or poor. The best things in life are free or close to it. I was reminded of the "cheap date" concept when I read a recent e-mail from a self-employed multimillionaire "right on the mark . . . balance sheet affluent." In it, he wrote:

"[I] ride my bike to work, 12 miles round trip . . . been doing it for the last 8 years. . . age 59, married 38 years, no inheritance . . . 3 adult children, all successful . . . we paid for three private colleges . . . no mortgage . . . own a business . . . no debt. . . . My career is demanding (60 hours per week) but I have coached kids' sports, I sing in the church choir . . . have a garden . . . annually make many gallons of apple cider . . . keep honey bees . . . attended 6 homebuilding trips to Mexico and serve on a variety of professional committees. . . . Wife and I share many Christian values . . . This has contributed to our long-term marriage. All of our friends seem to have similar values to ours."

He mentions that he has no burning desire to drive a new car. As he said, "We are satisfied. Our cars tend to last a long time, 2002 Tahoe—90,000 miles, 1995 Buick purchased 3½ years ago for $3,500."

This millionaire spends his time and money in ways that give him great satisfaction. Being a "cheap date" doesn't bother him in the least.

The Goods of Consumers

What many people loved (and some people loathed) about *The Millionaire Next Door* was the focus on living frugally. Throughout the years since its publication, individuals from around the world commented that they finally felt vindicated for their chosen lifestyle: one that eschewed the consumption machine. They described in detail their habits, from seemingly small behaviors like clipping coupons to how they purchased their latest automobile. The case studies in *The Millionaire Next Door* confirmed for them that they were not alone.

Compared to 1996, the cycle for consumer trends is faster, our social connections include nonstop information about what our neighbors are doing and buying, and marketing looks like journalism. Marketing and consumerism have all changed dramatically in 20 years, changing the nature of what is presented to consumers and how easily accessible shopping is, as discussed in Chapter 2. Despite those changes, and despite the influences of media, social and otherwise, we see consistency in the moderation of millionaires over the past 20 years. Prodigious accumulators of wealth continue to describe themselves as frugal more often than those who are under accumulators of wealth, and they recognize that they are more economically successful than their neighbors. While there is little difference in budgeting, there is a difference in overall wealth and frugality.

Table 4-7. Budgeting & Frugality of Prodigious Accumulators of Wealth vs. Under Accumulators of Wealth

Statement	Percentage Strongly Agree/Agree	
	UAW	PAW
I have always been frugal.	40.7	57.0
In terms of accumulated wealth, we are much better off than most of our neighbors.	42.9	72.5
My household operates on a fairly well-thought-out annual budget.	58.0	61.6
I know how much our family spends each year for food, clothing, and shelter.	69.0	63.2

Does it take more to be disciplined in the area of spending today than in the 1980s or 1990s? Certainly the advent of social media and the advanced ways in which marketers can track and remarket to us requires more discipline to ignore them.

For now, we'll look at some similarities over time. The most millionaires will pay for consumer goods today hasn't changed much from 1996. In 2016, millionaires spent about the same amount on suits, shoes, and watches as they did in 1996. The median price paid for suits decreased approximately 18% between 1996 and 2016, most likely due to the decrease in apparel costs as well as the increase in informal business attire allowed today. But the important point here is that consumption, at least for these categories of consumer goods, continues to show that millionaires, next door and otherwise, are not consumers of top luxury items within conspicuous categories. In other words, even for those who wish to emulate the wealthy, the answer, as it was in 1996, is to not shop at the high end. Are your spending behaviors more like millionaires or more like what you perceive to be the wealthy in this country?

Table 4-8. Most Paid by Millionaires for Clothing and Accessories: 1996 to 2016 (in 2016 Dollars)[12]

		Suits		Shoes		Watch	
	Median:	$612	$500	$215	$200	$361	$300
% that spent less	% that spent more	1996	2016	1996	2016	1996	2016
10	90	$299	$200	$112	$97	$72	$50
25	75	$437	$300	$152	$120	$153	$100
50	50	$612	$500	$215	$200	$361	$300
75	25	$919	$1,000	$305	$300	$1,726	$2,500
90	10	$1,533	$1,500	$457	$500	$5,831	$8,150
95	5	$2,148	$2,000	$512	$600	$8,132	$12,000
99	1	$4,296	$4,720	$1,023	$1,656	$23,016	$25,260

Playing the Part? A Lawyer's Guide

Ned Davis, 36, is a successful trial lawyer. Even at this early stage in his career, his tally of legal victories places him in the exceptional category. Ned was kind enough to share some of his insights about the importance of accessorizing when in the courtroom environment:

I'm not a big watch guy, but I had wanted to buy a leather-banded, gold watch for some time. I have a silver/metallic Rolex watch that I received as a gift about 15 years ago and I wanted a gold watch to wear on occasion. I thought that I could justify spending a couple grand on a new watch because I had never bought one (and my wife even offered to get it for me as a Valentine's Day present). After reading Stop Acting Rich, *however, I decided that I would not go out and blow several thousand bucks on a fancy gold watch. I ended up finding a Timex at the antique dealer/thrift shop at the end of my street. The one I found had a vintage look (it was from the 1970s) that made it look like a nice dress watch. The Timex label, however, made it extremely affordable—$40!*

Not long after purchasing it I realized how useful it was to have a modestly-priced watch to wear on those occasions when I didn't want to seem like a fancy-pants lawyer. When I'm in front of a jury or meeting with a client or witness of modest means, I now prefer to wear the trusty Timex. I think our clothes and watches (and cars) do send a lot of messages that can be good or bad. I find that it is better not to have your clothes or watch or jewelry stick out too much in court, and I tell all my witnesses the same thing. By the way, Stop Acting Rich *has also reinforced my decision to keep driving my 2004 Volvo. I figure I'm saving at least $500–$700 every month I keep driving my seven-year-old car!*

Ned's many successes and the well-earned respect that goes with them are true badges of achievement. Uniforms and accessories can be bought in stores, but they're not the same as a list of genuine triumphs in legal (or in any other form of economic) competition. Also, note that nationwide the typical millionaire paid at most $300 (median) for a watch. About one in four paid $100 or less. Note here, though, that in our survey we didn't distinguish between traditional watches and smartwatches or other wearable technology which some argue may replace the traditional watches featured in *The Millionaire Next Door*. Even so, the median price paid is the approximate price of smartwatches.

Luxury Jeans

Let's take a look at the new staple of "business Friday" offices: jeans. The US denim industry is a $13.7 billion one,[13] and a recent study reported that on average, Americans own seven pairs.[14] While the average American pays under $50 per pair,[15] the millionaires in our study paid just over that mark, spending at most $50 on denim. In the luxury realm, though, we know that designer jeans can cost much more than that: simply type in "jeans" into Amazon and sort from highest price to lowest, and you'll most likely see an opportunity to purchase a pair of Dolce & Gabbana jeans for more than $8,000.

Only 25% of millionaires spent more than $100 on a pair of jeans, a far cry from the inexpensive jeans of one millionaire we interviewed, an attorney who left the corporate world to help with a family business:

I buy $12 Wrangler jeans at Walmart. They fit great and last forever. Now, I realize they are not necessarily the most stylish. So when Costco puts Levi's on sale, I buy three pairs of those to have some nicer jeans. My five pairs of jeans will last me 10 years.

Note that at the time of this writing, Wrangler jeans had more than 4,000 reviews and an average rating of 4.4 out of 5 stars on Amazon.com.

Table 4-9. Most Spent by Millionaires for Jeans, Sunglasses, and Furniture

		Jeans	Sunglasses	Furniture
	Median	$50	$150	$3,800
% that spent less	% that spent more	Most Spent	Most Spent	Most Spent
10	90	$30	$20	$1,200
25	75	$40	$50	$2,000
50	50	$50	$150	$3,800
75	25	$100	$250	$6,000
90	10	$195	$350	$10,000
95	5	$200	$500	$15,000
99	1	$300	$800	$39,000

Clothing Tips from "Mrs. Point"

Today Americans go through clothing faster than ever before. In 2015, the per capita consumption of apparel was 67.9 garments and 7.8 pairs of shoes, returning to pre-recession levels according to the American Apparel & Footwear Association.[16] We also throw clothing away at a breakneck speed. According to the

High-Quality Furniture: Less Costly in the Long Run

There are certain quality consumer goods that can be used, passed down, resold, and used again for years to come. In many cases, they are often higher in price but ultimately are only purchased once. My father wrote this piece in 2013, highlighting his lifelong hobby of woodworking and the concept of quality in consumer goods, quality that perhaps doesn't lend itself to a room redesign shopping spree every two years:

Omitted from my online resume is the heading of hobbies: "avid woodworker since age 12; builds rustic tables, cabinets . . . carves ducks, many from first growth white cedar. . . ." As a woodworker, I often make judgments about the quality of wood and workmanship in new and used furniture, even some antiques. My admitted preference is for traditional solid wood furniture. Well-made, traditional furniture is preferred by many millionaire-next-door types who see it as a lifetime investment.

One of my favorite brands of furniture is Henkel Harris. The quality of its wood and craftsmanship are grade A+.

I was saddened to learn that in 2013, Henkel Harris had closed its doors. I said to myself, "Just not enough wood-oriented traditional furniture buyers in America today." Through billion-dollar marketing campaigns consumers have become part of the disposable society. Some in the furniture industry are certainly a part of this culture. As consumers, we are being trained to buy and replace, buy and replace again that which is "trendy" or so-called "fashion furniture." All too often this kind of furniture is made from particle board, some even from saw dust held together with glue. And don't forget Brand X, which is composed of cheap veneers with painted stains nailed together instead of pegged. How long will this furniture be trendy?

Because we are the world's greatest economy, it shouldn't surprise anyone that we have the very best and most aggressive marketers in the world. They are successfully convincing more and more people that furniture is no longer really a durable good that might last through several generations, but is a disposable consumption item heading in the direction of plastic razors!

Admittedly high-quality furniture is expensive. But because of quality, previously owned Henkel Harris, for example, can be a great value for those on a limited budget. On my last visit to the Scott Antique Fair in Atlanta, I noticed a Henkel Harris dining room set in mahogany (table, eight chairs, sideboard and breakfront) for $899! Today the raw wood alone that would be required to construct this set would cost at least that much. Even if this furniture was professionally refinished you would still be paying less than 20% of what a new set would cost.

And here is some good news. By chance I Googled "Henkel Harris" and found the following message: "We at Henkel Harris are delighted to say, 'Henkel Harris is back'. . . . After only a few months of closing the Henkel Harris doors in early 2013. . . ."

Council for Textile Recycling, every year, every man, woman, and child in the United States throws away 70 pounds of clothing and other textiles.[17]

First interviewed for *The Millionaire Mind*,[18] Mrs. Point and her husband live in a four-bedroom home in one of Austin, Texas's nicest neighborhoods. "I believe in living in the best section of the city . . . location, location, location. . . . I will do without fine cars [plus a lot of other luxuries], but insist on having the best home possible," she says.

Mrs. Point understands the value of clothing. She never wants to spend big dollars on clothes—they depreciate too rapidly and put a hole in one's net worth. But she always wants to look well dressed. Here is her solution: "Oh, yes, I wear couture clothes [previously owned] that I buy at the Junior League shop." (Yes, there is even a hierarchy among thrift shops!) Many of the clothing items she purchases still have the original sales tags attached. In other words, they had never been worn. It seems that Mrs. Point's clothing expenditures are being subsidized by some of Austin's "glittering rich." Unbeknownst to them, these "aspirationals" are also enhancing her ability to transform income into wealth. If some of the clothing doesn't fit perfectly, she and Mr. Point do what about 4 in 10 millionaires do: They have their clothes altered instead of buying new ones. Mrs. Point uses the money saved to purchase quality stocks. "I am mindful of the fact we live in a time of medical miracles. . . . I . . . invest in stocks related to medicine. We have land . . . [and] mining operations and oil leases. We do not tell our friends about our holdings because many of those we associate with do not have as much as we do." Could she be talking about the income-statement affluent?

Cars: The Ultimate Test in Consumption?

It's not often that *one* consumer decision makes or breaks one's ability to build wealth over time; patterns of behavior are a better indicator of the likelihood of building and sustaining long-term wealth. But buying a car is a major financial decision that can have a significant long-term impact on wealth.

In 2016, the median amount our millionaires paid for their most recent car purchase was $35,000. The median high price paid for a car was $40,000. Most millionaires do not drive luxury automobiles. Rather Toyota, Honda, and Ford top the list. These three manufacturers were reported by nearly one-third of all millionaires in our sample. Note that some of the top manufacturers from 1996 (Oldsmobile, Cadillac, Lincoln, Jeep) aren't represented in the top 15 for 2016.

Nonluxury makes have consistently been at the top of "cars of millionaires" lists over time. The most popular brands among millionaires are Toyota, Honda, and Ford, followed only then by BMW. So, for those who want to emulate the rich or show their millionaire status, consider the top three choices of millionaires today.

Table 4-10. Top Makes of Motor Vehicles of Millionaires (1996 & 2016)

Make	Example Models	1996 %	2016 % (Rank)
Toyota	Camry, Corolla, Highlander, Prius	5.1	12.5 (1)
Honda	Accord, Civic, CRV, Odyssey, Pilot	1.6	11.4 (2)
Ford	Edge, Escape, Explorer, F-150, Focus	9.4	9.0 (3)
BMW	325, 535, 328, 428, X3	2.2	6.4 (4)
Chevrolet	Equinox, Silverado, Tahoe	5.6	5.9 (5)
Lexus	ES 350, RX 350	6.4	5.6 (6)
Nissan	Altima, Maxima, Rogue	2.9	4.8 (7)
Subaru	Forester, Outback	-	4.2 (8)
Dodge	Caravan, Grand Caravan, RAM	2.2	4.1 (9)
Mercedes	C300, E350, S550	6.4	3.9 (10)
Audi	A4, Q5, A6, A7	1.8	3.7 (11)
Volkswagen	Jetta, Passat	1.1	3.0 (12)
Hyundai	Elantra, Santa Fe	-	2.8 (13)
Acura	MDX, TSX, RDX	1.6	2.7 (14)
Kia	Sorento	-	2.0 (15)

High satisfaction in life abounds among those who focus on what is inside a person and not on what they drive, wear, or where they live. Even for those who love cars, like my father did, the economically successful are more interested in what can help them build wealth over time. When we asked one millionaire next door from outside Winston-Salem, North Carolina, what he gave up in order to achieve significant wealth, he replied, "A new car every few years. I drove a well-maintained car for 21 years. I think that decision saved me about $250,000 in repeated car payments. The end game is financial independence."

The Consistency of Quality

In order to drive a car for 20-plus years, it will need to be of the highest quality. This is the reason the economically successful tend to buy based on this factor. The luxury automobile is still the calling card of those who are income-statement affluent. But the table above shows that Toyota and Honda topped the list of cars driven by millionaires. Here is an interesting piece that my father wrote a few years ago about Honda, number two on our list of millionaires' top choices for automobiles:

A 2011 advertisement for the Honda Accord describes it as having the highest resale value within its class. I'm not surprised. How well a motor vehicle holds its value depends on several factors. Of course, reliability is important no doubt, but there is something else. It has to do with retail versus fleet sales. What if the car that you are contemplating buying is sold in the hundreds of thousands under the heading of Fleet Sales? Most of these fleet purchases are made by rental car companies who demand very deep discounts from manufacturers. Later, these one-, two-, or three-year-old cars are "dumped" on the used car market.

I learned this firsthand when Leigh, a friend of the family, asked me to help her sell her grandfather's car, a three-year-old sedan purchased new for $25,400. The car sold for $7,000 (she was lucky) even though it only had 14,000 miles on the odometer and was in excellent condition. Why so little? It was the number one make and model of car purchased by rental car companies during the year it was originally purchased.

Leigh's grandfather thought at the time that he was getting a good deal, a deep discount on his purchase. So much for "first cost" when buying a car. He paid dearly in terms of life cycle cost, losing more than 70% of the purchase price. Maybe he should have purchased a Honda! If he had he would have netted at least $5,000 more.

According to a 2011 article in *Automotive News*, Honda America accounted for only 1.6% or 33,000 of all the fleet sales (2.1 million) in 2010.[19] In contrast, Honda sold 1,197,500 of its vehicles to retail customers. In sharp contrast in terms of fleet sales, General Motors accounted for 29.2% or 609,000 motor vehicles; Ford accounted for 29% or 604,900.

Ironically, I recently bumped into the owner of a large Honda dealership. I hadn't seen him since we were in graduate school together. I praised his reputation as a quality dealer. He responded, "They are great cars and Honda, wonderful people to work with. But once you sell a Honda to a customer, they'll hold onto it or at least keep it in the family. I never have enough Honda trade-ins to keep my lot filled."

Table 4-11. Model Year Cars by Percentage Owned by Millionaires (1996 & 2016)

	Percentage of Millionaires	
Latest Model Year of Car	1996	2016
Current Year	23.5	15.5
One Year Old	22.8	17.8
Two Years Old	16.1	15.1
Three Years Old	12.4	10.2
Four Years Old	6.3	7.6
Five Years Old	6.6	6.2
Six Years Old or Older	12.3	27.7

In 1996, those purchasing motor vehicles accounted for 81% of this sample of millionaires; those leasing accounted for 19%. In 2016, 86% of millionaires purchased their motor vehicles, while 14% leased their latest car.

Leasing, Luxury, and Aspirationals

It's very easy to judge others by the car they drive. Marketers count on it and spend billions of dollars so you have a certain (somewhat inaccurate) view of luxury car owners and drivers. But you cannot judge the wealth of your neighbors, friends, or family members by what they drive. And often those luxury cars are leased. Income-statement affluent consumers are especially prone to leasing during periods of economic prosperity.

In 2010 *Automotive News* reported that the vice president for Mercedes-Benz Financial Services indicated that leasing accounted for half of all sales of new Mercedes-Benz vehicles.[20] Further, this 50% figure is rather consistent in good times and in bad. How does this 50% figure compare with the lease versus purchase ratio for all those passenger vehicles acquired in America? It is much higher than the norm. Over the past decade leasing accounted for approximately 20% of all new passenger vehicles that were acquired.

Aspirationals—people who aspire to be rich and play the part by consuming as if they are already wealthy—are much better at spending income to look wealthy rather than actually accumulating wealth. If this group was really interested in emulating those who are truly rich, they might wish to purchase instead

Who Buys a 13-Year-Old Toyota?

Nearly 28% of millionaires in our latest study drive a car that is at least six years old, and of course, we know anecdotally that many millionaires drive cars into the double digits of years. In what you might call a field study, my father profiled the prospective buyers of his 13-year-old Toyota to examine anecdotal evidence about buying habits. He wrote this piece in 2010:

When I sold our family's mainstay, a 1997 Toyota 4 Runner 4 X 4, the car was like a good friend; it never let our family down. Even though it had 180,000 miles on it, everything worked. The paint was still nearly perfect.

We were surprised with the large number of prospective buyers who contacted us shortly after it was listed on the Internet. Two of the potential buyers are worthy of discussion here. Prospective buyer #1 was male, age 36, married, father of 3. He and his wife both work full-time. The couple was in the process of discarding the two late model vehicles which they currently owned. Why were these people interested in buying a 13-year-old, $5,000 used Toyota? It was not because they were in dire financial straits nor were they depressed about the prospects of "downsizing." As the young man explained, he and his wife had good-paying jobs, but they were on a treadmill making loan payments including one on each vehicle. At the end of each month after paying all their bills, they had little or nothing left to invest. The couple was determined to become financially independent. Selling their two expensive vehicles and investing the more than $30,000 in equity that they would receive was a start. According to the couple the encouragement and method for doing this came from the Financial Peace University program they attended at their church.

Prospective buyer #2 was a male, age 26, engaged, who had just sold his late model, fully loaded pickup truck. He walked away with over $20,000 equity in the truck that he wanted to enhance his nest egg for his upcoming marriage. He was a civil servant for the federal government and a moonlighter. He felt that in the small college town where he lived he could get all or most of his money back on the 1997 4 Runner even if he sold it in two years.

Prospective buyer #2 bought the car within five minutes of seeing it. The first prospective buyer did not buy the car because he wanted a seven passenger SUV for carpooling use and he bought one.

Not all people who "trade down" like these two buyers feel ego deflated or encounter loss of self-esteem. Those who plan to build wealth by downsizing and investing encounter enhanced pride and new confidence. It is all part of taking control of our lives and not being controlled by consumption and the hyper-use of credit. It took billions in advertising and marketing dollars to convince us that happiness and self-esteem can be purchased in stores with loans and credit cards. And such beliefs cannot be changed overnight. It is important to have a mentor who can help you change and then guide you to financial freedom.

of lease their motor vehicles. In our latest survey, only 14% of millionaires leased their cars, and the median value of those vehicles was $46,000, whereas millionaires who purchased their new cars did so for a median value of $35,000. Of those who leased, 25% of the cars leased by millionaires in our latest study were luxury cars, whereas 75% of the leased vehicles were nonluxury cars (e.g., Honda, Toyota).

My father profiled aspirationals in *Stop Acting Rich*. Perhaps Shakespeare was referring to these people when he wrote, "All that glitters is not gold." Yet many Americans are guilty of judging the wealth of others based on whether they drive prestige makes of motor vehicles. Judgments of this type are often inaccurate and can have a dampening effect on prudent consumption behaviors. My father received an e-mail from a man who expressed cynicism about the subject of consumer purchases and wealth:

> . . . *having a hard time not being cynical about people based on where they live or what types of car they drive. We go to a church that is considered "rich" . . . a lot of people drive the nicer vehicles, Escalades, BMWs, etc. . . . we jump to the assumption that they are hyper spenders not wealth accumulators. [Our children] go to the church's school . . . hard to tell them that they don't need all the status items, North Face, Abercrombie, expensive shoes, etc. that the other children have. . . . My wife looks at these people and wonders where they get all their money to purchase expensive items. How do you not become cynical?*

My father's advice to him? First, never judge the true quality of a person by what can be purchased. Second, as the reader suspects, often people who dress and drive as if they are rich are not.

In our latest study, across all respondents in our affluent sample, not surprisingly we found a correlation between purchase price of one's latest vehicle and net worth. And the combination of age, income, and net worth accounted for almost 25% of the variance in purchase price. From a practical perspective, the price of our cars has more to do with factors beyond how much we make, how old we are, and our wealth, including attitudes, influences about luxury, and what our neighbors are driving. These sociometric and psychological factors may be at play. And we found that *income* did a much better job at predicting how much you would pay for your next car than your *net worth*. This is particularly true for leasing: we found that *net worth* added very little when trying to predict the price of a leased vehicle above and beyond income.

For our cynical reader, the answer is clear: The purchase price of cars (and therefore the makes and models he sees in his community) has more to do with factors other than wealth or income than most of us believe. And if we are considering the financial side of why we drive what we drive, income level, not wealth, is more important.

Perhaps it is best said in the Old Testament: "Man looks at the outward appearance, But the Lord looks at the heart." —1 Samuel 16:7

How to Buy Used Luxury

What if you want to drive luxury? The "used-vehicle-prone shopper" category of the millionaire-next-door population provides a guidebook to those who choose to have luxury in a pre-owned state. One engineering professor detailed his latest car purchasing experience with my father:

> *The sight of cash has a powerful effect on some people. Accordingly, I took $2,000 in twenty dollar bills from my emergency cash reserve. I put $500 of it in my right trouser pocket and the remaining $1,500 in my left shirt pocket. After arranging to come and see the car, I got an old Navy shipmate of mine to drive me to the appointment. The seller lived in a pricey neighborhood with equestrian trails. He had a new Jaguar sedan, a Toyota sedan, and a Cadillac Escalade SUV in the three-car garage. His oldest daughter had been using the Mercedes to drive to [her college] classes. . . . She was moving [out of state] . . . and he had just bought her a new Toyota. He also said, "I don't need four cars for just me and my wife." This passed the "smell test" and it indicated that this was probably not a "lemon" he was trying to unload on someone. After test driving the car, I took out the wad of twenty dollar bills from my shirt pocket, laid it down on the hood of the Mercedes and asked, "Would you be willing to entertain an offer of $1,500 cash?" He was. Thus, it came to pass that I drive a 1980 vintage luxury Mercedes Benz [every day] to work and back. It runs quite well, gets 25 miles per gallon, and I enjoy driving it. This car was made back when Mercedes Benz had a well-deserved reputation for exceedingly high-quality manufacturing standards and for designing their cars to last. Plus, my inner 20-year-old kid is delighted that he finally got his wish, even if it took 38 years for it to come to pass.*

Too many Americans may believe that by driving a new car they are emulating economically successful people. But only 16% of millionaires drive this year's model motor vehicle. Don't ever feel degraded if you are riding around in a used motor vehicle.

Car Buying for Professional Advisors

John, a financial advisor, was relocating to a south Florida affluent enclave. He sought my father's advice concerning the "ideal" motor vehicle. John, who valued the millionaire-next-door concept, was seeking "special dispensation." He was fearful that he would alienate prospective clients by driving a "normal" (i.e., non-luxury) make of car.

Countless times people in John's position had tried to convince my father that driving an expensive motor vehicle is part of the required uniform for those who provide professional services to the rich. But he was never persuaded. Instead, he insisted that the key to success is to provide a high level of core service that is way beyond expectation. In other words, it was more important that John manage the money of his "glittering rich" clients successfully than worry about the make of car he drove.

Here's what my father wrote about the glittering rich in *Stop Acting Rich*: "These people are prodigious spenders on every form of prestige products and services. Yet they live below their means because to qualify they must have a minimum net worth of $20M. The glittering rich . . . own . . . a top of the line BMW, Mercedes, Lexus. . . . Most have at least one SUV. Yet many of these SUVs are not in the luxury class. Full size SUVs . . . are extremely popular among the glittering rich."[21]

My father had a compromise solution for John. Since full-sized SUVs seemed extremely popular among the glittering rich, why not purchase a previously owned one? He recommended something within the GM family because they were big, comfortable, safe, and considered by many to rank first in quality among all full-size SUVs. And John wouldn't have trouble finding one. My father found 93 pages of previously owned, full-size GM SUVs for sale in John's trade area.

Big-Ticket Spending

Besides purchasing consumer goods, cars, and homes, how do millionaires allocate their income? As we will cover in Chapter 7, most millionaires we surveyed spend 1% of their annual household income on financial advice, but one-third pay nothing. One out of three millionaires allocates none of his household income to "economic outpatient care" (aka big-ticket financial gifts to relatives), whereas one-third gives approximately 1% of their income to this cause. Thirty-six percent of millionaires give 5% of their income to charitable organizations; approximately one-fourth of millionaires give 10% or more of their annual household income away to noble causes.

Table 4-12. Percentage of Income Spent on Categories by Millionaires

Spending Category	Percentage of Income Spent by Category							
	0%	1%	5%	10%	20%	30%	50%	75% or more
	Percentage of Millionaires							
Income Taxes	0.8	0.6	1.8	5.8	21.8	50.1	18.0	0.3
Interest on Credit Card/Installment Loans	71.7	16.4	8.4	3.1	0.2	0.3	0.0	0.0
Cash/Equivalent Charitable Contributions	3.1	37.0	36.1	19.8	2.6	1.4	0.0	0.0
Fees for Financial Advice/Management/Transactions	32.7	56.3	8.3	2.5	0.2	0.2	0.0	0.0
Education/Tuition	47.6	12.2	16.2	14.8	5.7	2.6	0.6	0.2
Gifts of Cash, Securities, Property, Vehicles, etc. to Relatives	33.6	33.9	23.2	7.3	1.4	0.3	0.2	0.0
Pension/Annuity Contributions	35.1	7.2	19.8	24.3	12.0	0.9	0.5	0.2
Investments (other than Pension/Annuity Contributions)	20.3	10.8	27.4	19.2	13.8	5.2	2.2	1.1
Mortgage Payments	32.6	6.6	14.6	21.8	15.1	8.3	0.9	0.2
Club Dues/Fees/Expenses	68.1	19.5	9.8	2.1	0.5	0.0	0.0	0.0
Motor Vehicle Purchase and/or Lease Payments/Services/Fuel/Insurance	14.8	34.3	37.2	11.3	1.7	0.5	0.3	0.0
Clothing	1.8	59.7	32.3	5.5	0.5	0.0	0.2	0.0
Commercial Loan Payments	83.8	5.2	5.5	4.0	0.8	0.6	0.2	0.0
All Other Categories (not listed above)	14.2	8.5	19.5	15.9	17.6	12.9	9.2	2.2

What Gifts We Give

The billionaire businessman and former mayor of New York City, Michael Bloomberg, has been documented as only possessing two pairs of work shoes. And it has also been disclosed that he routinely has them resoled so he can wear them for longer periods of time. Our data indicates that of the top 1% of wealth holders in America, 70% regularly have their shoes resoled or repaired. This supports our general thesis that people who have a propensity to build wealth tend to be quite frugal in allocating their dollars for consumer products. Mr. Bloomberg is quite obviously a prodigious accumulator of wealth: a balance-sheet affluent type. And yet Mr. Bloomberg—consistent with the broader sample of prodigious accumulators of wealth—tends to be quite generous in donating his wealth to noble causes. Conversely, the data indicates that people with high incomes and significantly lower levels of wealth accumulated for their age or income cohort tend to spend big on themselves but donate relatively little to noble causes.

In our 2016 survey result, our sample indicated that 52% of the under accumulator population donated 5% or more of their annual household income to charitable causes, while nearly 70% of the prodigious accumulator population donated 5% or more of their annual household income. At first glance, this data may appear counterintuitive (shouldn't the prodigious accumulators be giving *less* away to others?), but upon reflection it makes sense. The income-statement affluent types don't give as much away because they need more of it to fuel a high-consumption lifestyle. The prodigious accumulator group has more to share because their fixed lifestyle costs are lower. The IRS estate tax data also shows that as estate size increases, charitable giving increases dramatically.

Table 4-13. Charitable Deductions as a Percentage of Size of Estate[22]

IRS Estate Tax Data (2016 return filings)	
Size of Estate	Charitable deduction as %
<$5 million	2.71
$5–$10 million	3.91
$10–$20 million	5.84
$20–$50 million	9.75
> $50 million	15.80

In 2013 Mr. Bloomberg donated $350 million to Johns Hopkins University, his alma mater, thereby pushing his lifetime giving to the school above $1 billion. Let's translate that amount into consumer product equivalents: That's $500 million donated for each pair of work shoes he owns.

Our research indicates that recognition is not a major factor motivating affluent individuals to support noble causes. It has more to do with the satisfaction they receive from helping others, especially in terms of enhancing the growth and development of future generations.

That's Why They're Wealthy!

If you've decided that being frugal isn't for you and you want to consume with abandon, can you still build wealth? Ah, the ultimate question of the income-statement affluent. The trouble is that most average- to high-income-producing Americans burden themselves, their households, their children (and most importantly, their adult children) with expectations for a lifestyle that perpetually requires a high income, heavy amounts of economic outpatient care, or debt.

As we've already mentioned, the original title of *The Millionaire Next Door* was *That's Why They're Wealthy* until the editor, Suzanne DeGalan, suggested the new title. One of the main reasons that the "they" are wealthy is because they live below their means and shop for value. Those who are successful accumulators of wealth approach spending and consumption with consistent discipline, training for financial Independence Day, transaction by transaction. This allows them to build wealth in good economic times and bad. They research, evaluate, and scrutinize their purchases over a lifetime.

As my father wrote in *The Millionaire Next Door*, "How did the wife of a millionaire respond when her husband gave her $8 million worth of stock in a company he recently took public? . . . She said, 'I appreciate this, I really do.' Then she smiled, never changing her position at the kitchen table, where she continued to cut out 25 and 50-cents-off food coupons from the week's supply of newspapers."[23]

Ignoring trends, being indifferent to the views and influence of the herd, and living below their means are the hallmarks of those who are good at transforming income into wealth. As a result of this lifestyle, they have greater freedom and security to change jobs, start their own businesses, and take chances. In essence, a consistent and disciplined pattern of consumption behaviors is the marker of those who can be wealthy on their own, and those who are wealthy today.

Chapter 5

Strengths for Building Wealth

It is very confusing, all this information about the keys to becoming economically successful. How did millionaires become rich in America? The best way to answer this question is to ask them.

—from *The Millionaire Mind*

WITHOUT A HIGHER-THAN-AVERAGE INCOME, MOST INDIVIDUALS WORKING for others cannot amass wealth easily. And small business owners aren't universally successful. (In fact, the failure rate for small businesses in the US within five years as of 2016 was 50%.[1]) Finding great satisfaction in one's work, while important for long-term revenue generation, doesn't guarantee wealth. Put simply, the ability to transform any amount of income into wealth still relies upon the discipline and hard work associated with saving and managing one's finances effectively. This includes the mundane (e.g., creating budgets, paying bills) and the more complex (e.g., filing taxes, investment analysis).

To achieve financial independence, someone (or more than one someone, which is more often the case today) will have to assume the role and responsibility of "Household CFO" for budgeting, planning, and overall leadership related to all things financial. Just like the millionaires who are proficient in targeting market opportunities, most economically successful households have in them a leader or a team that is able to capitalize on their strengths for building wealth. They run their households like a business, assigning key tasks to the team member who can effectively do that job.

So the question becomes, what competencies or characteristics allow for better *personal financial management* than others? Studying the habits and characteristics of the affluent was the main focus of my father's lifetime of work. As I began to join him in his research efforts, I had to apply the type of science I had been trained to use to help understand if the characteristics of the wealthy were, in fact, related to net worth. Was it really the case that frugality always led people to be more financially successful than their peers, or was luck at play? Was it really possible that confidence and discipline could impact one's ability to transform income into wealth, or were the millionaires featured in 1996 financially successful because of the times and a few good choices along the way?

Much of our work examining the affluent had focused on demographics and consumer-related data: what they buy, where they live, what they drive, and how they spend their time. Some of that research included examining life experiences and characteristics, particularly in *The Millionaire Mind*. Beginning in 2010, we began to broaden the focus of our research, identifying common behaviors of individuals at various points on the wealth accumulation spectrum—those who are above average at the task of converting *income* into *wealth* (PAWs), and those who are below average at this task (UAWs). From this we can make certain inferences regarding the higher-level behavioral common denominators of successful wealth builders.

To study this critical *job*, one that to some extent all of us have, we began a series of studies back in 2012. Several of these included samples of mostly mass affluent Americans, selected from a crowdsourcing site.[2] These were Americans who were essentially freelancing or moonlighting to generate additional revenue for themselves or their families. This endeavor was in some respects a reverse approach to our other historical research efforts. In the past, we examined traits and habits of millionaire populations and at times divided samples into prodigious accumulators of wealth and under accumulators of wealth based on age, income, and net worth, and then identified significant behaviors in each group. Our main focus in recent years was to find out what other big-picture behavioral common denominators make prodigious accumulators of wealth better than their peers at converting their income into lasting wealth. These other behavioral characteristics that were imbedded in our survey research regarding purchasing decisions and career paths were not as obvious.

The Job Analysis of the Household CFO

If we forget about windfalls and inheritances for a moment, we can consider the characteristics that are most conducive to building wealth over time. What characteristics *predict* or are related to net worth, regardless of how old you are or how much money you make? To do this, we first considered personal financial management as a job, one that has a distinct set of responsibilities and activities that go along with it. To illustrate how this works, imagine you had to hire a professional to manage *every* financial transaction or task you had in your life, not just "financial planning" or investing. Everything from paying bills to interacting with your spouse or significant other about money would have to be done by this new hire. A combination of science and common sense would help guide your decision-making process to find the best candidate for the job. What would this job posting look like?

WANTED: Household CFO

Description: The role of the Household CFO is to ensure his/her household is building wealth in order to ultimately achieve financial independence.

The Household CFO will oversee the household's budgeting and financial planning. He/she will be required to create, manage, explain, defend, and negotiate household budgets annually, and monitor spending and saving related to said budget. He/she will be required to plan for the financial security and longevity of the family, focusing specifically on retirement planning, college savings planning, and other large expenses in the foreseeable future. The Household CFO will be required to balance checkbooks, file tax returns, pay bills on time, create financial plans, create estate plans, research investments, monitor investments, and generally run all financial matters for the household. The Household CFO will serve as a check on household spending, and thus will work closely with the following individuals: Household Chief Procurement Officer and his/her team members (read: spouse/self and/or children). The Household CFO may choose to outsource any number of his/her responsibilities to trusted advisors, and therefore, part of the Household CFO job may include the ability to research and hire quality professionals who act in the Household CFO's household's best interests.

After a thorough search and finding no suitable candidates, you decide that you or your significant other will take on the role, regardless of the nominee's qualifications.

The last piece above is the reality. This critical role is *always* filled by someone in the household even if partially (e.g., some of the tasks are outsourced to professionals), and even if not effectively or with any great attention. Regardless of whether there is interest, ability, or personality well-suited for it, *someone* is in the role, even if they are not actually *doing* the job. The difference between economically successful Americans and those who are not is often that they:

- Know the universe of tasks that are required to do the job.
- Understand what they can do well, what they need to improve on, and what needs to be outsourced.
- Demonstrate or work to improve in areas that are key to building and maintaining wealth.

As we discussed in Chapter 3, a combination of both nature and nurture gives us strengths that can allow us to build wealth or get in the way of us being economically successful. Every individual steps into the household CFO job with a unique set of experiences and competencies, behaviors, and attitudes. Despite these differences, unless our financial lives are completely cared for by someone else, we have to perform the role of managing our money.

Part of our research in the past few years has focused on an analysis of the tasks required for personal financial management. This was conducted in the same fashion that industrial psychologists study occupations. What are the requirements of someone who is in the role of household CFO? What does this person do to manage their finances? Once we know the requirements of the job, then we can examine what it takes to do it successfully. When an individual serves as the household CFO, his or her main tasks include those related to spending, budgeting, and doing administrative tasks, as well as making investment-related decisions, and finally, working with others (especially in the case of couples or households with children).

Presumably, if someone in the household is completing the most critical tasks for her household, then the household will be financially successful, assuming no one on the "team" (spouse, children) is actively working against the goals. These tasks require different skill sets to some extent, but, luckily, there is some overlap across them. The list can serve as a *what-you-need-to-know* checklist, especially for those who either haven't had to manage their own financial affairs in the past or are now able to do so without a team.

Critical Tasks for Household Financial Management[3]

General

- Consider the outcomes of potential actions before deciding on a course of action
- Make financial decisions based on household's budget, plans, and long-term goals
- Focus financial management efforts on becoming debt-free

Spending

- Live (spend) below means (income/net worth)
- Spend less on expenses than household's total income in a given time period

Budgeting

- Create an emergency fund
- Budget enough money for basic needs (e.g., food) before budgeting for optional purchases (e.g., entertainment)
- Account for important household needs (e.g., food, clothing, shelter) in preparing budget
- Analyze budget and financial goals when considering a significant life change (e.g., job changes, additional children, moving locations) that may impact goals

Administrative Tasks

- Pay bills on time to ensure no late fees or interest charges apply
- Complete and file tax returns on time (whether in-house or with assistance)
- Pay credit card bills on time to ensure no interest charges are incurred
- Pay entire balance of credit card each month

Working with Others

- Discuss unplanned or unexpected purchases with spouse/significant other prior to purchase

- Work with spouse/significant other as a team when managing household financial issues

Investing

- Understand the nature of investments and their risk and return profile
- Invest in employer-provided retirement savings accounts (e.g., 401(k)s)
- Understand the appropriate level of risk to take for own investment portfolio

Someone in the household must complete these tasks in order for the household to run effectively. Even if some are outsourced, part of the success of such an endeavor is hiring the right set of trusted advisors. And the tasks listed here are just the tip of the iceberg: We found a total of more than 240 potential tasks for the household CFO, some more critical (and frequent) than others.

Competencies for Wealth

Consider the tasks of the household CFO, and then think about how much you enjoy those tasks and whether you have the knowledge, skills, and abilities to carry them out. Now we're not discussing what the job of financial management entails, but instead the characteristics of how they are completed.

Perhaps one of the biggest steps to building wealth involves recognizing how one wants to live one's life, evaluating one's values and interests, setting goals, and achieving them. All of us have a wide range of competencies. These are personal characteristics that range from being detail-oriented and organized to leaving the details and organizing to others. They include interests that span from artistic endeavors to those focused more on conventional concerns like making lists and keeping track of daily routines. They also include values that are highly individualized to those that are more collective and team-based.

We know from years of research in predicting job performance, from the field of industrial psychology, that some of these same success factors predict future job performance as well as financial success. Conscientiousness, among the best personality-based predictors of job performance in almost any role[4], is also related to financial success. Particularly, *self-control* tends to be positively related to illiquid and liquid asset holdings, as well as net worth.[5]

The Importance of Responsibility

Assuming responsibility for the financial success or failure within a household relates to financial success.[6] In other words, individuals who view financial management as something they can impact and have responsibility for tend to have a higher net worth than those who believe that other factors (e.g., government, financial markets) play a large role in financial success. This is similar to the concept of locus of control in psychology: Those with external locus of control often assume that they cannot control or impact the outcomes in their lives, while those with internal locus of control view themselves as the ultimate source for success and failure. While living on either side of that continuum can have downsides, taking responsibility for financial outcomes, and acting accordingly, can positively impact wealth, and this same concept applies in other aspects of our lives, as well. My father highlighted the role of responsibility and leadership in an essay in 2012:

Ron Chernow's book, *Washington: A Life*[7], has been well received by most critics. In an interview published in the *Wall Street Journal* in 2012, Mr. Chernow said of President Washington, "You don't have to be the brightest or the most original mind on the block . . . but what Washington's life shows is the clarity of vision, the tenacity of purpose and character, and how much can be accomplished in life if you keep your sights on your ultimate goals."[8]

In *The Millionaire Mind*, I cite the work of Fred Fiedler and Thomas Link, two scholars in the field of intelligence and human performance. They concluded that "Cognitive ability tests [standardized intelligence tests] have been notoriously poor predictors of leadership performance. . . . Relations between intelligence and leadership and managerial performance . . . accounting for less than 10% of the variance. . . . Even these low correlations are likely to be overestimates of the true relationship. . . . Leader intelligence under certain conditions correlates negatively with performance."

It is unfortunate that counselors rarely tell students that 90% of the variation in leadership is not explained by standardized intelligence measures. How many kids gave up on themselves early in life because they did poorly in school or ranked low on the SAT totem pole? Perhaps they should have been told, "You still have a chance. You may have to work harder, but you may also have the ability to lead other people."

One of the most interesting millionaires that I ever interviewed never excelled in school or on any standardized test. During high school, his parents in frustration asked for a consultation with a seasoned guidance counselor. He told them, "Don't worry about your son; he is a natural born leader. What he has cannot be measured." The counselor was correct in his assessment of the young man, who today is an extraordinarily successful adult.

George Washington—like most successful people—took responsibility for being a leader at an early age. It is important to encourage young people to look for opportunities to lead and not follow.

Of course, much of financial management is in the details, so those who have administrative or clerical skills will be better able to keep track of the spending, saving, and other details. Economically productive households tend to have one member of the leadership team who can effectively track such details. Being detail-oriented, or conscientious, tends to relate to a person's financial success over time.

To identify the characteristics that were most predictive of net worth in broad samples, again assuming age and income were constant, we conducted a series of parallel studies designed to determine what the broad behavioral categories were that would relate to or predict one's ability to build wealth over time. Using two sets of broad samples of Americans, including those with a net worth ranging from $100,000 to $1 million as well as a sample of high- and ultra-high-net-worth individuals, we find that key areas of behaviors impact one's ability to transform income into wealth, regardless of age and income levels.[9]

Those behaviors and experiences tend to fall into six categories, both statistically and practically. Specifically, we find that the competencies related to discipline and conscientiousness (including frugality and social indifference, or not being influenced by trends) are positively related to net worth. In relation to discipline and conscientiousness, we see that financial planning behaviors and the ability to focus and not get distracted also impact net worth. Confidence in financial decision-making, and taking responsibility for one's financial success, also relate to net worth at any age or income level. It's never too late to learn, as one retired millionaire told us: "I lost my job . . . in 1982. Made me realize I was responsible entirely for my family and financial well-being. Became interested in my 457 at state of Illinois employment and learned the concepts of investing in mutual funds and buy and hold. We were prodigious savers and over time realized a $1M net worth."

Table 5-1. Categories of Wealth-Related Behavioral Patterns

Category	Definition	Example Question
Confidence	Demonstration of confidence and collaboration in financial management, investing, and household leadership.	*How comfortable are you making significant financial decisions for your household?*
Frugality	Financial behaviors associated with consistent saving, dedicated commitment to lower spending, and rigorous adherence to a budget.	*My friends and/or family members would describe me as frugal.*
Responsibility	Acceptance of the role of actions, abilities, and experiences in financial outcomes. Belief that luck plays a small part in achievement.	*I take responsibility for the financial outcomes of my household.*
Social Indifference	Spending and saving behaviors that reflect immunity to social pressure to purchase the latest in consumer and/or luxury goods, clothing & cars.	*How often do you ignore pressure to shop and spend as your neighbors or friends do?*
Focus	Demonstration of the ability to focus on detailed tasks through completion without becoming distracted	*I find it easy to complete tasks without becoming distracted.*
Planning	Behaviors related to goal-setting, planning, and anticipating future needs	*I have a clearly defined set of daily, weekly, monthly, annual, and/or lifetime goals.*

Taken together, these *wealth factors* are related to net worth regardless of your age or income. In our research, we divided our samples into groups of high, medium, and low potential for wealth accumulation and gathered relevant data for each group. Probably the most significant difference between these groups was the median savings rate for each (i.e., the amount of their monthly and annual income they were able to save rather than consume). The savings rate of the "high-potential" group was nearly 2.5 times that of the "low-potential" group. Let's say that again: The high-potential group saved 143% more every month and year than the low-potential group. Consider the power of this difference applied over a 30-year working career. And consider its relative power in Wall Street terms, where vast fortunes are earned by money managers who are able (to at least promise) to deliver portfolio returns that beat the market by a percentage point or two.

What does it mean to "hold age and income constant"? Are we saying that these factors did not affect financial outcomes? Of course not. Or to put it another way: Age and income have a significant effect on financial position and net worth. What we are saying is that our approach held those variables *constant* and then looked for statistically significant behavioral variables *over and above* any variation explained by age and income. Here's an example: While we all know that a 65-year-old individual who earned $1 million a year working as a surgeon is likely to have a higher net worth than a 23-year-old construction worker, our study sought to find behavioral differences that contributed to their economic results over and above the significant effect of age and income.

About Those Engineers

Those who are economically successful tend to be aware of their strengths and weaknesses when it comes to financial management, revenue generation, investing, and the like. They are aware that even if they do have the skills and abilities to manage their financial lives, they occasionally need to outsource some of the more complex or time-consuming tasks to professional experts.

The same can be said for those who tend to excel in their chosen career or vocation: They tend to be aware of their strengths and weaknesses, their interests, attitudes, and values, and find jobs that fit, that are congruent, with their own unique skills.

One vocation often tied to the ability to transform income into wealth is engineering. Many millionaires next door often come from this line of work. In *Stop Acting Rich*, the frugality associated with engineers was explained this way:

> *The frugal nature of wealthy engineers is certainly reflected in their demonstrated superior ability to generate wealth from income. On average, engineers produced about 22% more wealth per dollar of realized income than did millionaires in general.*
>
> *They have a higher-than-average propensity than others in their income/age cohort to accumulate wealth. They are less likely to favor expensive status-denoting products and brands than others.*[10]

What is it about the engineers that makes them astute at transforming their income into wealth? Is it their interest in engineering? Their attitude? Answer: It is the same critical skills that led them to be engineers. For example, think of the key work competencies required for a shipping engineer[11]: dependability, attention to detail, analytical thinking, independence, and integrity. Many of these same or similar competencies impact one's ability to build and maintain wealth over time.

When we examine our own *financial competencies through the lens of job-related behaviors, a few things happen*:

1. We recognize that one good decision or even a few good decisions doesn't a millionaire make.

2. We can identify where we fall short or where we need to improve.

3. We can *change* and improve over time.

These *wealth factors*, behavioral characteristics that are related to net worth, can be improved. It's possible to become more frugal over time. You can increase confidence in financial matters through building knowledge and having some small successes along the path to financial independence. Through those successes, you can begin to see the effects of your own financial behaviors playing out: slowly increasing your savings rate, adhering to a budget, and having more left over at the end of the month.

Millionaires Next Door . . . Today

We see the value in adopting a *pattern* of behaviors play out in real-life millionaires next door. In an upper-middle-class suburb of Atlanta, Georgia, live Mike and Hollye Wells. Their disciplined approach to location, careers, child rearing, education, and life has allowed them to achieve the distinction of millionaires next door in their early 40s. They own two older model cars, live in a modest home within an excellent public school district, and live a lifestyle on their own terms. They cite the application of many of Dave Ramsey's lessons on their approach to building wealth. Through a combination of setting financial goals, tracking expenses, and focusing on controlling debt, they have been able to become financially successful amid the hyper-consumerism all around them.

Even with that, Hollye shared her surprise about the likelihood of becoming economically successful via a slow and steady path: "I didn't know you could be a millionaire this way . . . [I] thought only if you inherited it or were in Hollywood or a CEO. . . . This was such a surprise." Indeed, Hollye saw firsthand that high incomes were not necessary for achieving millionaire status.

Mike's planning and intense focus on the family's financial goals set the family on a course to build wealth by finding a home they could afford, even in a sought-after school district. Mike was able to ignore some of the trappings that come with suburbia. Unlike his cohorts who hired a real estate agent to find their home, he ignored the trend and handled the sale on his own. He said, "[We] moved into an area without an HOA and not near the golf course. I didn't want to be tempted by the country club. We refused to work with a real estate agent."

One of their goals is to empower their children to have some of the same opportunities starting out. This required extreme planning on their part to ensure that each of their three children can go to college without the burden of student loans following them. They took on the responsibility for this task, while others in their community assume their children will take on debt to attend school (or just don't think about it at all). Of course, funding education *and* retirement requires planning and a correspondingly frugal lifestyle.

Discipline is also part of their daily lives. To ensure they are meeting budgets and sustain a frugal lifestyle, Hollye focuses on consumption in a way that is tied to their financial goals and not on having the latest and greatest. She explains it this way: "If it's not on sale or clearance, I don't buy it. I hate paying retail. . . . I'm willing to be patient with purchases. We have [boys and a girl] so I usually buy mostly black or neutral clothes and gear so we can pass it along to all of them. We buy [sporting] equipment secondhand—it doesn't need to be new. We don't compare ourselves. We're not trying to outrun anyone . . . but we have to balance [the children's] expectations for wants and needs."

Table 5-2. Discipline Related to Wealth Status: Under Accumulators of Wealth vs. Prodigious Accumulators of Wealth

Statement	Percentage Strongly Agree/Agree	
	UAWs	PAWs
Our household operates on a fairly well-thought-out annual budget.	58.0	61.6
I have a clearly defined set of daily, weekly, annual, and lifetime goals.	55.0	59.0
I spend a lot of time planning my financial future.	49.0	64.3
I have always been frugal.	40.7	57.0
I rarely get distracted when working on a project.	48.5	51.0

Like many of their Generation X cohorts, the Wellses tend to save for and spend on experiences with their families, such as traveling internationally to events with their children. The Wellses spend in anticipation of market ups and downs that they cannot control, rather than spending in anticipation of future financial success or assumed increases in income. They demonstrate a *consistent* pattern of behaviors, versus being frugal only when the economy tanks.

This disciplined approach to managing the household finances not only allowed them to reach millionaire status in their early 40s, but also allowed them margin when the environment around them was less than ideal. Mike says, "When the [housing] market crashed, we were immediately underwater in 2010, but we kept going with our plan. We used to monitor our balance sheet all the time. Now we don't check and overcheck. I changed jobs in 2013 so I would have more freedom and more work-life balance. I was able to [make a change] because we had our finances in order."

When we asked the Wellses for some advice for those who are transforming themselves from income-statement affluent to balance-sheet affluent, their comments were peppered with the discipline required to build wealth:

- Don't allow your lifestyle to dictate your financial goals. For the Wells, and others who seek to achieve millionaire status, the reverse must be employed.
- Have a "good enough" mindset about consumer items.
- Regardless of current economic conditions, always have a well-thought-out plan.
- Be open to learning how to do things differently, particularly when those around you are living a high-consumption lifestyle.
- Have open discussions about wants and needs.

The Wells' dedication may be in the 99th percentile on the discipline scale. They demonstrate an example of consistent hard work, tough choices, and discipline to set and meet a goal. They're committed to a lifestyle that provides just enough of what their family needs and some of what it wants, but not to the excesses of those around them. Because they do not live in a $700,000 house and drive a late-model year SUV, many of their neighbors, coworkers, and friends might be surprised at their balance sheet and the great freedom they have knowing they can withstand changes without having to adapt their lifestyle or give up the independence they worked hard to create.

The Marathon of Building Wealth

The idea that there is more than just smarts to building wealth or becoming successful in other endeavors pervaded my father's work. He wrote this in 2011:

In *The Millionaire Mind*, I said that the process of building wealth is a marathon. How well you do in this race involves much more than grade point averages. . . . Standardized testing (SATs, GREs, etc.) cannot be substituted for running the race. Otherwise our government could just redistribute our nation's wealth each year—give it to all those with high IQs. If they're going to end up with it all anyway, why not just speed up the process?

I was reminded of this after reading an article about the limitations of using standardized tests to predict variations in achievement over the course of an entire career. The author points out that "from the SAT to the NFL's 'Combine' the problem [is] with short term tests."[12]

"It turns out that many of the most important factors for life success are character traits such as grit and self-control, these can't be measured quickly. . . . grit . . . reflects a person's commitment to long term goal[s]."

And, as I discussed in *The Millionaire Mind*, Professor David C. McClelland, a Harvard-based distinguished scholar of intelligence and achievement, discovered that traditional measures of intelligence do not account for a substantial portion of the variation in achievement and success in life.

What have I found out about multimillionaires who were not A students and didn't generate high numbers on achievement tests? They never allowed "academic odds makers" to dictate their performance in life. They recognized that their creativity, hard work, discipline, and certain social skills, including leadership, were more significant than grades and aptitude tests.

The typical millionaire did not reach the 7-figure net worth threshold until he had worked for 59,800 hours [median]. Those are many more hours than it took him to complete his SAT.

Intelligence: Not Quite What Makes Us

We hear a lot about the importance of discipline in financial management, but typically it's without much research to back it up. The findings over the past 40-plus years of research regarding financially successful, self-made Americans consistently support the conclusion that discipline (e.g., frugality), hard work, and perseverance are factors in economic success. From studies of high- and ultra-high-net-worth individuals in *The Millionaire Mind* to the mass affluent studies conducted by DataPoints, we see that conscientiousness, whether in terms of how these individuals run their businesses or how they manage their family finances, comes into play. It's been cited as one of the most important success factors, and a relationship has also been demonstrated between conscientiousness and net worth, independent of age and income.

If you look at any publication related to how well we perform on any given job, you will undoubtedly come across the concept of *cognitive ability* being one of the major predictors or indicators of success on a job. In other words, most research finds that the smarter we are the better we can perform. Should this be the case for financial management at home?

One of the more interesting findings from the study of millionaires featured in *The Millionaire Mind* was the lack of support for the relationship between wealth and intelligence (measured by SAT scores of the respondents). The average millionaire from *The Millionaire Mind* had an average undergraduate GPA of 2.92, and an average SAT score of 1190. Was this a fluke?

Some researchers set out to examine the relationship between intelligence and wealth using samples that were broader in terms of their demographic characteristics than those studied in *The Millionaire Mind*. A study by Dr. Jay Zagorsky received quite a bit of press at the time of its publication.[13] Dr. Zagorsky examined the National Study of Youth 1979, trying to answer the question: Was IQ related to net worth? From his review of nearly 7,500 individuals, ranging in age from 33 to 41 years old, he did not find support for the hypothesis that intelligence and wealth were related.

Instead of cognitive ability, perhaps we should consider financial literacy or the knowledge of or ability to use personal financial management practices and methodologies. Approximately 57% of Americans are financially literate[14], typically measured by answering simple financial literacy questions correctly.[15] The work of Anna Maria Lusardi and her colleagues has demonstrated the woeful state of financial knowledge and education in the United States and around the world.[16] Often, this group of researchers measures financial literacy with a few questions. Even with what might be considered basics of personal finance, just over half of Americans can answer them correctly.

Financial literacy is related to a host of financial "success" outcomes, leading to better decision-making about a variety of investment-, debt-, and spending-related issues. But to build wealth, financial literacy is not enough. Think about the last time you worked with a brilliant colleague who couldn't or wouldn't show up on time, consistently pushed the boundaries of behavior that are appropriate at work, or missed deadlines. Something else is at play when it comes to success at work: conscientiousness. One of what's known as the "Big Five" personality characteristics, *conscientiousness* includes aspects of

- industriousness (working hard, confidence)
- virtue (doing what's right morally or socially)
- self-control (being cautious, delaying gratification)
- order (the detail-orientation component)
- responsibility (doing what's right for others, community)
- traditionalism (adhering to authority and rules, disliking change).

It has been consistently tied to job performance and retention in a variety of jobs and organizations. If you're in the position to hire someone and you can only measure one aspect of personality, this is the one you want (with some key, artistic exceptions).

So, too, it goes with financial management. Many of the behavioral components that impact net worth, regardless of how old we are or our income levels, including frugality, planning, and responsibility, tie into this personality characteristic, and help us understand why it is so critical in the creation and maintenance of wealth over time.

In another study that examined the National Longitudinal Survey of Youth, researchers found that conscientiousness, specifically self-control, was related to illiquid and liquid asset holdings, as well as net worth.[17] Financial literacy had some effect on net worth, but only in relationship to self-control, a key component of conscientiousness. The study found that "Financial literacy by itself is not

Integrity: The Benefit of an Open Book Policy

Another psychological characteristic tied intimately with conscientiousness is integrity: being honest and truthful with others, doing what you say you're going to do, and generally acting in a manner that is beyond reproach. Integrity is often cited by millionaires as one of the main factors that led to their success, in our latest sample of millionaires as well as those profiled in The Millionaire Mind. *My father highlighted the importance of integrity during the housing market crash a few years ago:*

Mrs. Lang, my first Sunday school teacher, often said, "You should always do your best. Everything you do in this life is recorded in a big book. . . . and some day in the next life you will be judged on how you behaved on this earth."

And success often goes to those whose business practices are "an open book." I was reminded of this as I read an article in the *New York Times* about the current state of the residential real estate market here in Atlanta[18]: "A dismal distinction in housing: with worst market in 2011. . . .That distinction goes to Atlanta . . . Luxury homes that never sold . . . inundated with foreclosed properties. . . . Atlanta has the most government owned foreclosed properties for sale. . . ."

The journalist also highlighted foreclosures not only in the Atlanta area in general but more specifically in Cobb County/Marietta, Georgia. Ah, Marietta, that rings a bell with me as part of my research of high-income-producing, extraordinary sales professionals. Some suggested that Mr. M, a home builder, be added to my "must interview" list of economically successful people. Mr. M's profile is more important today during this down market than it was even when I first interviewed him.

There is a special kind of builder who can succeed even in a depressed market. According to an article published in the *Atlanta Journal-Constitution*,[19] there were 53,410 new homes sold in 2005. In 2011, there were only 7,664 new homes sold.

While I was digesting these facts, I thought of Mr. M. On my daily commute with my dog, Lily, to our favorite park, I see signs and building permits at construction sites which read "This Home Being Constructed by Mr. M and Company." How can it be that Mr. M's business is flourishing? Even in a down market some people have more than enough money to have homes built for them. Mr. M has a reputation for building homes of very high quality.

One of Mr. M's competitive advantages is his "Open Book Policy." All his prospective home buyers receive more than a building proposal. They are given a complete list of the names, addresses, and phone numbers of every family for whom Mr. M has built a home. Yes, all 163 of his growing list of customers.

A long track record for delivering a quality product, combined with his outstanding reputation with those in his "open book," explains how Mr. M succeeds in a miserable market. Also, it has something to do with how Mr. M looks at a so-called down market. Call it adversity. View adversity as an opportunity to strengthen your resolve and enhance your reputation.

The Limits of Metrics

In large organizations (schools, companies, government agencies), making hiring, placement, or admission decisions often requires some type of metric to make those decisions more convenient and cost-efficient. Who is succeeding? Who might be leaving next? Who is falling behind? For organizations making decisions about large numbers of people, standardized testing and other metrics (like GPA) are a legitimate business necessity. However, not everything that is critical to future success can be captured by standardized tests. And, these tests are not often useful for the individuals who take them: They are used to help the organization, not to propel us to greatness. Often, though, we apply too much to those numerical values, insisting that a high GPA, for example, dictates the rest of one's life or is an indicator of more than just succeeding in rote memorization and academic endeavors. My father wrote this piece in 2015, highlighting how more than GPA is required in leadership:

The archetype millionaire next door is an economically successful self-employed business owner. In other words, he is an employer not an employee. He is in essence a leader. This fact has much to do with understanding something important about millionaire business owners. There is little or no significant correlation between cognitive intelligence test scores and demonstrated leadership performance. I'm of the opinion that the SATs, ACTs, GMATs, GREs, and the like are essential measures of cognitive intelligence.

Along these lines, I cited the related findings of two eminent scholars, Fiedler and Link, in *The Millionaire Mind*:

Cognitive ability tests have been notoriously poor predictors of leadership performance. . . . accounting for less than 10% of the variance. . . . [20]

As an example of this consider Dave; today he is a decamillionaire. He had already read *The Millionaire Mind* before he asked me the following question: "Of all the college graduates in my office building who would you think had the lowest grade point in college?"

You guessed it! It's Dave who had a "low" C average in college. Dave owns the building that houses his very successful investment management company. And unlike all of the college graduates he employs, Dave graduated from a college that ranks in the bottom quintile nationally in academic standings. Plus he never scored above the 900s on the combined SAT (original version).

Even today Dave continues to be amazed that each week he receives: "a stack of resumes from kids with Phi Beta Kappa keys, summa cum everything who want to work for me. Very intelligent young men and women from great schools."

But what Dave lacks in academic credentials he makes up with demonstrated high scores on scales such as discipline, integrity, initiative, risk-taking, ability to judge others, vision, tenacity, empathy, perseverance, and social skills. In essence he possesses excellent leadership skills.

What do all Dave's Phi Beta Kappa employees think of his college grades? Surely they have some concerns about working for a C student. No employee ever asked to see Dave's academic transcript. It is irrelevant as long as Dave continues to pay them very well for their work and provide an exceptional work environment.

significant, but when paired with conscientiousness it seems to help those low in conscientiousness to increase net worth." The authors of this study called on early intervention as well as the financial services industry in general to focus efforts not only on education but also on self-control: "perhaps the concept of 'financial education' should be interpreted more broadly. Interventions to increase conscientiousness and self-control could be more innovative approaches to 'education.'"[21]

The authors of this study suggested that financial professionals should focus efforts on helping to improve their clients' ability to be disciplined when it comes to spending. They stated, "financial planners and educators can serve consumers by making them aware of their self-control shortcomings and providing tips and practices to help increase financial well-being. Suggesting practices such as cash-based spending, automatic savings plans, or automatic bill-pay may help consumers reign [*sic*] in some of their negative spending patterns."[22] This counsel is critical to anyone building wealth, not just those providing advice to others.

Strength Beyond Schooling

The national survey which served as the basis for *The Millionaire Mind* represented a fraction of the top 1% of the wealth holders in America. Some of the myths about these people are that they were all straight-A students, scored at the top on the SAT, and attended elite private schools. The average SAT score for the sample was 1190. Their most frequent grade in both high school and college was "B." Their GPA in college was 2.9. They typically did not qualify for admission to an "elite" college or university. Many a millionaire has told us that their experiences with rejection compelled them to succeed. Gaining access to an elite college does not ensure success. Only about 1 in 10 (11%) of decamillionaires rated "attending a top-rated college" as a very important factor in explaining their socioeconomic success. Overall out of the 30 success factors, "attending a top-rated college" rated 29th or just above "graduating near or at the top of my class." As one eminent scholar has said, "Your degree will get you your first job, but after three years nobody will care where you went to school." Even in America not all opportunities are equally distributed. Recognize it, deal with it, and overcome it.

Consider instead an anecdote of intelligence versus confidence in reaching career-related goals. Take two children from seemingly similar advantaged, affluent backgrounds. Perhaps they have parents with similarly prestigious jobs, the same type of family structure, high SAT scores, same GPAs, even the same

Grades Don't Make the Leader

Those numerical scores we receive growing up, and perhaps even today in well-meaning but often useless performance appraisals in organizations, can affect each of us differently. Some of us, regardless of the rating or score, will ignore it. Others will feel as if our future success has somehow been bolstered or hindered by the value. Still, others of us will use a negative rating as a means to push us forward, not necessarily ignoring the number but instead using it as a force to do our best work. Millionaires, particularly business owners, often had the latter reaction, as cataloged by my father in 2012:

In *The Millionaire Mind* I wrote that "millionaires . . . [are] often . . . labeled by some authority figure or some standardized test result as being 'average' or 'inferior.' But as the results of this research point out, such evaluations make some people all the more tenacious. Some millionaires thrive upon such judgments, as they have made very clear to me. Where did they get their resolve? It was a direct result of their earlier experiences in deflecting negative judgments."[23]

Ralph de la Vega was the CEO of AT&T Mobility. This company had annual sales of $63 billion and employed nearly 50,000 workers. According to an article in the *Atlanta Journal-Constitution* on March 18, 2012, Mr. de la Vega immigrated from Cuba to the United States when he was 10. The Castro regime would not allow his family to accompany him. He lived here for five years until his family was finally allowed to join him.[24]

While in high school and struggling with English, he told a counselor that he wanted to be an engineer someday. The counselor discouraged him from this goal because of his grades and his family's lack of finances. Mr. de la Vega states, "He killed my dreams right there." He dropped out of an academic high school and started mechanic's school.

But Mr. de la Vega had his dream rekindled when his grandmother arrived in the U.S. and told him, "Ralph, don't let anybody put limitations on what you can achieve. If you want to be an engineer, you can be an engineer."

And so, he did. And he continues to offer his grandmother's advice to young people who wish to achieve.

interests and career plans. Why, in the future, would one end up with a significantly higher income than the other?

It may be self-concept, or more specifically, core self-evaluations (CSEs): a set of psychological characteristics that include a belief in one's worth and one's overall efficacy for being effective in new situations, a belief in having control in the decisions and outcomes of decisions, and lower levels of stress and anxiety.

Examining sets of data from the National Longitudinal Survey of Youth, Drs. Timothy Judge and Charlice Hurst demonstrated that the advantaged childhood to income relationship is not simple.[25] As expected, children from more advantageous backgrounds had higher income levels. But, they found that children with a high self-concept with advantageous backgrounds had very different income levels (that is, much higher) than did their low self-concept, but equally advantaged, peers. Judge and Hurst state, "These resources [family advantages, high SAT, GPA] barely seemed to make a difference to individuals with low CSE and, in some cases (i.e., SAT scores) actually seemed to have a slight negative impact." They conclude, "It seems that resources, such as family advantages, and positive CSE together are necessary to the attainment of above average levels of income."

Considering net worth instead of income for a moment, we again see that how we feel about ourselves and our abilities related to financial matters significantly impacts net worth, regardless of age, income, and percentage of inherited wealth. While self-concept is generally a stable or unchanging trait, understanding self-concept and changing financial-related behaviors may have benefits to income and net worth in the long run.

The Case for (Thoughtful) Higher Education

A reporter contacted us wanting to know how educational costs are impacting the ability for young Americans to become wealthy on their own. Can anyone become the millionaire next door today with the high costs of education? Education costs have risen since 1996 by almost 400 percent. High education debt puts adult children behind the starting line financially. Even well-meaning, planning-focused parents can't often fully fund college. One study indicated that while 43% of parents want to pay for all of college for their children, only 29% will have done so by the time their children are freshmen in college.[26]

The value of education still holds: In most cases, higher education still has benefits in building wealth, even if those benefits have more to do with the level of income you can achieve by having certain degrees. The median net worth of a college graduate (approximately $292,100) is more than four times that of high school graduates ($54,000).[27] In our current study, those with college or graduate degrees have higher income levels and net worth than those with some college or high school diplomas (although the difference in net worth was not significant). Of course, that income level matters little without frugality, but the relationship between level of education and income persists.

More than 75% of millionaires in 1996 and 2016 both had college and/or graduate degrees. In a way, education could be considered a "minimum qualification" for building wealth: a qualification, yes, but not a guarantee. It is a factor, even if only to ensure a high-paying job at first. And only 20% of millionaires said attending a top-rated school was important to their success.

Table 5-3. Education Levels of Millionaires (1996 & 2016)

Education Level	1996 (%)	2016 (%)
None	1	0
High School Degree	6	4
Associate's Degree/Some College	16	2
College Degree	38	36
Graduate Degree	38	58

Table 5-4. Percentage of College-Educated Millionaires by Type of College

Higher Education	Percentage of Millionaires
Private	30
Public	55
Both	15

Alternative Approaches to Designer Education

In 2016 nearly 78% of undergraduate students attended a public institution, while 22% attended private colleges and universities.[28] How does our millionaire population compare? In our latest study, approximately 55% of millionaires attended public colleges and universities, 15% of millionaires attended both public and private institutions, and 30% attended private institutions. The costs for all institutions are on the rise, as is student debt to cover those costs. Some well-meaning but uninformed parents have decided that debt is an expected and acceptable part of higher education. Unfortunately, in their effort to get their children the minimum qualification of education that they need, they are also setting them back significantly on the net worth scale. Why aren't parents telling kids to find alternatives to traditional routes to a four-year degree that often require borrowing heavily? Why the push to obtain college degrees and run up hundreds of thousands of dollars in college debt?

Perhaps we should consider the impact of sociometrics and the Joneses on the way in which we encourage students to achieve higher education. Colleges, for some parents and students, have to have an Instagram U. factor. With echoes of what the Joneses are doing, or where they are sending their children to school, many an income-statement affluent family is feeling the pressure to send their children to brand-name schools. Going to a name-brand college is a status symbol like wearing designer clothes or owning a luxury vehicle. You can advertise your entrance and matriculation on social media, and friends and neighbors will tell you that it's so great that your daughter is going to a school with an NCAA Division 1 football team. But if that college comes with 5 to 10 to 20 or more years of debt afterwards, the short-lived rush of telling others you're going to a school you cannot afford is financially dangerous.

Many of these same families will tell you that they are frugal or shop only when there are sales for clothes, groceries, and household items, but yet they will set back their children by insisting on a name-brand college that leads to high debt.

To avoid these costs, it will require a shift in mindset. Are state schools now "aspirational" like a Mini or entry-model BMW? Are any of these luxury schools worth the cost? Is starting behind the finish line worth it? Does that value of the degree outweigh the debt carried throughout early adulthood? It's hard to know.

Consider alternatives before assuming that a four- to five-year stint at a name-brand university is worth the cost. Millionaires have shared with us a variety of experiences related to how they obtained their education. Doing so without debt will require going against the tide, like so many other financial choices economically successful Americans make.

Owing It All to Community College

One alternative to at least the first two or so years of a traditional four-year stay at a traditional university is community college. My father wrote this commentary in 2015, highlighting how one famous American obtained his education:

Tom Hanks's movies have grossed over $8 billion worldwide. If you read his op-ed "I Owe It All to Community College" in the *New York Times*[29] you might understand why he should be nominated for an honorary membership in the millionaire-next-door club.

So, what if he graduated from a public high school? He describes himself as, ". . . an underachieving student with lousy SAT scores. . . . I couldn't afford tuition for college anyway. . . . [So it was off] to Chabot, a community college . . . which because it accepted everyone and was free, would be my alma mater." According to Hanks, he received an excellent education "all free but for the effort and the cost of used textbooks . . . that place made me what I am today."

Hanks may not have aced the SAT but he was extremely creative and insightful about gathering resources at Chabot which were used in perfecting his chosen occupation. I stated in *The Millionaire Next Door*, economically successful people demonstrate an uncanny ability to select the right occupation, i.e., one that they love and that is financially rewarding as well.

Hanks obviously had a great deal of discipline in terms of selecting specific courses and professors on the basis of his chosen vocation. As evidence of his discipline, he invites the reader to examine Chabot's library take-out slip on the celebrated actor Jason Robards's monologues of Eugene O'Neill's *The Ice Man Cometh*. Hanks listened to these recordings at least 20 times. "Classes I took at Chabot have rippled through my professional pond," he says.

In fact, Hanks gives credit to his history professor "whose lectures were riveting" for the outline format he adopted for his HBO miniseries, *John Adams*.

If you follow Hanks's lead in taking advantage of the resources available at the majority of community colleges and four-year colleges and universities in America, you can get an excellent education.

Subject Matter Experts: Millionaires

When we group some of these wealth competencies from current and past surveys as well as other research, we see similarities between what it takes to build wealth (which could be considered a job), and how successful someone may be in a traditional job. Being aware of our own competencies not only allows us to pursue the right type of occupation (which we'll discuss in Chapter 6) but also allows us to capitalize on those strengths when it comes to managing our own household affairs (or, if we have the means to do so, to hire those who can be trusted advisors).

While *The Millionaire Next Door* focused on targeting market opportunities and selecting the right career, *The Millionaire Mind* focused on the mindset, or psychology, of high-net-worth and ultra-high-net-worth individuals. In the chapter on success factors, seven different categories of what we might call "wealth competencies" are featured. The profiled millionaires had a median net worth of $4.3 million in 1998 (which is roughly equivalent to $6.3 million today). For this book, the millionaires we've studied have a median net worth of $3.5 million. Despite the difference in median net worth, there are similarities that seem to be timeless when it comes to becoming financially independent. These millionaires serve as *subject matter experts* in the field of building wealth.

Today, as in 1998, we find that millionaires continue to rate *discipline, getting along with others, integrity,* and *hard work* as critical to their success. We see the factor of *resiliency and perseverance* as well, most likely because of what these individuals experienced as they climbed the corporate ladder, built a business, or navigated managing their household affairs through different seasons of their lives.

Table 5-5. Success Factors: Percentage of Millionaires Endorsing as Important or Very Important (1998 & 2016)

Success Factor (1998 statement)	Percentage of Millionaires	
	1998	2016
Being well disciplined	95	91
Resiliency/perseverance	-	88
Being honest with all people	90	86
Getting along with people	94	83
Having a supportive spouse	81	81
Working harder than most people	88	80
Being very well organized	85	74
Loving my career or business	86	70
Having strong leadership qualities	84	68
Having a very competitive spirit/personality	81	63
Living below one's means	43	61
Having a clear vision of my future	-	61
Having supportive parents	-	59
Recognizing unique opportunities in the marketplace (seeing opportunities others do not see)	72	58
Having high intellect/IQ	67	53
Having a great teacher/mentor (having good mentors)	73	53
Having original ideas	-	50
Ignoring the criticism of detractors	51	45
Having engaged/involved parents	-	42
Investing in the equities of public corporations	42	37
Having strong religious faith	33	32
Having excellent investment advisors	39	29
Internship during college or immediately after graduation	-	22
Graduating near/at top of one's class	33	21
Attending a top-rated college	48	20
Attending private schools	-	8

Note: An (-) indicates the statement was not included in the 1998 study.

Discipline and Wealth

Success in life and work has been consistently tied to conscientiousness whether it's being disciplined, having and meeting plans, or focusing on details. As we discussed earlier, research in the field of psychology shows a relationship between this personality characteristic and how well someone will perform on the job.[30] The research conducted on those with high net worth the past several decades also provides insight into why they are balance-sheet affluent: They have a long-term, disciplined approach to saving, spending, and investing. These individuals are not distracted by what "the Joneses" are doing.

More than 9 out of 10 of the top 5% of wealth holders in America reported that being well disciplined was very important in explaining their socioeconomic success. This finding is consistent over time. From *The Millionaire Mind*, we are reminded that "a disciplined person sets his or her sights on a lofty target, then figures out productive ways to reach the target. Disciplined people are not easily sidetracked. . . . They could live in a French bakery and not gain weight or they could encounter hundreds of economic opportunities and then select one or two that are best suited to their strengths and the market's needs."[31]

It's no wonder discipline is rated among the most important factors in becoming financially successful. Managing one's financial life to ensure money-related goals are met *requires* high levels of discipline, routine, and conscientiousness.

Discipline in building wealth also means setting our own goals. Take for example graduate education: a gauntlet that requires self-directed study and large-scale, independent project management. Sadly, half of all graduate students drop out before completing their PhD.[32] How can this be possible? It's not about a lack of intellect. From my father's experience as a professor for more than 20 years, he had his own views about why students bailed out of PhD programs. There are several reasons, but he believed the most important was a lack of self-discipline. As undergraduates, these students were told specifically what to do, what to study, and what tests to take. It was all programmed on the syllabus. Later, in graduate school, these same students did well in terms of classroom assignments. But when it came to proposing and completing a dissertation, an activity that by its nature requires those who undertake it to create their own project plans and execute those plans with little external reinforcement, he found that many of these students were unable and possibly unwilling to do it on their own. Completing a dissertation is akin to being self-employed. In both instances, it is the individual who must allocate time and energy in the most productive way. There is no job description or curriculum given by the employer.

Most of the millionaire-next-door types we've interviewed would not qualify for entrance into the typical PhD program. They did not have A averages as undergraduates nor did they score high on standardized tests. Yet they had a great deal of self-discipline, which along with integrity is one of the most important ingredients in becoming economically successful.

Resiliency and Perseverance

Another component consistently cited by financially successful individuals is resiliency. To build wealth, to build one's own business, to ignore critics and media and neighbors, you must have the resolve to keep pursuing your goals past rejection and pain. Millionaires and other economically successful Americans who pursue self-employment, decide to climb the corporate ladder, or strive to create a financial independence lifestyle early do so by perpetually pushing on. It's not for the faint of heart. We see this resiliency illustrated in those who pursue the early retirement/financial independence path (FI/RE as we alluded to earlier). Those who pursue this path to economic freedom meet daily hurdles to becoming so thanks in part to their neighbors, community (both in-person and virtual), and companies pursuing them for their financial and cognitive resources.

Alan DeMarcus had the resiliency to build a successful refrigerant recovery business, sell that business, and then become a millionaire eight times over. He is now worth between $8 and $10 million.

Starting in his uncle's HVAC business when he was 14 years old, Alan learned the trade and what it meant to work hard. During college, he returned to his uncle's business, landed a sales role, and ultimately quit school after two and a half years. From that point on, Alan's track to becoming successful took some unanticipated twists:

> *After two years working in the sales role, my uncle sold the business to a publicly traded company—sold it under condition of an earn out. I got a job offer but decided not to take it. In early 2000, that company went bankrupt, and my uncle lost everything. I decided to start my own business, pooling money together and partnering with my uncle. We started with $180,000 that we had to borrow from friends and family members. I made a promise to honor each loan. It was so scary. We grew really fast on paper, but were*

cash poor. It's an asset rich business. We were living in a too expensive condo in San Francisco, my wife was making $26,000 a year, and I was making $0. We were starting with nothing. As the business grew fast, it would run out of money all the time. We had to have faith. I'm a believer and that is interwoven in my business today. But starting out, I was too cocky . . . had to rely on prayer to get through. I realized frequently that everything I own could be gone tomorrow. What do you do when you don't have cash and you own the business? You dump your own money in. We would use our personal emergency fund to fund the business and pay employees.

While the world of business was crashing in 2008-2009, Alan's prudent business practices ensured his business was successful despite the industry trends:

The entire industry, the HVAC industry, had a 65% decline in 2008. Our total gross revenue was down 18%. We had to borrow some money, but we had good advisors, including good legal advice and accountants. We're now in 43 markets with 165 employees.

His prudent practices were also reflected at home, and his wife had much to do with Alan's perseverance and success:

My wife and I were a team. I could never have done this without my wife. She is my sanity, rockstar . . . We had a solid home life. I believe that chaos at home is reflected in chaos at work. We spend less than we make . . . consistent. But, cash flow doesn't always match. So, we'd fund the business with our personal emergency cash. Started once with $150,000. The business cash flow problems became our problems. We never had to sell assets or anything but had to deplete our savings regularly.

Having left college after two and a half years, Alan's perspective on education, and feedback from a wise CEO, give us an interesting perspective on the importance of building wealth and leadership:

Our society places a lot of emphasis on education. But people are still so rudderless when they come out of school, just like when they went into school, but now they have tons of debt, too. This is fine if you want a corporate America job. It's a prerequisite. But, learning more, knowledge . . . is needed for a business. Trying more things helps you find a sweet spot in the market. You don't have to have a degree. There's too much emphasis on the degree. You just

Hard Work in Academia: Lots of Wealth with Lots of Discipline

Teaching at a research-focused, higher-level institution requires consistent production of peer-reviewed journal articles, which is the reason for the common phrase "publish or perish." My father spent the first half of his professional career in this environment and knew well the personalities and pressure of this type of culture. He wrote about this in 2013 after a former professor wrote him to share his experiences:

As stated in *The Millionaire Mind*, a distinguished scholar once told me, "If you don't publish, you may not get tenure at a good school. But you will have a lot of friends. Publish a lot and you will not be really popular among your colleagues."

I received an email from a former college professor we'll call "Dr. F. O." In it, he told me, "just a few years after I resigned a full professor position at the university to begin my own . . . business. . . . I was 51 years old and virtually all of my colleagues thought I had lost my mind to give up the security of tenured university life, but it turned out to be the best thing I have ever done."

Nine years after he started his own business he reached near decamillionaire status. He is now retired and has had the time to reread *The Millionaire Mind* and shared some of his experiences related to discipline in the pursuit of financial freedom. "Many things in the book," he said, "describe my experiences from the living beneath our means (I was worth more than $1 million before the business), to taking risks, the frustrations of working for others (in this case university administrators and tenured colleagues), to a supportive wife of 42 years, to my religious beliefs, to believing in myself, to finding a business niche. . . ."

Some of his "friends" told Dr. F. O. that he was just lucky, and he pointed out that he was "very insulted" by their comments. In the survey of 733 multimillionaires that was the base for *The Millionaire Mind*, luck was rated among the least important success factors, while being well-disciplined was at the very top along with integrity. Discipline and integrity continue to top the list of critical success factors in our latest survey. Dr. F. O. explained his path to success in this manner:

"I come from very humble beginnings, and from educational institutions at the bottom of the university food chain. Like the findings in the book [*The Millionaire Mind*], I was rejected by top tier institutions, but outpublished all of my colleagues. The idea of luck denigrates the hard work and preparation I put into everything I have ever done. Even though many of them [his colleagues] come from elite educational institutions, none of them ever worked as hard or as smart as I did for many years, and they would never have jumped at the opportunity like I did if it came their way. In fact, they never even looked for any such opportunities. I have been blessed in many ways, but luck had very little to do with my success. . . . I want you to know just how true I think your research findings are. I made this money in my fifties. It can still be done in America with the right attitudes, beliefs, and hard work. Unfortunately, this is not the message society is sending to our young people.

After nine years in business on my own I have more money than I ever dreamed of and loved the experience of running my own business. I love a comfortable retirement even more. Since retiring a few years ago I have had time to reflect on my university and business experiences, and this reflection included rereading *The Millionaire Mind* over the last few days. It resonates with me now more than ever.

I have not had one cent of debt for fifteen years and I now have a net worth of $8-9M. I have never revealed this amount to anyone before this moment. I don't think any of our friends have any idea we have this much money. Other than considerable overseas travel the last few years, we don't live appreciably different than we did previously. Costco and Walmart are our favorite stores."

Dr. F. O. used his prolific publishing in academia to create his own business. Like building wealth, publishing in academia or creating a business has metrics by which you can judge success and work toward. Hard work pushed him over the finish line of economic success.

need to try more things. People who have money don't care about your degree. Investors don't care—they care if you can do it. I know way too many Harvard MBAs with luxury cars and tons of debt.

Alan had created margin in his business by building up cash over time and not following each "must do" idea. He made sure that each decision was made with calmness.

The more economically successful you become, the more critics you will attract.

A Marine's Life

Are the personal characteristics of millionaires next door the same today as they were more than two decades ago? Have the significant changes in technology and increases in the cost of education and health care had a significant effect on what it takes for individuals to build real wealth on their own?

In our two major samples of the top 5% of wealth holders in the United States from 1998 (the study featured in *The Millionaire Mind*) and 2016, integrity and discipline were consistently ranked among the top of the 30 success factors they rated. These factors play in to a full range of areas related to managing one's household finances, from making investment decisions to simply paying bills. A millionaire next door consistently applies discipline to building wealth, regardless of the times, the economic conditions of the day, or technologies available.

As described in *The Millionaire Mind*, "It is hard to overemphasize the importance of discipline in accounting for variations in economic success. If you lack discipline, the chances of you ever accumulating wealth are very, very small. Yes, you can win the lotto. But in most cases, you have a better chance of contracting leprosy."[33]

Interestingly the three success components that come under the heading of intellectual orientation are nowhere near as important as discipline in explaining one's socioeconomic success. Having a high IQ or superior intellect, graduating from a top college, and graduating near or at the top of the class were consistently at the bottom of success factors.

Congruent with these findings is a recent case study we received from a lawyer who had benefited greatly from his Marine Corps training. Keep in mind that discipline is a major component of the Marine Corps experience.

Dr. Stanley,

I've read The Millionaire Next Door *and* The Millionaire Mind, *and I loved them both. I just finished* The Millionaire Mind. *The book spoke to me because although I am not a millionaire . . . I plan to be. I am like your main character, the millionaire next door . . . I went to Officer Candidate School in the Marine Corps; I went to college; I went to law school. I am not highly intelligent and I am not "gifted" with a high IQ. I am disciplined and I work hard. I also happen to have a twin brother and we are identical in every way. We both opened a law firm about five years ago; we practice real estate. We are social; we get along with people; we have a high degree of basic common sense. Also, we practice in real estate so we are not competing with the prototypical high IQ people. We are doing well . . . last year both of us made over $250k.*

As far as personal consumption, I follow the "Dave Ramsey" plan and maintain a cash budget. I drive a 98 Honda Accord with 247,000 miles on it. Every time I get behind the wheel, I smile as I drive the beast as a badge of honor. All my friends are buying big homes they cannot afford and luxury cars that they lease or purchase with loans. They are Income Statement Affluent. They earn fairly large salaries and they spend it all. One of my best friends says that he takes out loans to buy things because it puts pressure on him to earn more money. I cannot think of a more flawed logic. My intention is to do the exact opposite. I am 37 and I have no debt. My goal is to invest as much as possible in mutual funds and to accumulate commercial and residential real estate over my lifetime. I will do this without ever having taken out a mortgage!

I love reading your books so if you keep writing them, I will keep reading them.

All the best. Semper Fi—S.

Resiliency in Action

My father wrote this piece in 2012 in response to a Forbes *online article by Clare O'Connor about Spanx founder Sara Blakely. The article stated that "Sara Blakely is the youngest self-made woman to join this year's billionaire's club—turning $5,000 in savings into a new retail category: shapewear.*[34]

Ms. Blakely once had her heart set on going to law school, but according to the *Forbes* article, she performed poorly on the LSAT exam for law school admission. So what if she lacked high analytic intellect? Only 9% of decamillionaires, both men and women, indicated that their choice of career was based upon aptitude test results.[35] Like most people who are destined to succeed, she took another route. Before Ms. Blakely started her own business, she spent seven years as a cold-calling fax machine sales professional. She said, "I'd get business cards ripped up in my face because I was so soliciting."

According to my database, the profession of selling is the most often mentioned first job of self-made millionaires (14%). Selling is a great way to both enhance and test your self-discipline and tenacity.

As a salesperson, Ms. Blakely understood that her appearance was a very important part of her profession. As such, she wanted to look her best at all times. She realized, however, that some of the foundation products on the market were lacking both in style and in function. After much trial and error, she invented Spanx, a slimming undergarment. This product along with her high creative intellect and enormous drive has made her a billionaire!

After reading the full article, I noted many similarities between Ms. Blakely and other successful people. As part of my research for *Millionaire Women Next Door*, 313 women nationwide who own and operate successful businesses wrote an essay, at my request. The title of the essay was "Suggestions about How Young People Might Become Successful Adults."

In essence, they actually wrote "How I Became a Successful Business Owner Myself." After completing an exhaustive content analysis of the central themes and components of these essays, I determined that perseverance was the factor most often attributed to success (51% of these women stated as such). In the book, I wrote, "Most respondents reported success only after initial failure and after strong discouragement from family and friends. There is a sense in which these individuals seem driven to overcome obstacles and to prove their critics wrong. Most felt that a key subcomponent of perseverance was having strong aspirations, a strong desire of ambition as for advancement, honor, etc. Respondents stressed that staying focused on the desired result (persevering) over extended periods of time is the key to success."[36]

Perseverance Required

Spirit and ideas abound, but turning those into reality requires a dose of resiliency and confidence that must be present not just in the beginning stages of any type of change, but more importantly, when a dream seems out of reach. Consider this vignette my father wrote in 2014 on how resiliency and confidence are required for the inevitable challenges one will face in creating a business:

Roy is considering a transition from being an employee to a self-employed business owner. He has many of the characteristics which are important for succeeding in business. He is very knowledgeable in his field, he is well-disciplined, he has excellent work habits, and he has a stellar credit rating. He and his family live well below their means. Yet I should wonder if Roy's proposed business venture will ever get off the ground.

Roy's enthusiasm has dampened since all three of his applications for business loans have been turned down. He has difficulty with those who criticize his business proposal. He found loan officers to be condescending, aloof, and even insulting. Even his in-laws have no desire to lend him money. They told him that it was much too risky and that he lacked business aptitude.

I suggested that Roy reread the topic of "dealing with critics" in *The Millionaire Mind*. Here are just a few quotes that I hope Roy will find comforting:

"There are countless examples of critics who try to destroy the dreams of ambitious men and women. But critics are a necessary part of our social system in America—they screen out those who lack the courage and resolve to take criticisms and triumph despite them."

"Even steel cannot be hardened unless it's hammered, and it's no different with people. Self-made millionaires report that degrading evaluations and comments by certain authority figures played a role in their ultimate success in life. Hammering built the antibodies they needed to deflect criticisms and temper their resolve."

"Life is not one short race—it is a marathon of marathons. Labels come and go. If you believe that you can succeed in life despite degrading labels that predict your failure, you are likely to win most of the marathons. This is the common experience among millionaires."[37]

And Roy needs to understand that the length of the line of his critics will get longer as he becomes progressively more successful.

Occupying Our Minds and Time

How we spend one of our most valuable nonrenewable resources, time, can either support our financial goals or detract from them. What activities occupy the time of millionaires? How do these activities compare for prodigious accumulators and under accumulators of wealth? Prodigious accumulators, those who are adept at transforming their income into wealth, spend considerably more time reading business articles and reading in general than their under accumulating peers, but perhaps it is because our under accumulating friends are working more than the prodigious accumulators. Our research has shown that under accumulators must keep the revenue engine turned on to keep up with their consumption lifestyle, leaving little time to plan, read, and contemplate their investments. We see, too, that the under accumulating affluent in our latest study are spending more time on social media sites (approximately 14 hours) as compared to prodigious accumulators (9 hours). Could it be that those extra 5 hours could be put to use elsewhere, perhaps toward planning for one's financial future?

Table 5-6. Hours Spent Per Month in Selected Activities for Under Accumulators of Wealth vs. Prodigious Accumulators of Wealth (1996 & 2016)

	1996		2016	
Activity	UAW	PAW	UAW	PAW
Studying/planning future investment decisions	5.5	10	8.7	11.3
Managing current investments	4.2	8.1	8.6	11.3
Exercising	16.7	30	19.5	25.0

Table 5-7. Hours Spent Per Month in Selected Activities for Under Accumulators of Wealth versus Prodigious Accumulators of Wealth

Activity	UAW	PAW
Reading trade journal articles	10.7	10.5
Reading business articles other than trade journals	10.8	16.5
Reading for pleasure	17.0	22.8
Working	184.6	140.9
Spending time on social media sites (non-work-related)	14.2	9.3
Shopping (in person, in store) for clothing, accessories	3.7	3.6
Playing games on a mobile device or other technology enabled system	3.2	2.5

Table 5-8. Hours Spent Per Week in Selected Activities: Millionaires vs. American Population

Activity	Millionaires (Hours per Week)	Average American (Hours per Week)[38]
Working	38.4	32.1
Reading for pleasure	5.5	2.0
On social media	2.5	14.0[39]
Exercising	5.8	2.5
Caring for family	8.5	3.6
Playing video games	0.8	1.7
Sleeping	53.6	61.5

Time Spent

Consider any number of technological distractions today: From social media to texting to gaming, how many hours a day do you spend on your devices? Distractions are a significant reason why many struggle to become financially independent or achieve other goals. We know that the more we're able to focus without distractions, the better we're able to build wealth long term. How much time do millionaires today spend on the so-called "excitement" of the day? Consider this: most millionaires in our latest study reported only spending 2.5 hours per week on social media, versus the average American who spends almost six times more (14 hours per week). How many hours did you spend thinking about the most recent presidential election and the outcome? Most millionaires spend less than an hour thinking about political elections (and about 10% spend no time at all). That time and worry can be better spent on areas that will allow you to reach financial or career-related goals.

We can easily shift our attention to the strife, challenges, pain, and other emotions of watching others compete in politics, sports, reality shows, and even in our social events. By becoming engrossed in ongoing competition, you're necessarily taking time and emotional energy from something else: your business or education or some other productive activity. If that competition lives out on TV, you may be spending more than the average two hours that Americans watch.

Table 5-9. Time Spent in Previous Week on Selected Activities by Percentage of Millionaires

Activity	No Time	One Hour or Less	One Hour or More
Listening to music	13.0	42.9	44.1
Watching sports	32.2	24.5	43.0
Playing sports	52.2	8.2	37.6
Watching political TV	42.8	32.6	24.5
Listening to political radio	52.9	29.8	17.3
Playing video games	77.4	16.4	9.3
Online shopping	30.2	60.9	8.9
Listening to sports radio	68.4	22.9	8.7
Watching sports talk TV	72.7	23.6	3.8

158

Table 5-10. Time Spent Thinking About Selected Topics by Percentage of Millionaires

	Percentage of Millionaires				
Loss	No Time	Minutes	Hours	Days	Weeks, Months, Years
Favorite candidate loses state or local election	17.9	56.6	13.7	6.8	5.0
Favorite candidate loses national election	9.4	35.5	25.3	12	17.7
Favorite sports team loses	22.7	46.8	18.6	8.2	3.6

Successful individuals are keenly aware of how they spend their resources, including their emotional and cognitive resources. The time between each "every once in a while" is getting smaller . . . and the more distractions we add to that list, the fewer meaningful things we're going to be able to accomplish. If the distraction is a *habit*, then we will be even more challenged to avoid it. Changing behaviors requires more than listing out resolutions: New habit formation can take approximately 66 days and also requires rewiring our brains.[40]

Making resolutions work involves changing behaviors—and in order to change a behavior, you have to change your thinking (or "rewire" your brain). Trying to change that default thinking by "not trying to do it," in effect just strengthens it. Change requires creating new neural pathways from new thinking.[41]

Focusing on goals is related to building wealth, regardless of age and income.[42] But of course we all have worries that can occupy our time and cognitive resources. We see some differences in the worries of those who are prodigious accumulators of wealth versus those who are not. Specifically, the worries of the under accumulators tend to include:

- Lackluster sales profits
- Job being eliminated
- Never achieving financial independence
- Having to retire
- Children with little initiative to become financial independent
- Not enough wealth to retire in comfort

Table 5-11. Percentage of Prodigious Accumulators of Wealth and Under Accumulators of Wealth Spending Time Worrying About Selected Topics in Past Week

Fear/Worry	Percentage That Spent Any Time in Last Week Worrying About Topic	
	UAW	PAW
Not having time to shop to take advantage of sales	23.5	11.8
Having your family argue over your wealth	22.0	15.3
Having your job/occupational position eliminated	36.6	17.7
Depletion of the ozone layer	29.5	24.1
Never achieving financial independence	55.7	27.0
Having a child with an unproductive spouse or significant other	25.8	28.6
Having adult children who are undisciplined	37.9	28.8
Having to retire	61.1	33.9
Extinction of certain wildlife species	44.5	35.7
Having lackluster profits from your business/employer's business	58.3	37.8
Not having enough wealth to retire in comfort	78.6	41.1
Having adult children who spend more than they earn	43.2	43.4
Having children that show little initiative to become financially independent	60.6	44.6
Increasing concentration of wealth held by the rich	52.3	51.4
Having visual or hearing problems	58.8	57.3
Increased adverse global climate change	62.8	58.0
Spreading of diseases from other countries	50.4	58.4
Memory loss	56.8	60.2
Having cancer and/or heart disease	62.0	61.8
Increasing governmental control of citizens' rights	56.1	68.1
Increasing size and scope of the federal government	61.5	70.5
A decrease in your general level of physical health	71.2	76.1
Increased government regulation of business/industry	64.9	76.6
Increased government spending/federal deficit	70.5	77.7
Paying increasingly high federal income taxes	80.9	80.5
The state of the US economy	93.2	92.0

The decisions we make, particularly related to the allocation of our time, energy, and money, impact our ability to become financially independent. Coupled with the patterns of behaviors we exhibit are the topics that occupy our cognitive resources. Those who are effective at transforming their income into wealth spend those cognitive resources in ways that are conducive to building wealth. The activities and topics of concern may not be tweetable or make it into Instagram feeds, but over time, those behaviors will allow you greater freedom to pursue life in the way you want, versus in the way you want to have others believe you want.

Chapter 6

Getting to Work

They chose the right occupation.

—from *The Millionaire Next Door*

THE TIME WE SPEND TOILING AT AN OCCUPATION, WHETHER WE ENJOY THAT occupation or not, is a valuable resource, a resource that unlike (to some extent) money, is nonrenewable. Time spent generating revenue either working for someone else or ourselves cannot be retrieved and cannot be used for any other endeavor, which makes the discussion of work and careers critical for anyone who wants to be economically successful; even more so for those wanting to be financially independent.

The world of work, like technologies that enable us to manage investments on our own, has changed in the past 20-plus years since *The Millionaire Next Door* was published. Consider again our friends in the FI/RE community: We may have marginalized them in the 1990s as being eccentric, but we now celebrate their independence. And that independence makes more sense today as working for large organizations is no longer a guarantee of pensions and long-term financial support.

Still, most of us want to skip past vocations and go directly to the exciting world of investing (addressed in the next chapter). Indeed, if you were to Google "investing tips," approximately 656 million sites would pop up to provide you with insights into the world of buying and selling securities. Compare that with career search tips, which only provides one-seventh of those results (87.7 million sites). Compared to the stock market, or managing money, or to discussing behavioral finance, "work," "careers," and "vocations" seem immeasurably dull.

There isn't a career development-exploration-search movie equivalent of *Wall Street* or *The Big Short*. Maybe *Forrest Gump* qualifies, but his career experiences and the ultimate success in his own business are closer to the myths we covered in Chapter 2 than to reality. My father wrote in 2013:

> *A newspaper headline once proposed that "the best way to get rich is the stock market."[1] Building wealth via stocks or other investments is akin to growing trees. You can't grow oak trees if you don't have enough money to buy acorns. So, suggesting that the stock market leads to wealth is putting the cart before the horse. It is not just about being frugal. Frugality has its limits. Some people misread the material in* The Millionaire Next Door. *In the book, I mention that most Americans are not wealthy. This is especially interesting among those who earn incomes in the good to great categories: "many of these people live from paycheck to paycheck. These are the people who will benefit the most from this book." So in essence the book is designed to help those who make a better than average living.*

At some point, without windfalls and rich uncles, without lottery winnings or discovering a Liberty Head V Nickel in vending machine change, we all must work to generate revenue that then allows us to live (and consume) and ultimately provides for savings, which in turn provides additional revenue over time. Even for those who choose an early, purposeful retirement, generating revenue is a requirement at the early stages of one's economic path. Fortunately, we have great freedoms and opportunities in the United States and other parts of the free world to pick and choose our careers or jobs. In that effort, good defense (how we refer to managing spending and consumption), stable surroundings, and a loving childhood can only go so far. Recognizing our strengths and creating goals can only serve as a starting point. We must use these strengths in ways that allow us to generate income in order to have the seeds of wealth that can then be planted. How do economically successful individuals do this?

When we hear from readers and critics of *The Millionaire Next Door*, *The Millionaire Mind*, and other works, frequently we see some confusion over the possible paths to wealth and/or financial independence. Many assume that only three paths exist: (1) the frugal, steady-as-she-goes journey; (2) the high-income-producing, high-level leadership path; or (3) the self-employed, risk-taking, investing-in-my-business approach. The truth is, no path is that simple. They are all unique and they all require discipline.

As stated in *The Millionaire Next Door*, economically successful individuals tend to choose (or create, or eventually find) a career that is "right" in that it provides ample income while also providing satisfaction. Today, though, we expand this to include those who retire from the world of work relatively quickly by amassing savings early in their careers. The "right" career may be one that only lasts 10 to 15 years while a frugal lifestyle ensures a high savings rate that can then generate revenue through investments. It is a contrarian idea, but it is possible, as illustrated in the FI/RE community.

Economic success doesn't require that you have extraordinarily high intellect in America, as we discussed in Chapter 5. If you have great discipline and leverage your creative intellect, you will likely become an achiever. Under the heading of creative intellect are two factors that underlie the millionaire-next-door profile. These include two main factors related to vocation from *The Millionaire Next Door*: Factor 6, *they are proficient in targeting market opportunities*, and Factor 7, *they chose the right occupation*. Economically successful Americans choose the right approach to earning revenue and working. They experience "work" and thereby find and choose a career or business that is conducive to building wealth. They determine, early on, if they can amass wealth over a lifetime, starting early, and find ways to grow that wealth over time without being beholden to a traditional career. They start businesses that make the best use of their talents.

The millionaires profiled in *The Millionaire Next Door* seemed out of the ordinary because often they were either small business owners in mundane businesses (e.g., heavy equipment leasing companies) or they had amassed wealth slowly in careers like teaching or accounting. There were also doctors, lawyers, and other professionals. The typical millionaire next door is given this label because he doesn't appear to be wealthy but is, notwithstanding his vocation. His simple lifestyle allows him to transform household income, an income which is usually above the national average, into wealth. The simple truth is:

Job titles are better indicators of income than wealth.

In our most recent study, we found that millionaires spanned various industries and job types, just as 20 years ago (see Table 6-1). Millionaires (with on average $3.5 million in net worth) included a higher concentration of professional occupations than the millionaire-next-door population from twenty years ago, but also included job titles outside of what might be expected. The job titles of the millionaires in our sample included government employees and small business owners, managers and vice presidents, accountants and IT directors. Some millionaires reported owning multiple businesses at once, while others were consultants.

Table 6-1. Selected Millionaire Job Titles

Accountant	Federal Agent	Orthopedic Surgeon
Airline Pilot	Financial Advisor	Owner, Multiple Businesses
Architect	Financial Analyst	Physician
Assistant Vice President	General Manager	Physicist
Attorney	Graphic Artist	Pilot
Banker	Health Care Consultant	President
Business Analyst	Human Resources Director	Product Manager
Business Consultant	Insurance Broker	Real Estate Agent
Business Owner	Investment Advisor	Real Estate Appraiser
CEO	IT Consultant	Real Estate Developer
CFO	IT Director	Regional Sales Director
Civil Servant	Lobbyist	Restauranteur
Computer Engineer	Management Consultant	Risk Management Consultant
Consultant	Manager	Sales Associate
CPA	Manufacturing Representative	Sales Executive
CTO	Marketing Research Consultant	Scientist
Defense Consultant	Medical Director	Security Consultant
Dentist	Medical Sales	Software Engineer
Dietician	Middle Manager	Systems Consultant
Economist	Military Officer	Teacher
Educational Consultant	Nurse Anesthetist	Trainer/Consultant
Engineer	Oil and Gas Explorationist	Upper-Level Manager
Executive Vice President	Operations Manager	Veterinarian

The studies of the affluent over the past two decades are perhaps most useful to those who make a better-than-average living. However, as we saw in Chapter 5, successful financial behaviors, those that allow the transformation of income into wealth, transcend income levels.

Without a consistent source of revenue, there is little to invest. And having something consistent, or at the very least, relatively stable, requires finding a career in which one's skills, knowledge, and abilities can be put to use, in which one can find a passion, or one that provides income enough to meticulously save and exit the traditional world of work early. Finding a career that makes full use of one's competencies is often a reward in and of itself. And becoming financially independent may also prove to be even more rewarding.

Even so, many millionaires today continue to work into their 60s. Millionaires spend on average approximately 38 hours per week working (or 45 hours per week if you exclude retirees). In comparison, about two-thirds of millionaires we surveyed in 1996 spent between 45 and 55 hours per week at work. Overall, nonretired millionaires earned 75% or more of their gross income from their salary.

In 1996, 20% of affluent households were headed by retirees, and this number has not deviated much (19% of millionaire households are headed by retirees today). Of the remaining 81%, just over 42% of these millionaires are self-employed. In 1996, two-thirds of affluent households not headed by a retiree were headed by a self-employed business owner. This difference, 66% in 1996 compared to 42% in 2016, is similar to changes in self-employment in general. In 1996, about 18% of American heads of households were self-employed. In 2015[2], that number was 10%. This number has been on the decline, partially due to decreases in agricultural self-employment.

As we discussed earlier, this is only one path to financial success. If you love your job, if it provides you with the lifestyle and level of freedom you desire, then working is less a chore and more of a pastime. If this doesn't describe you, millionaires next door before you, and today, have alternatives to suggest.

Benefits of Early Experiences

The challenge of careers (and for those in the field of career development) is that rarely do we know everything required to make perfect career choices when we begin working. Many millionaires shared with us that their parents provided them with early and frequent realistic previews of the world of work. The parental emphasis on career exploration in financially successful individuals hasn't changed since *The Millionaire Next Door* was first published. Early experiences continue to allow self-made Americans to hone their ability to target opportunities and find careers and jobs that give great satisfaction.

For example, imagine as a student you had the opportunity to work one summer in mineral engineering, spending time with others in the field, learning what it's like to put in 60 hours a week in the dirt. At the end of that experience, you would be able to determine (a) if the field was of interest to you, (b) if you could "survive" in the type of environments that mineral engineers often find themselves, and (c) if you, in general, liked the work you were doing. These early experiences would allow you to make thoughtful decisions about the way in which you were going to generate revenue in the future. We see these early experiences and their impact on millionaires particularly with early sales experiences, which we'll discuss later.

Some of us were lucky to have had early experiences that helped us decide what we liked and didn't like about working, as well as what we were interested in and able to do. When we asked one of our samples of mass affluent Americans about their career experiences, and what they had hoped for in their career experiences (that is, what would have allowed them to be more successful), here's what they shared with us:

> *I was taught to work hard, and that no job is beneath me. It has become very beneficial to me especially in my current situation, where I had to take a step back in my career path while I start a business, while working in a menial labor position to help pay the bills.*

> *I was responsible for helping to replace and repair fire hydrants. This job was essential to teaching me a solid work ethic, teamwork, and doing a good job. It was also more enjoyable than a grind type job like office/retail work.*

> *Having a set allowance, and then working. My parents only supported me financially in terms of what I needed, and not what I wanted. I had to plan to get what I want. One specific experience was figuring out how to save enough to go on a ski trip with friends.*

> *I had multiple jobs and was required to save and invest my money. I learned in high school about mutual funds, etc. and was made to choose ones to put my money into.*

My father forbade me from working. That put me behind my peers in many ways, including work experience and financial matters. I wish I had a job like my peers.

The part-time jobs I had in high school did not pay very much, and my parents required me to be responsible for a lot of my own expenses. I had to learn to save and budget my money in order to get by.

Having part-time jobs taught me how hard it was to earn money.

I believed in working as a teenager toward a goal. I wanted a car, and as soon as I turned 16, I got a job and worked for 6 months to save $1,000 for a piece of junk. It did not matter it was junk, because it was mine. I earned it.

Early career experiences, early failures, and early tightrope walking without safety nets provide necessary fuel for long-term career success.

The Upside of Less Than Ideal Careers

There are still some parents out there who are doing a poor job preparing their children for the world of work, not only through a lifestyle of consumption, which requires constant, high levels of income to sustain, but also through sugar-coating the typical problems that go along with working for a living or, perhaps worse, insulating their children from early career experiences altogether.

How do you know if you will love a big national sales manager job that requires 50% travel time? What about teaching? Enjoying children and managing a classroom are two different animals. Maybe a career in technology is for you. But the reality is these jobs require sitting and staring at a device, or two, or three all day, which may not suit your interests or disposition.

The benefit of having multiple career experiences is that someone is able to discern the market opportunities that are best. For some, a single career experience can dramatically alter the degree of someone's socioeconomic achievement. And here is just one example:

I had dropped out of college and was working as a cocktail server at a casino. The sections that we served rotated daily so I would work with different girls every day. I walked into my designated service bar one night and saw that

I would be working with all older servers. As I looked around the bar at the women in their sixties wearing miniskirts and carrying heavy trays of drinks I decided that wasn't going to be me. I got back in school the next semester, graduated, and I am now employed as a tax accountant with a local accounting firm. I'll finish up the CPA exam this fall. I look back at that moment in the service bar as the turning point in my professional life.

For this young woman, even the rigorous requirements of studying accounting somehow seemed less demanding when compared to a job that didn't match her interests or desires for long-term employment.

Influenced Out of Real Work

Consistent over time, millionaires tend to be a satisfied group: a full 90% of millionaires in our sample reported being extremely satisfied with life, which typically correlates at some level with job satisfaction. How many Americans are satisfied with their jobs? The Conference Board[3] suggests that less than 50% of Americans are very satisfied with their jobs, and the Pew Research Center[4] says it's about 52%. The Society for Human Resources Management suggests the number is higher, reporting that 86% of workers are satisfied, although this number includes those who indicate they are "somewhat satisfied."[5] We would argue the practical difference of someone being "very satisfied" and "somewhat satisfied" with their job is fairly significant. A 2017 Gallup poll on the state of the US workforce included this finding: "While 37% of engaged employees are looking for jobs or watching for opportunities, higher numbers of not-engaged and actively disengaged employees are doing the same (56% and 73%, respectively). Actively disengaged employees are almost twice as likely as engaged employees to seek new jobs."[6]

Maybe our expectations about work are too high, especially for those of us who have never experienced real work, or hardship, or been required to be disciplined to reach a goal. As with spending, we are guided by what those around us are doing. Many Americans are indoctrinated into a casual, or carefree, version of the world of work, courtesy of the media. As an example, my father once asked readers to consider how sitcoms often portray the world of work. From 2003 to 2015, the television series *Two and a Half Men* had its share of controversies (primarily due to its original star) and its share of awards and accolades for its cast and production team.

Required for Career Success: Sell Something

The early part of my father's career studying the affluent involved helping financial institutions and other related companies target wealthy Americans for their services and products. Part of this research focused on extraordinary sales professionals—individuals with seemingly endless resilient passion and assertiveness, coupled with respect for those to whom they were soliciting, particularly the affluent. The excerpt below combines material from two essays (one written in 2010, one in 2013) he wrote on the benefits of sales experience:

I recently asked nearly 1,000 millionaires nationwide "What was your first full-time job?" Out of those 1,000 respondents, 137 answered, "sales/marketing professional." In fact, this proportion places the "sales/marketing vocation" as the #1 first full-time job. Does this mean that people in this profession have a significantly higher probability than those in other jobs of becoming wealthy? No! There is a smaller proportion of millionaires who are sales professionals than would be expected given the large size of the sales professionals category in general employed in America.

Only about one-half of those millionaires who started with a career in sales remain in that profession today. Those who moved on are highly concentrated in two areas: they are either owners/managers of successful businesses or they are senior executives of public corporations.

This in no way should discourage people from entering the sales profession. For this vocation is often the incubator for future corporate leaders and entrepreneurs. Given the right sales position, you may be given the opportunity to interact with possibly thousands of key people in other corporations and businesses. This often stimulates one's creative side in finding opportunities that have not been exploited. One of those opportunities is to be hired by one of the organizations that are among your customer base. If you are successful in selling for others, you may be able to sell your own product via your own company someday. Most millionaires are leaders. And most leaders must sell their ideas to their troops.

When considering career paths, one should look at the tradeoffs between income and other factors such as responsibilities and GROWTH OPPORTUNITIES. But understand that building wealth is highly correlated with the size of one's income. Ideally, you will find a job that pays well and has great opportunities.

. . . I mentioned that the profession of selling was the most frequently cited "first job after college" by millionaires. And today many are either senior corporate executives or successful self-employed business owners. In fact, according to my calculations, there are more sales professionals with annual incomes of $200,000 or more than there are physicians and surgeons who generate this high level of income.

Too many people shy away from the opportunities that are provided by selling. Some fear they will not be able to produce at a level that is required in the job description: no sales, no pay. However, if you can succeed in sales you are likely to be able to succeed among the ranks of the self-employed. Look at the profession of selling in another way. Some sales positions actually pay you for constantly enhancing your image. In essence your description is to contact people who may ultimately offer you a great position and/or become patrons of the business that you may start one day.

The benefits of experiencing and developing skills in sales transcend a *sales job*, and prepare the economically successful small business owner for selling his own ideas, services, and products in the future.

Over the past 40 years, what have millionaires shared with us about the benefits of sales?

- Sales roles are unique in their compensation structure: There is no upper limit to what you can make.
- Sales roles are the ultimate in pay for performance. There are few politics, and numbers don't lie. Pay for performance allows for proof in the pudding.
- Extraordinary sales professionals are always in demand since they pay for themselves many times over.
- Sales gets you great exposure. You are getting paid for doing interviews for jobs you may have in the future.
- Sales roles allow great freedom. In some ways, a sales role is the closest role to that of an entrepreneur.
- Great sales numbers cover most all other metrics and demographics. With excellent sales numbers, your employer will give little attention to your college GPA, SAT scores, or even if you graduated.
- Sales roles require less education than becoming a doctor, lawyer, or other professional, but still can provide a high level of income.
- In sales, you are really an intelligence officer looking for great strategic opportunities.

The show, still in syndication, featured a character named Charlie, whose lifestyle suggested that he could afford to hyper-consume without working very hard or at all. He was a composer of advertising jingles, but we rarely saw him sweating at the piano hour after hour to come up with the songs. Somehow, he supported a multimillion-dollar beach house in Malibu, his brother and his nephew, and a housekeeper. Most of the time he could be seen at home entertaining guests and distributing one-liners.

Often viewers of shows such as *Two and a Half Men*, as well as other mass media, are unknowingly conditioned to believe that most successful people are like Charlie. Somehow these people are so talented and gifted that they can make a great living working five minutes here and there. It is easy to become discouraged if you think that Charlie's method is the formula for success in America. Clearly it is not. Feel-good television, and now social media, is filled with depictions of people who succeed without really working. This, of course, is fantasyland.

Excluding heirs, lottery winners, and other folks who receive windfalls, building wealth typically requires that someone starts with a self-generated source of income. Our research on economically successful people differs widely from dramatic fantasy. Most people in America must hunt and gather every day. Without an alternative form of income, which most in America do not have, they rely on their jobs, day in and day out, to provide income to survive, as 78% of American workers live paycheck to paycheck.[7] Even most millionaires we have interviewed or surveyed work nearly 40 hours a week. More than 90% are married and typically have two children to support. Most did not become wealthy until their late 40s or early 50s. And very few of them were ever leisurely entertaining throughout the day.

Table 6-2. Sources of Income for Millionaires

Sources of Income	Income Source Percentage							
	0%	1%	5%	10%	20%	30%	50%	75% or more
	Percentage of Millionaires							
Salary	24.1	1.9	2.5	3.3	4.5	5.8	16.3	41.6
Pension/Retirement/ Annuity Income	64.9	2.7	4.3	5.2	3.7	4.9	5.7	8.6
Business Profits	66.7	2.9	6.2	5.4	4.0	4.9	4.5	5.4
Professional Fees/Sales Commissions	79.5	2.5	4.4	3.4	2.7	2.4	1.5	3.7
Commissions/Bonuses/ Profit Sharing	51.6	6.2	7.7	10.1	9.9	5.1	6.2	3.2
Dividends	20.7	32.8	23.6	12.3	5.5	2.4	1.1	1.6
Rental Income from Real Estate	68.6	7.2	9.1	6.3	3.6	1.8	2.6	0.8
Realized Capital Gains – Securities	45.1	18.5	19.4	10.2	3.7	1.8	0.6	0.8
Income from Trusts or Estates	86.2	3.8	2.7	2.8	1.8	1.3	0.7	0.7
Savings/CDs (interest)	38.4	39.9	13.1	6.5	1.0	0.5	0.3	0.3
Realized Capital Gains – Other Assets	75.6	9.5	6.2	5.1	1.3	1.5	0.7	0.2
Alimony or Child Support	99.2	0.0	0.3	0.2	0.2	0.0	0.0	0.2
Royalties from Intellectual Property	97.4	1.3	0.6	0.3	0.2	0.0	0.0	0.2
Gifts of Cash, Securities, Property, Vehicles, etc. from Relatives	90.3	6.8	1.9	0.8	0.2	0.0	0.0	0.0
Other Sources Combined (not listed above)	73.4	4.9	8.5	6.4	2.7	1.4	1.7	1.0

Millionaires and Working . . . Today

One hallmark of those who have become economically successful is that they are congruent or have "high fit" with their careers. In other words, their skills, abilities, knowledge, interests, and other characteristics match the requirements of their jobs. The income from a career can't last if you cannot last in the career. Without fit or congruence with your occupation or chosen career, the prospects of long-term income are murky—or laden with stress and strife.

Today's millionaire next door continues to find opportunities, despite the governmental, social, and economic conditions of the day. Awareness of one's own skills and the corresponding market for those skills is still required. Millionaires and those who become economically independent and successful on their own are able to (a) assess their own skills, abilities, and characteristics *and* the environment/market, and (b) choose an occupation that makes the most of both. The 733 millionaires surveyed in 1998 nationwide for *The Millionaire Mind* were asked about their important choice factors regarding their selection of vocation. Four out of five (or 81%) indicated that they chose their vocation because "it allowed full use of their abilities and aptitudes." Seventy percent of millionaires in 2016 stated that loving their career or chosen business was important in their economic success (for small business owners, three out of four stated it was important). The experience of jumping out of bed each morning and loving your job requires alignment.

Millionaires . . . in a "Regular" Job?

Just as in 1996, it is possible today, with an average to higher-than-average income, to become a millionaire through steady, prudent, disciplined financial management and regular income—regular meaning not extraordinary commissions from sales roles or extremely high salaries like those of attorneys, doctors, and CEOs.

How can this be? This is the most pressing question for those who cannot imagine or want to challenge the idea of building wealth with a slow and steady career. From the research conducted for *Stop Acting Rich*, we know the typical balance-sheet affluent millionaire had an annual realized median household income of $89,167 when he first became a millionaire. In other words, one-half of the balance-sheet affluent had incomes that were less than this figure. What does this tell us about building wealth and becoming financially secure? For most Americans one's desire, discipline, and intellect are more important factors in accumulating wealth than earning a high income. The problem today among many high-income earners is that they think that money (income) is the most easily renewable resource. Consequently, they act according to the principles found in the "Handbook for Hyper Consumers."

But not all Americans follow these principles or the path taken by the modal crowd (that is, the group we see around us most frequently) in America. They think for themselves. And most rich people in this country become rich and remain that way because they receive much more satisfaction from building wealth and financial security than displaying expensive store-bought badges. So it is with Mrs. C.C., who was kind enough to share some of her thoughts in a letter to my father about becoming financially independent without ever earning a high income:

Dear Dr. Stanley,

When my friends read your "Millionaire" books they always say, "C.C., it's you he's writing about." I attended public schools where the teachers were role models and mentors. I have had the benefit of knowing many strong women, some who did well financially. From them, I learned to rely on myself and not wait for "Mr. Right" to support me. I was a scholarship student at a small liberal arts college. I had many mentors whose examples shaped my life.

While my net worth can be attributed to frugality and canny invest-ing, my lifestyle is shaped by an excellent education. I have always tended to wander away from the herd in my thinking, but my education taught me self-discipline, independence of thought, and strong ethics.

I am the child of a single, working mother, and my early years were fraught with financial uncertainty. I learned by watching my mother that women have to work harder and longer to achieve financial success.

While I am not as wealthy as most of your subjects, my net worth is above $1 million, and like most of your subjects, I started with nothing more than a college scholarship and a good mother. The thing that you may find interesting about me is that I have never earned more than $60,000. I have worked in middle management in state government most of my career.

I have accumulated most of my net worth by living below my means. I have everything I want, but I have learned not to want too much. Also, I avoid debt. Midway through my career the state government was being downsized and I was in danger of losing my job. I told myself I wanted to get into a position where I would never again be faced with that uncer-tainty. First, I stopped giving myself raises. All new money went into invest-ments. Then I paid off my house loan, and the house payments could go into investments. I am fairly conservative in my investment but not afraid of risk. Most years, I saved 30 percent of my income, if not more.

My net worth is my own, separate from my husband's, and I manage it myself. Recently, I "semi-retired." It was satisfying to know I could afford the pay cut. While I have no biological children, I have had many foster children. I notice that they have learned from me the ability to manage money well, as I learned from my mother.

Sincerely,

Mrs. C.C.

Mrs. C.C.'s story highlights how one can succeed in the creation of wealth despite an income that isn't in the six figures. Her steady source of revenue was transformed into wealth via disciplined saving and investing, and living below her means. If this is the path you're taking, one that is connected to an employer, then transforming income (which is relatively consistent, except in a few cases) into wealth requires heavy doses of discipline and restraint.

Enjoy the Safety . . . and Always Be Looking

Working for someone else provides benefits beyond career experiences and income. It affords some level of safety: an office, maybe collegial coworkers, and a 401(k). This safety might also include leaders to guide you, equipment paid for with someone else's money, and office Christmas parties flowing with gift cards. Safety is Ping-Pong tables, health care, wellness benefits, and onsite gyms. What we pay for those benefits, though, is our time, and as many have come to realize perhaps too late, the majority of our lives. And they don't always stay safe. Obtain and save not only income from your employer, but the skills, opportunities, and experiences that will allow you flexibility and resources in the future.

It's still the case that transportable skills and experiences set up a good defense against job elimination, economic woes, and even geopolitical upheavals. When catastrophe strikes, the knowledge, skills, abilities, and other characteristics that someone has can be transferred to new industries, countries, and opportunities. While perhaps the millionaires from a few decades ago knew this well, many having lived through the upheaval and horrors of World War II, even economically successful individuals today recognize the need to prepare regardless of the times.

For those who experienced job loss, those memories last, but the experiences can be used to compel action. Consider this Minnesota millionaire next door's experience during college and his attitude toward it:

> *I was laid off from my part-time job working as a blackjack dealer while attending college. It was a large publicly traded company back in 1989. I needed the job to pay for rent, tuition, etc. I asked my supervisor why I was being let go since I always volunteered to work overtime, received excellent reviews from customers, and was considered a solid employee based upon my employment reviews. He basically said the other people had families and I was young and could find something else.* This was the best thing that ever happened to me. *As a result of being laid off, even though I was considered a solid employee, I learned at an early age that you cannot depend on a company to take care of you, no matter how hard you work your job. Since that experience, I have structured my life so that I never have to depend on an employer ever again. I've always been self-employed and could retire today (at age 49) if I didn't have so much fun working on my business.*

Economically successful individuals use challenges and career setbacks as springboards for greater experiences in the future. They spend little time blaming others. That valuable resource, time, is used to contemplate, plan, and execute their next career move, be it self-employment or employment in some other capacity (or, as we've seen, early retirement along with a less consumer-focused lifestyle).

Three Components for Escaping the Trap

After years of education, and perhaps years working in a career, what if you find yourself trapped by the time and effort you've spent building, networking, and climbing within an organization in which you no longer want to work? Particularly, if you're relying on paychecks, this is a source of dissatisfaction and stress that can permeate the rest of your life. Or what if you decide you want to join the ranks of the self-employed?

Being in the business of studying the wealthy, we talk to many individuals who ask us about our research and data, about the books, stories, and survey responses. Many times, the first part of the conversation sounds a bit like this: "I loved reading *The Millionaire Next Door*. I love reading those stories, especially the stories of business owners . . . doing it all on their own. You know, I've thought a lot about going out on my own." But the end of the conversation usually sounds like this: "I don't want all that responsibility of owning my own business" or "I need the security of a full-time job and benefits."

Millionaires have shared three themes related to removing yourself from the trap of working to live: creating margin in their lifestyle to allow for career moves, particularly significant ones (e.g., living off of savings while starting a business); exploring career opportunities while generating revenue from a traditional job (i.e., moonlighting); and making a move to self-employment.

Margin Required

Most millionaires we interviewed highlighted the great freedom that comes from spending below their means. The freedom translates into opportunities to make career changes that provide either (a) more time and flexibility to pursue efforts outside of work, and/or (b) the potential for increase in revenue. Of course, it's hard to see the future, particularly when you're starting out and your lifestyle and choices about spending have been affected by a high income. A millionaire biology instructor from California told us, "When I got my first teaching job at the community college, I was hired on a part-time basis. One older and seasoned instructor said I needed to learn to save and invest my money because one day 'you may decide you don't want to teach anymore. That money will give you the independence and, more importantly, options to choose, rather than to continue working. Money isn't about being rich. Money is about giving you choices. You are young and may not be able to see this now, but someday you will.' It has been 25 years since that day and I can say that I took his advice to heart and I have both the money and choices!"

Others realize this later . . . but if it's later, and there isn't any margin, what happens then?

Mr. Lionel's Lack of Margin

As in the case of where you live, one's vocation can have a significant impact on lifestyle and the freedom or flexibility you and your household have in making significant career-focused changes. Consider for a moment the lifestyle of a former high-level senior sales executive at a midsized business, Mr. Barry Lionel. His parents were government employees, but he generally had a loving and warm home life. Armed with an excellent college education and scrappy early career experiences, Mr. Lionel began climbing the ladder.

As the business he worked for succeeded and his income rose, so did his and his family's consumption. From a small, three-bedroom home in a middle-class neighborhood, Mrs. Lionel decided the family needed a house to reflect her husband's success. Once his income went into the solid six figures, $180,000 a year, the Lionel family moved to a $935,000 home in a luxury neighborhood, a home they purchased that was more than five times Mr. Lionel's income at the time. But it was similar to the homes of the other chiefs in his company. The new neighborhood in which the Lionel family lived required homeowner's association dues of nearly $1,500 per year, but even with that, most of Mr. Lionel's neighbors were members of the nearby country club which charged initiation fees of $80,000 and monthly dues of $650. Everything seemed rosy for the Lionels.

But the Lionels were living paycheck to paycheck keeping up with his colleagues and the Joneses in their new community. And then, Mr. Lionel's company was acquired! Hooray? Yes, he made approximately $1.4 million on the sale. But with little else saved, this essentially became his household's net worth. And he was not included in the company moving forward. More importantly and significantly, perhaps, was that the Lionels' consumption habits were firmly established based on his past income level.

Now, the dust has settled, and after a few failed attempts at going out on his own, Mr. Lionel's skills have atrophied, while his family's consumption habits, including those of his adult children who are starting high-consumption households of their own, have only increased. Despite the incredible amount of hard work during those early years at the company, he cannot enjoy the fruits of his labor because they were eaten away as soon as they were produced. He is firmly in the income-statement affluent camp, and he is setting his children up to be the same.

What type of career path is this? It is truly a lifestyle-driven path. Consider how Mr. Lionel's lifestyle necessarily changed at each level: the car he drove, where he dined, the friends he kept, and the vacations he took were in some ways dictated by the combination of his income and his career community.

So if you do not like to deprive yourself of whatever consumer good is available, that is your choice, but simple and immutable *math* dictates the result.

Spending above your means, spending instead of saving for retirement, spending in anticipation of becoming wealthy makes you a slave to the paycheck, even with a stellar level of income and a once-in-a-lifetime opportunity like the sale of a company.

The hyper-consumption lifestyle of this once young executive wasn't detected until his options ran out, as did time. Ratcheting up spending along the way isn't noticed or is easily dismissed because of the time saved or the "necessity" of having "it." Can you last in this role? What else will you need to survive? Do you want this path for yourself? Are you strong enough to create a path where there is none today? Or can you continue working for someone else *and* maintain your own sense of self and goals? Learning the answers to these questions *early* in one's career can help to ensure satisfaction later in life.

Some of this goes back to an understanding of our own strengths and weaknesses. But most of it relies on being disciplined throughout our lives, regardless of our income level or success in careers or what our neighbors, family, and coworkers are doing. Indeed, financial margin is required for freedom in career choice.

Changing Your Work/Family Balance

Having margin, or creating it through prudent saving, is often required when our work life begins to interfere with more critical aspects of our lives, including our families. Consider the following example from this North Carolina millionaire next door with a net worth of between $1 million and $1.5 million who shared her experience of breaking free of a trap of a high-income and requisite lifestyle:

> *I was working for a very large global company, managing a large group of people across seven countries and three continents. My children and husband [were top] priority, but I kept hearing myself say, "I have to work" on the weekends, in the early morning, in the late evening. I realized one day that the company was becoming too demanding when I was on a 7 a.m. conference call, one organized by my executive team. One that "I had to take." My three-year-old was crying on my lap, my five-year-old was knocking on the door, and my husband was running out of the house to work for a meeting of his*

From the start, Ms. Meehan and Mr. Redding were well aware of the allergic reactions many women encountered with traditional shampoos and related beauty products. Many other people realized this too, yet only Ms. Meehan and Mr. Redding saw this as a significant market opportunity. Both obviously had entrepreneurial vision or, alternatively, what some call creative intelligence. Plus, they had the courage to launch a line of products that addressed allergy-related problems of women in 35 countries.

Distributing Redken products exclusively through salons was a brilliant and novel strategy at the time. In essence Ms. Meehan had a sales force of tens of thousands of high-end hairdressers promoting Redken products to clients who were a captive audience "while sitting in the chair."

Ms. Meehan was the marketing force behind Redken. She had the enormous energy that was required to aggressively build a business, sell products, and work as an actress. And she took "night classes in management, accounting, and law" to learn to build and operate an entrepreneurial enterprise.

Her boundless energy came from her conviction that the Redken product had enormous potential. She absolutely believed that there were significant benefits afforded by her pH-balanced beauty product line. Ms. Meehan predicted that millions and millions of other women had the same sensitivity she had.

Like most successful entrepreneurs Ms. Meehan "had great affection for her product as well as for her job description. As stated in *The Millionaire Mind*: "select a vocation that is not only unique and profitable, but one you love."[9]

Confidence Required to Moonlight

A high school teacher named Murray is an example of having confidence in choosing how to generate revenue.

Murray taught for several years in a school district that did not have a true commitment to academic achievement. So when he was given the opportunity to teach in a district where students ranked in the top tier in regard to SAT scores, college-bound graduates, etc., he jumped at the chance. By making this change, Murray also encountered a significant increase in salary. Taken away by the euphoria of teaching in such a prestigious school and the upswing of his cash flow, Murray made a mistake. He bought a house in the lovely village where his school was located, but it was a house in a neighborhood he could barely afford. Typically, educators are a frugal bunch. In many ways, Murray and his family were frugal. But when you live in an affluent village, everything costs more. It did not matter that Murray ate peanut butter sandwiches out of a brown bag every day or that he did all of his own home maintenance and repairs. Great defense was not enough. And when Murray's third child was born, his wife stopped working to be a full-time homemaker.

Given these circumstances, the family was not able to contribute to a college fund for their children or to save meaningful amounts of money. These are some of the same problems that millions of people are facing today.

One summer day while Murray was painting his house, his next-door neighbor stopped by to chat. "I wish I could paint my own house like you are doing, but I just don't have the time; I travel so much with my job. The estimates I just got from three housepainters took my breath away." When Murray heard how much these painters were charging, he nearly fell off his ladder.

The next morning, Murray had a revelation. Genius is often defined as seeing opportunities that are so obvious they go unnoticed by 99% of others. Murray realized that he could paint his neighbor's house for a fraction of what the professional housepainters had proposed and still make a sizable profit. He already had the knowledge and the equipment to do the job. And he was a very good painter for an amateur. But, he thought, should an educator in an affluent community be out painting houses during the summer recess? What will people say? In the end, Murray decided that the economic welfare of his family was more important than what the neighbors might think about his moonlighting venture.

He went next door and proposed to paint his neighbor's house for two-thirds of the lowest bid given by the professional housepainters. The neighbor took a chance and hired Murray. At this time, he never envisioned starting a house painting business; he was just trying to make some extra money. But while painting his next-door neighbor's house, another neighbor came by and asked him for an estimate. He painted that house and then another and then another. In short order, Murray became overwhelmed with business. The next summer he hired several of his colleagues to help paint. He also hired his best and most conscientious juniors and seniors to earn extra money. And they continued to work for him during their summer breaks from college.

Murray kept his "day job" with all of its benefits. He enjoys teaching, but today he makes a lot more money from his summer work. He is successful because he didn't let his perceived middle-class status prevent him from earning a living in what some people might consider a "blue-collar" vocation.

Build Wealth to Control Your Destiny

The concept of a "go to hell fund," a savings amount that would allow for you to live for 10 or more years without having to work sounds like a fantasy, particularly to those just starting out in their careers. But, as we discussed in Chapter 1, an entire community is growing around this concept. Indeed the financial independence's go-to-hell fund lasts them a lifetime, once invested. In 2012, my father wrote about the benefits of such a fund on the heels of a reader's e-mail regarding being trapped in a career:

In *The Millionaire Next Door* I profiled a millionaire corporate sales professional. He, like other self-made millionaires, said that he had a "go to hell fund . . . just in case my employer suggests (insists) that I leave Austin for corporate headquarters in 'Rottenchester.'" He never had to leave Austin and he added, "PTL" (praise the Lord). In other words, the millionaires next door have accumulated enough wealth to live without working for 10 or more years.

Those words still ring true today, as we were reminded of this wisdom after reviewing an email from Ms. F who currently resides in a lovely community in the southern United States:

> I went to my local library this morning, hoping to borrow *The Millionaire Next Door*. However, the only available book was in Spanish, so I borrowed *Millionaire Women Next Door* instead. By the time I completed the second paragraph on page 8, I had collapsed in a fit of "craughter"—simultaneously crying and laughing at my sad truth. My newest work assignment is no less than 8,200 miles, 18 hours of flying time, and 12 time zones away from everyone who means the most to me in this world. Simply put, the situation stinks, but I had convinced myself that it was necessary to pay the bills. Suffice it to say that I have renewed my concerted efforts to become a cultivator of wealth, and I plan to share my transformation with you soon. Thank you for creating this compilation of evidence-based encouragement!

What precipitated Ms. F's "craughter?" Consider the words I wrote in *Millionaire Women Next Door*:

> Aren't you growing tired of being among the ranks of hunter-gatherers? Do you enjoy your hyper consumption lifestyle so much that you must fly out of town every week to earn a paycheck to pay your bills? . . . Begin making the transformation to a cultivator of wealth. Think about that the next time you are ten thousand miles from home, surrounded by strangers, and flying in dreadful weather. It is up to you. Those financially independent folks. . . . make their own decisions about their next destination. Right now, you and your career are essentially corporate property. Neither one of you has the luxury of self-determination.

I also wrote, "The [millionaire business] women profiled herein will not tolerate such an existence. They are free. They are cultivators of wealth and satisfied with life. They are in control of their own destiny."[10]

Case Studies in Moonlighting

The benefits of moonlighting include the ability to transfer one set of experiences and knowledge gained in a "regular," full-time job to a new way in which to approach problems within your same field or industry. Appendix C includes some of the job titles of moonlighters from our research with the mass affluent/high-net-worth samples. While being paid in your current role, you can catalog the knowledge of your industry and field, using it to apply to a new and potentially more profitable endeavor. Consider these examples my father shared a few years ago:

Seeing Opportunities in the Dental Office

The *Atlanta Journal-Constitution* once profiled a woman named Tonya Lanthier who was trained as a dental hygienist (one of 192,330 in this country) and built a multimillion-dollar business based upon, what I believe, is her extraordinary creative intellect.[11] Dental hygienists make approximately $71,530 a year, median income, but she came into contact with hundreds of potential clients as well as job seekers.

Dentists with jobs to fill constantly asked [her] to recommend good workers. They knew the dental hygienist pulled shifts as a temp in lots of offices and had plenty of friends in the business.

Because she had so many requests, she decided "to launch a national online job site for the dental industry." The site now has more than 400,000 registered users.

How does someone with no previous business experience, no business degree, no marketing background or previous computer experience build a successful Internet business? People with these skills can be hired, but it was Tonya's creative intellect (or vision) which is reflected in her company's offerings. Also, as highlighted in the article, Tonya has demonstrated tremendous perseverance and leadership qualities.

Moonlighting: From Nurse to Sales to Self-Employment

A registered nurse asked me where people in her profession ranked in their ability to transform income into wealth. Highly compensated RNs are in the average range of productivity, ranking 88th among the 200 occupations studied.

But her question reminded me of several case studies of RNs who leveraged their rigorous training, extraordinary work ethic, and considerable experience into a variety of lucrative businesses. Plus, all of them ranked high on Factor 6, a key characteristic of the millionaire next door: They are proficient in targeting market opportunities.

Kay, for example, was a surgical nurse for nine years. Then she took a job selling surgical equipment. While in sales, Kay found that she spent a lot of time in one particular activity that was not part of her traditional job description. She became an amateur headhunter for hospitals and medical practices that were in need of physicians, nurses, and medical technicians. This "fringe benefit" provided for free to her many clients had much to do with Kay's designation as a top producer. Eventually she recognized an opportunity to fill a market need. Plus, she had much goodwill and many contacts in the medical field. Accordingly, as I wrote in *The Millionaire Next Door*, "Most successful business owners had some knowledge or experience with their chosen industry before they ever opened their own business."

Kay left her sales job and began her own employment agency specializing in the medical field. Much of her motivation to go out on her own was the need to be self-employed. She previously had high job satisfaction being a nurse, but she found that being self-employed did not require any more hard work or responsibility than being an RN had.

Other former RNs have also opted for self-employment. Among the types of businesses they chose are management consulting/medical science administration, in-home health care services, employment agencies for home health care professionals, owners/managers of nursing/rehabilitation facilities, and owners/managers of mental health facilities, day care centers and preschool facilities.

Making the Move to Self-Employment

The millionaire next door of tomorrow can play it safe while playing good defense. The self-employed millionaire next door of tomorrow will take considerable risks, working to create something of value from the extraordinary resources given to him or her. Nearly 30% of self-employed millionaires say most of their career decisions throughout their lives were "risky" or "very risky." Contrasting that with all other millionaires, only 15% said the same. As an Austin millionaire's wife shared with us, "My husband decided to start his own business: I was nervous, but we made a plan. We downgraded, scrimped, saved, and sacrificed for several years to prepare for him to leave his salaried job and go out on his own. We lived on my income . . . and banked all of his. It paid off nicely for us."

While it is not the case that all millionaires are self-employed business owners (42% of millionaires in our sample are), it is the case that extraordinary success in terms of revenue, and reinvesting in one's business, can be found in being a business owner. As my father wrote in *The Millionaire Next Door*, "Fear abounds in America. But, according to our research, who has less fear and worry? Would you guess it's the person with the $5-million trust account, or the self-made entrepreneur worth several million dollars? Typically, it's the entrepreneur, the person who deals with risk every day, who tests his or her courage every day. In this way, he learns to conquer fear."[12]

The potential payoff for those career risks, specifically for the risk associated with starting one's own business, is the ability to generate revenue, more revenue often than would be possible working for someone else. Self-employed millionaires in our latest survey have over 1.5 times the median income of those who work for others. On average, their actual net worth minus their expected net worth is more than twice those who work for others.

When it comes to their finances, self-employed people are often extremely well disciplined, just as most economically successful people are in general, as discussed in Chapter 5. They have a daily routine that maximizes output for every moment of work. They write their own job description. Eighty-one percent said that the job they designed allowed full use of their abilities and aptitudes.

Table 6-3. Career Strategies & Choices of Self-Employed Millionaires vs. Other Millionaires

Millionaire Group	Current Career Strategy (%)			Majority of Career Choices Throughout Lifetime (%)		
	Very Risky/ Risky	Balanced	Conservative/ Very Conservative	Very Risky/ Risky	Balanced	Conservative/ Very Conservative
Self-Employed	20.8	45.9	33.3	28.9	42.3	28.8
All Other	5.7	48.1	45.2	15.2	46.7	38.1

The probability of becoming a millionaire is quite low for those who generate low levels of income. The median household income in America was about $60,000 in 2016 according to the US Census Bureau.[13] With this level of income, a married couple with three children would have a difficult time becoming millionaires. Of the thousands of interviews that my father pored over during his career, one of the most interesting involves a multi-decamillionaire who expressed how most millionaire-next-door types feel. He described making money in stocks, commercial real estate, cattle, oil fields, even high-grade antiques and precious metals. Yet he eloquently summed up what most millionaire-next-door types believe: "[It is] hard to be knowledgeable on a great many [investment] topics. The best thing that I have done has been my own business and to be as good as I can in that. That's the mother lode that supports everything else."

In other words, the major-league revenue generated from his business funded all his other investments, as in the acorn analogy earlier. But self-employment does not automatically translate into big income and wealth. Consider the following: Of the more than 23 million small business owners who are self-employed sole proprietors in 2015, their average annual net income was only $11,637.

Investing in one's own business has been one of the hallmarks of those who have become economically successful, provided they have the strengths, including perseverance, resiliency, and discipline, to get through the inevitable highs and lows of the business. The ease with which you can start a business today is unfathomable to those who grew up 20 or more years ago. Starting a business just by spending a few hours on a laptop was not possible in 1996, and certainly not in 1976 when the average millionaire in our sample was 17 years old. None of these individuals were being told by their parents, mentors, coaches, teachers, or guidance counselors that the way in which they could generate income and make a mark in this world was entirely up to them and there were resources literally at their fingertips. But today, in just a few hours (or even minutes), you can create a business online and run it with little overhead. The Internet and its related technologies for running a small business have leveled the playing field in many ways, allowing those who have challenges with steady employment to create their own opportunities, regardless of what might have held them back before. For example, among the self-employed there is a greater percentage of disabled Americans (11%) than the regular population (6%)[14], in part due to the accessibility that technology brings.

See and Create Value

Of course, income from small businesses varies considerably across industries and over time. Not all types of businesses are equally profitable (for an example, see Appendix C) and not all businesses with any net income can cover living expenses for their owners. Take dentist offices (where 89% of the offices are profitable) and restaurants (where 66% of them are profitable). For the 69,364 dentist offices that were profitable in 2015, that income was on average $118,676. Contrast this with the over 400,000 people who own restaurants and/or drinking establishments. Their net income was just above $7,000 from a gross of $129,304. Selecting the right business is a major factor in explaining profitability and ultimately wealth.

Regardless of tools, technology, and smarts, business success still requires focus and creativity, hard work and discipline, and analysis and foresight. There are a great many businesses that *begin* and few that actually succeed. My father often quoted fighter pilots and generals, citing the focus and awareness they require to become successful at their professions. He wrote:

> *A great fighter pilot once said about inexperienced combatants, "They see but they do not see." In other words, despite having better than 20/20 vision (like being born with high analytic intellect) it does a combat pilot little good if he never looks in the right direction. The same is true in targeting market opportunities and selecting the right occupation. Those who are self-employed*

tend to be contrarians, as they think differently about business, generating revenue, and using creative intelligence to solve a market need. This helps to explain why many of them are in niche, backwater, low status type businesses where competition is light or nonexistent, offering them better chances of succeeding. In addition, as we saw in The Millionaire Mind, *four out of five (or 79%) of millionaire business owners indicated that they chose their specific business type because it gave them a high probability of becoming financially independent.*[15]

In both *The Millionaire Next Door* and *The Millionaire Mind*, my father listed the types of businesses owned by the millionaires surveyed. These businesses ran from the "dull normal" to the unique. For example, in *The Millionaire Next Door* under "Businesses of Self Employed Millionaires," you will find "'bovine semen distributor."[16] Interestingly a 2013 *Wall Street Journal* article mentioned: Julio Moreno, of Oakdale, California, has a freezer full of the bull's semen that sells for at least $3,000 per unit."[17] If asked how he became wealthy, would Mr. Moreno say stocks or bull semen?

Of course, the failure rate for small businesses is roughly 80%[18], and, as also mentioned in *The Millionaire Next Door*, there are certain types of sole proprietorships and small businesses that are extremely low on the success ratio.

Not for the faint of heart, or those who are unwilling to roll up their sleeves, owning your own business can lead to autonomy and independence. The key differentiators of those who can become successful in these endeavors include a combination of creativity, hard work, and perseverance. In the case of the latter, of the self-employed millionaires in our latest study, nearly 93% of them cited resiliency or perseverance as their top success factor (rating it very important or important), followed by being well disciplined (90%) and being honest with all people (87%).

Perseverance Required

It's often said that a successful business becomes that way because the owner had two important ingredients: time and money. Often an individual must have the financial wherewithal to survive without a steady paycheck for many months and even years before his business takes off.

Who Do You Work For?

Who is really in charge when you have large chunks of your equity held by others? Do you really own it anymore? The glamour and glitz of venture capital companies and startups like the ones portrayed on the television series Shark Tank *are intriguing. And maybe those lights are calling you. But being funded via debt is still working for others in some way. Consider this story regarding funding that my father wrote related to small business owners, and ownership, in 2014:*

Davis is a millionaire business owner. Earlier in his career he was asked, "Where do you do your business banking?" He responded, "I bank at the bank of abuse." It seems that Davis encountered an ever-occurring change in loan officers who were constantly condescending and aloof. And no matter how often he repaid his business loans, he was required to update his financial data frequently. During this time Davis was dependent on credit to keep his business going. But more recently he made sacrifices and did a better job using the company's profits to further its growth. This was done shortly after Davis heard a speech given by Gene, an extraordinary millionaire-next-door type I profiled in *The Millionaire Mind*.

Gene's revelations and contributions to my research placed him in the top 10 of all the millionaires I have interviewed. His main vocation was "owner of a salvage business." He became extremely wealthy by purchasing or salvaging distressed real estate from a variety of financial institutions.

But Gene was also a mentor to aspiring entrepreneurs. His fire and brimstone sermon warned against the heavy use of credit. Part of his sermon, which I understand was highly persuasive, details an experience that Gene had while cutting a deal with a large commercial bank. Immediately after the deal was signed, ". . . the senior credit officer of the institution signaled to Gene and walked him over to the large window in the officer's top floor office. They could see for miles . . . thousands of commercial buildings all around . . . the officer pointed to all the buildings and said the words that made a lasting impression on Gene, 'We [the lenders] own it all . . . all of it. The business out there? . . . You [borrowers] just run these businesses for us. You guys run them for us, the financial institutions."

Gene told me how angry he was and "couldn't see straight" after hearing those words. He used this scenario in his sermon to emphasize that if one is addicted to credit he has little or no control over his own business: "Bankers don't respect you, why should they? They've got you trained like a seal act in a circus."

One of the main reasons that people become self-employed or entrepreneurs is that they want to become independent, to run their own ship. Going solo takes a lot of courage and initiative. Yet according to the senior bank executive above business owners don't really own their own businesses. They are controlled by lenders. Certainly, credit has a place in the world of business ownership. But over time business owners should strive to be less and less dependent on financial institutions for their existence.

We suggest, as research has shown and the millionaire business owners in our studies have suggested, that perseverance is the third necessary ingredient. Success in any meaningful endeavor, but particularly in creating a business, is more akin to a long-term journey than a leisurely night out. That long journey requires time, resources, and the ability to manage the inevitable pits of despair and highs of running a business and presenting one's ideas to the marketplace. In fact, for many, success only emerged after they were able to negotiate their way through a series of gauntlets of adversity.

A 2014 article in the *Wall Street Journal* outlined how adversity can be overcome to create a successful business.[19] The article profiled the trials and tribulations of Kevin Hartford. After his once-successful consulting business went belly up, Mr. Hartford began searching for a white-collar corporate job. During years of searching he never found one. He maintained that prospective employers were turned off because of his "stuttering problem." The article reported, "For several years he did odd jobs . . . delivering packages, gluing together medical supplies . . . sorting mail . . . and mowing lawns."

He and a partner took over a struggling small business that made metal parts. Today the business is thriving; sales in 2013 were $6 million. Mr. Hartford overcame adversity including an early business failure and a speech disability. And according to the article (it cites Labor Department data), workers with a disability are nearly twice as likely to be self-employed than those without disabilities. Many self-made millionaires who own businesses report that they selected self-employment because it allowed them to capitalize fully on the abilities and aptitudes that they possessed (that is, 83% of millionaires in *The Millionaire Mind*). Mr. Warren, a self-made decamillionaire profiled in *The Millionaire Mind*, eloquently stated, "Frankly, had I been able to get a decent job, I would have never gone into business for myself . . . I was forced into self-employment. I didn't opt for self-employment. If I had the credentials (to be an executive/employee) I would have accepted mediocrity."

Making Your Own Destiny

Consider this case study, first presented in *The Millionaire Mind*. Given his less than stellar academic background, W.K.'s job prospects were limited. Consequently, he realized that he would have to become his own employer. In that way, he would be evaluating his own job application.

Today he is quite successful as a self-employed mortgage broker. According to W.K., age 43, not one of his $1.7 million net worth clients ever asked him about his SAT scores or class. In other words, his reputation for his work was the reason he was sought out, rather than a score or grade or fact about his family. People who seek mortgages want mortgages. They are not interested in the fact that he was raised by a single mom who immigrated to America at age sixteen carrying a plastic bag. She worked 80 hours a week while raising 5 children. As he puts it, "She did a great job in raising her kids. The greatest lessons I have learned from her . . . hard work, live within your means, and treat people right. . . . With my SAT scores in the 800s [combined] I'm telling you that anyone can make it. My theory is most people don't get it. They live for the wrong reasons, the big house, the fanciest cars, and consume as much as possible. My number one goal is to be the best dad."

W.K. is yet another member of what my father called the "900 Club." As described in *The Millionaire Mind*:[20]

> Only those millionaires who scored below 1000 on their SATs are admitted. Life is a marathon. How well you do in this race involves much more than grade point averages. . . . Standardized testing cannot be substituted for actually running the race. [People like W.K.] never allowed academic "odds makers" to dictate their performance in life. They recognize that creativity, hard work, discipline and certain social skills including leadership were more significant than grades and aptitude test results. These are the people who confound their teachers and other fans of aptitude and intelligence testing.

So what if your resume, academic credentials, or what's on your job application are not outstanding? Be determined to move to the other side of the negotiating table. Change roles. Become the actor in the human resource drama that evaluates the applicant's credentials.

Still Required: Sacrifice and Hard Work

Research from Tufts and Stanford's Young Entrepreneurs Study found four common traits in founders: innovative thinking, drive and control, business focus, and having business-focused mentors in their lives.[21] The study's authors stress that entrepreneurs "are made, not born" and that parents, mentors, and teachers can support these traits, but that as a country we are often missing the opportunity to

Entrepreneurial Lessons from the Rolling Stones

Coming of age in the 1960s, my father was a huge fan of the rock that came out of that era, whether it was Led Zeppelin, the Rolling Stones, or Derek and the Dominos. While he loved the music, it was often the stories behind the artists that he found even more compelling. He especially loved the Rolling Stones and often commented on the history of Mick Jagger and Keith Richards as they navigated becoming essentially small business owners, which my father described in 2011:

Are you contemplating a career as a small business owner? If so, you may wish to read Keith Richards's book, *Life*.[22] I believe that the Rolling Stones band is the single most productive small business in the free world! Often public corporations brag about their average revenue per employee—in the hundreds of thousands of dollars. For the four full-time employees of the Rolling Stones, it is in the hundreds of millions.

Let's cut away the "bad boy" personas including bad hair, bad behavior, bad outfits . . . These personas sell records and concert tickets. Yet there is an explanation for how this group has produced major hit after major hit and generated billions of dollars in revenue—an explanation that goes beyond having extraordinary creative intellect and talent.

Consider this: After completing their first grueling 1,000 gig tour, Mick Jagger and Keith Richards made one of the best business decisions of their short careers. They hired a manager, Andrew Oldham, for the Rolling Stones. Mr. Oldham informed them that musicians, no matter how talented, are a dime a dozen, and unless they begin to write their own songs they will soon be out of business. He even locked them in a kitchen and told them not to come out without a song! Jagger and Richards became cultivators of wealth by composing their own songs starting in their early twenties. These new songs acted as the base generator for all other revenues including the tours by the Rolling Stones. The royalties earned from these songs are a perpetual source of income for the composers and eventually their heirs.

Of course, not everyone has the creative talent of the Rolling Stones. But most people have the ability to start building their own "royalties" for the future. Consider some of the cases I have written about in the past, like J.T., the Texas forest farmer. He started with "just a few acres" and then kept adding to this inventory. Today he plants 3.5 million trees a year and is worth over $30 million. Take Brian, who was profiled on thomasjstanley.com. He failed his high school equivalency exam several times. As he said, "If I can become a multimillionaire anybody can . . . sold all my toys . . . and bought my first 4-plex." Today he owns seven of them. And finally, there's the moonlighting firefighter Malcolm, who realized early in his career that fighting fires is something that cannot be inventoried. He started with one fixer-upper house and rented it to students. And the constant student demand for housing is nearly a guaranteed source of wealth from his real estate holdings.

Two quotes from Keith Richards's *Life* illustrate the amount of work that it takes to become successful, the amount of work that not everyone is willing to do:

"Every waking hour of every day . . . you collapsed on the floor with a guitar in your hand. That was it. You never stop learning an instrument."[23]

"The work was always intensely hard. The gig never finished just because you got off stage. We had to go back to the hotel and start honing down these songs. It was nonstop high-pressure work. Which was probably good for us."[24]

It is obvious to me after reading his memoir that Keith Richards also has high analytic intellect. Mr. Richards spent thousands of hours studying all the great blues artists and rock virtuosos and integrated this knowledge into his musical compositions. He even kept a diary of audience response to each new musical riff introduced by the Stones for future adjustments. In other words, he was collecting and analyzing market research information. His passion was to elicit the same deep emotional response that he felt from the Stones' music from his audiences.

Like the Rolling Stones, almost all self-employed people are tested. Multiple early setbacks and seemingly lack of market response must be overcome. Richards especially had tremendous tenacity, focus, passion, physical stamina, and toughness. He writes, "For three years we played . . . every day . . . well over 1,000 gigs . . . barely a break . . . ten days off in that whole period."

In one-half of the 1,000 gigs in which the Stones performed prior to coming to the U.S., they netted nothing. How would you feel if "only 2 people turned up [in the audience]"? But they continued their musical mission despite their precarious financial situation, inhuman living conditions, and predatory advisors and managers. Richards explains why: ". . . my idea has never been to make money. Originally it was do we make enough to pay for guitar strings? . . . later do we make enough to put on the kind of show we want to? Initially . . . the money was . . . most of it plowed back into what we want to do."

No doubt Mr. Richards helped sell millions of guitars to kids who thought they could easily match his success. But they quickly found out that it is much easier to buy a guitar and play the part by visual cues than it is to practice for thousands and thousands of hours while working for nothing.

do so. Every time we as parents complete the long-term project, fulfill orders for cookie or popcorn sales, or bring forgotten items to school, we're demonstrating that our children have security, yes, but that also something or someone will be there to catch them when they fall to prevent failure. This denies them the chance for learning self-reliance and perseverance in the face of adversity.

Determination for Careers

As in the case of managing our financial lives, the way in which we approach work is influenced by our early experiences. Millionaires often share that having supportive caregivers or mentors made the difference in the way in which they became successful in their careers or built their businesses. And early experiences, particularly challenging ones or failures, can sharpen the way in which we approach the next opportunity and the next.

And what if you find yourself trapped today? What does it take to begin again, to be able to leave a job for another, or to create one's own business? How have many made the transition from one career to the next, or from employment to self-employment?

In the same way we approach managing our personal finances, building work-related resources in the forms of experience and reputation are critical. Continuing to seek out opportunities regardless of employment status, including moonlighting, builds knowledge and experience capital that can then be used to make a move or create your own opportunities. But perhaps more important is ensuring continued financial margin to make career changes when needed or wanted.

In the past 20-plus years, the world of work has changed, more so than my father suspected when we began work on this book several years ago. True, the concept of lifetime employment and pensions to take care of us in retirement had long disappeared. And the types of industries in which millionaires find themselves is expanding. Continuing to view employers as a guarantee of safety and security is naïve and can dampen your ability to build wealth on your own.

The traditional notions of work are slowly disappearing, and the millionaires next door of tomorrow are embracing new concepts of generating revenue, both in terms of how they approach employment and how they generate experience and knowledge to make the next move.

Chapter 7

Investing Resources

Risk comes from not knowing what you are doing.

—Warren Buffett

ECONOMIC SUCCESS IS DEPENDENT UPON EFFECTIVELY MANAGING RESOURCES. Those who can transform their income into wealth allocate their time, energy, and money in ways that are conducive to long-term financial success. This finding hasn't changed in 20 years, and we suspect it won't change anytime soon.

Economically successful Americans *do not do this* by following the crowd, and by this we mean the crowds that shop on Black Friday in person, the crowds that spend any and all free time ingesting and fuming over politics, or the crowds that spend more than two hours a day on social media. As we've seen throughout the years, and continuing today, most millionaire-next-door types are contrarians. They think and act differently than others when it comes to how they make purchases, how or whether they allow others to influence their spending and living habits, and indeed, how they invest. They are savers and investors in a population of hyper-consumers. They study their investments, including their own businesses and industries, and make educated and wise decisions about how to use the resources they have to invest and grow.

The success factors listed in Chapter 5 not only impact our ability to determine ways to generate revenue, create jobs, and find careers, but also impact the way in which we manage the income we make. Generating revenue through a career we are passionate about, as we saw in Chapter 6, provides resources. Beyond the consumption areas in Chapter 4, how do economically successful individuals grow and utilize the wealth they bring in and accumulate over time? What, in the past 20 years, has impacted how they invest?

At the time of writing, there were more than 1,000 financial technology companies that provided services for both financial professionals and individuals.[1] Many of these companies offer consumers ways to manage their financial lives efficiently, with little to no help from a financial advisor or wealth manager (or, in the parlance of *The Millionaire Next Door*, stockbrokers). For better or worse, we can save, buy options, and invest in exotic foreign stocks all from the comfort of our smartphones. We don't have to call our broker to make trades (although some still do, as there are approximately 631,000 stockbrokers in the United States).[2] More sophisticated actions—such as "tax-loss harvesting"—are also being automated thanks to robo-advisors, algorithms, and similar technologies.

But in the face of these advances in technology and a tide of changes in how advice is provided (e.g., the rise of the fiduciary standard), the hallmarks of prudent investors haven't changed much in 20 years. Attitudes toward investing shift with the times[3], but those with a disciplined approach to investing tend to remain steadfast in the face of economic adversity and fluctuations in the market. Whether that prudent behavior comes naturally or is something that investors learn from caregivers, mentors, or advisors, the investing decisions we make can impact our ability to build wealth long term.

Where It's Invested

Perhaps because of their reliance on self-study and on close examination of markets and investment opportunities, millionaires typically invest in more conventional types of investments (see Table 7-1). More than 60% of millionaires have 30% or more invested in retirement accounts. Nearly 33% of millionaires have some investment in real estate. Millionaires in our latest study rarely invested in exotic or unusual investment products. Approximately 6% of millionaires have any portion of their assets held in land use rights, for example, and very few millionaires (4%) have intangibles (e.g., copyrights or other intellectual property) as a portion of their portfolio.

Table 7-1. Percentage of Assets Held by Millionaires

Asset Type	Asset Allocation Percentage							
	0%	1%	5%	10%	20%	30%	50%	75% or more
	Percentage of Millionaires							
Retirement Accounts	2.0	3.2	7.1	12.1	13.5	23.4	28.2	10.5
Cash	3.5	19.6	35.7	25.2	9.8	4.5	1.2	0.7
Cash in Value - Life Insurance	49.6	22.8	13.0	6.9	4.9	1.0	0.8	0.8
Closely Held Private Business or Partnership	58.8	5.6	6.9	8.1	5.4	5.4	4.6	5.1
Securities	16.7	7.5	12.5	15.2	15.9	15.9	9.4	7.0
Stock Options	80.6	5.4	5.7	3.2	2.7	1.8	0.2	0.4
Real Estate (Personal; Equity Only)	3.6	2.4	8.2	19.8	27.3	21.3	15.0	2.4
Real Estate (Commercial/Investment)	67.7	2.7	7.1	7.3	6.0	3.9	4.3	1.1
Motor Vehicles	13.1	54.0	26.8	4.0	1.9	0.3	0.0	0.0
Tangibles/Collectables	37.9	39.5	16.8	4.4	1.0	2.0	0.0	0.2
Land Use Rights	94.4	3.7	0.9	0.7	0.2	0.0	0.0	0.2
Intangible Assets	96.2	2.7	1.0	0.0	0.0	0.0	0.0	0.0

Table 7-2. IRS Estate Tax Data Comparing 2016 and 1996 Estate Tax Returns

Asset Type	Size of Gross Estate (Return Filed in 2016)				Size of Gross Estate (Return Filed in 1996)			
	>$5 million	$5-$10 million	$10-$20 million	>$20 million	>$5 million	$5-$10 million	$10-$20 million	>$20 million
	% of Gross Estate Value*							
Personal Residence	8.70	7.93	6.43	2.77	8.68	4.66	3.58	1.16
Other Real Estate	11.67	14.84	14.24	12.43	13.34	12.49	11.44	6.42
Closely Held Stock	2.87	4.61	7.33	19.25	3.03	8.70	11.99	20.27
Publicly Traded Stock	24.16	22.85	25.81	24.43	21.87	28.96	30.94	35.12
State & Local Bonds	10.39	7.89	9.35	6.47	12.04	14.98	16.01	10.29
Federal Bonds	0.91	0.77	0.75	1.17	0.89	3.76	3.26	5.91
Corporate & Foreign Bonds	1.60	1.48	1.52	1.31	0.72	0.68	0.56	0.42
Bond Funds	0.94	0.48	0.52	0.37	4.03	0.30	0.15	0.08
Unclassified Mutual Funds	1.34	0.90	0.66	0.39	4.03	1.05	0.64	0.29
Cash Assets	11.81	9.60	9.43	6.06	13.66	6.84	6.38	4.72
Net Life Insurance	1.30	2.61	1.61	0.51	0.09	0.10	0.07	0.02
Farm Assets	3.72	5.79	3.95	1.63	0.49	0.28	0.18	0.23
Private Equity/Hedge Funds	0.37	0.32	0.69	3.70	n/a	n/a	n/a	n/a
Retirement Assets	9.62	11.59	7.58	2.14	n/a	n/a	n/a	n/a
Intangibles	0.49	0.47	0.40	0.12	0.31	0.56	0.55	0.46
Art	0.37	0.28	0.52	1.83	0.11	0.36	0.47	2.56

*Does not total 100% because certain asset classes excluded from table.
n/a = not separately disclosed in the 1996 data.

Here are some points of interest in this data that compare the composition of gross estates of various sizes in 2016 versus 1996:

- It appears that at a gross estate of $20 million or greater, both hedge funds and fine art become much more attractive as investments. In 2016, hedge fund composition jumps to 3.7% at $20 million, as compared to only 0.69% for estates between $10 and $20 million (and even less than that for smaller estates). (Hedge fund/private equity data is not available for 1996.) Similarly, art as an asset class comprises 1.83% and 2.56% of total gross estate value for estates north of $20 million in 2016 and 1996, respectively, and is almost nonexistent in the smaller estates. These data points seem to support the notion that at a certain point of extremely high net worth (i.e., $20 million or above), more exotic and complex investments become unavoidably attractive.

- In both the 2016 and 1996 data sets the "closely held stock" composition of the estate jumps dramatically at an estate size of $20 million or more. Family-run businesses would fall into this category.

Indeed, it's the exotic investments, hedge funds, and private equity that are at the bottom of the list, so to speak. One of the myths of the wealthy, a myth perpetuated by the media and lack of awareness, is that those with any wealth have exotic investments. Based on the IRS estate tax data highlighted above, it appears that this exotic-investment phenomenon sets in at around a net worth of $20 million or more . . . that is, after you have made your fortune and can afford to pay more in fees for less return. Most individuals who are the millionaire-next-door types do not put money into these types of exotic investments.

In his 2016 letter to Berkshire Hathaway shareholders, Warren Buffett explained this behavioral phenomenon to perfection:[4]

Over the years, I've often been asked for investment advice, and in the process of answering I've learned a good deal about human behavior. My regular recommendation has been a low-cost S&P 500 index fund. To their credit, my friends who possess only modest means have usually followed my suggestion.

I believe, however, that none of the mega-rich individuals, institutions or pension funds has followed that same advice when I've given it to them. Instead, these investors politely thank me for my thoughts and depart to listen to the siren song of a high-fee manager or, in the case of many institutions, to seek out another breed of hyper-helper called a consultant.

That professional, however, faces a problem. Can you imagine an investment consultant telling clients, year after year, to keep adding to an index fund replicating the S&P 500? That would be career suicide. Large fees flow to these hyper-helpers, however, if they recommend small managerial shifts every year or so. That advice is delivered in esoteric gibberish that explains why fashionable investment "styles" or current economic trends make the shift appropriate.

The wealthy are accustomed to feeling that it is their lot in life to get the best food, schooling, entertainment, housing, plastic surgery, sports ticket, you name it. Their money, they feel, should buy them something superior compared to what the masses receive.

In many aspects of life, indeed, wealth does command top-grade products or services. For that reason, the financial "elites"—wealthy individuals, pension funds, college endowments and the like—have great trouble meekly signing up for a financial product or service that is available as well to people investing only a few thousand dollars. This reluctance of the rich normally prevails even though the product at issue is—on an expectancy basis—clearly the best choice. My calculation, admittedly very rough, is that the search by the elite for superior investment advice has caused it, in aggregate, to waste more than $100 billion over the past decade. . . .

Human behavior won't change. Wealthy individuals, pension funds, endowments and the like will continue to feel they deserve something "extra" in investment advice. Those advisors who cleverly play to this expectation will get very rich. This year the magic potion may be hedge funds, next year something else. The likely result from this parade of promises is predicted in an adage: "When a person with money meets a person with experience, the one with experience ends up with the money and the one with money leaves with experience."

Compare this exotic-investment mindset that Buffett describes to the approach employed by the famed Fidelity stock-picker, Peter Lynch. Mr. Lynch's axioms about companies whose stocks he bought are congruent with the philosophies held by many of the millionaire business owners we've studied over the years. Much of Mr. Lynch's success in selecting stocks was predicated on the enormous number of personal interviews he conducted with key players and the visits he made to corporate headquarters. Some of his most colorful conclusions or "Lynchisms" included:[5]

> *One way to judge a company's commitment to frugality is by visiting the headquarters. The extravagance of any corporate office is directly proportional to management's reluctance to reward the shareholders.*

> *If you could tell the future [performance of a stock] from a balance sheet then mathematicians and accountants would be the richest people in the world.*

> *The amateur investor . . . can beat the market by ignoring the herd.*

> *All else being equal, invest in the company with the fewest color photographs in the annual report.*

Especially noteworthy are some of Mr. Lynch's observations about several companies that he correctly predicted would become winners:

> *At corporate headquarters . . . no executive dining room . . . no limos in the parking lot . . . no corporate jet at the airport.*

> *Avoid[s] spending money on a Greek temple for the main office, Queen Anne furniture for the lobby, blimps, billboards, celebrity sponsors, and original artwork for the walls. Travel posters . . . suffice.*

> *Executives get no bonuses unless the company does well in a particular year. Success and not [occupational] status is the basis for rewards.*

This last Lynchism is in close harmony with Factor 3 from *The Millionaire Next Door* that underlies the lifestyle of millionaires next door: They believe that financial independence is more important than displaying high social status.

But more often than not, the income-statement affluent equate "exotic" or "expensive" with "better"—maybe consciously or subconsciously because putting money into these types of investments implies a certain status. The income-statement affluent types may presume that they need these exotic and expensive investments because they are consistent with their income levels, their other status purchases (expensive houses and cars), and their economic status. But the hard data shows that most of them would fare better by implementing a simple and solid investment plan that was diversified, covered the market, and kept costs low. But that may be too much like buying a Toyota instead of a Lexus.

A recent prominent example of the exotic-investment philosophy trap is the performance of university endowment funds. The missteps of the Harvard University endowment—the largest of its kind—have been well publicized. In fiscal 2016 the endowment fund returned a loss of 2% during a period when the S&P 500 index was flat (no gain or loss). And while Harvard may be the most famous endowment falling victim to what Ben Carlson at "A Wealth of Common Sense" blog has dubbed an "ego premium," it is certainly not alone. In 2017 Mr. Carlson wrote a piece that compared the annualized returns of a simple three-fund portfolio of Vanguard funds (that he calls the "Bogle Model") to the average annualized returns of the nation's college endowment funds. The 10-year returns of the Bogle Model portfolio (6.0%) ranked in the top 10% of the endowment returns (an annual return of 5.4% scored in the top decile). So to translate this data: If you sat at your computer and invested your portfolio in three of the most widely held Vanguard funds (or ETFs)—with a blended cost of somewhere around .10% per year—you would have fared better than 90% or more of the college endowment funds out there. And understand how these endowment funds operate—as Mr. Carlson wrote, "These funds are invested in venture capital, private equity, infrastructure, private real estate, timber, the best hedge funds money can buy; they have access to the best stock and bond fund managers; they use leverage; they invest in complicated derivatives; they use the biggest and most connected consultants, and the vast majority of these funds still fail to beat a low-cost Vanguard index fund portfolio."[6]

In sum, these status-seeking, exotic-investment income-statement affluent types end up paying more . . . for less. But why? These are smart people. And yet they are willing to pay an "ego premium" even in the face of evidence that these investments often deliver less in value than a cheaper alternative. The psychoanalytical part of our team wonders whether it's possible that there is some complex (potentially subconscious) signaling taking place here, with the income-statement affluent types sending a message: "I have enough to burn."

Most Millionaires Own No Works of Art

Many people in this country are ambitious, and they want to emulate those who are economically successful. Marketers spend billions of dollars trying to convince people that most successful and rich people own a large portfolio of so-called upscale artifacts. This is as much a myth today as it has been throughout the history of our economy. High-income-producing households may view art as a way to signal to others they are rich; however, only their income levels are above average. Their net worth typically tells a different story.

Art comes under the broad heading of tangibles or collectibles. My father once wrote an article about this for *American Demographics*. In it he said, "Surprisingly under 6% of the typical millionaire's assets are held in such tangible or collectible forms such as antiques, coin and stamp collections, precious gems or *works of art*."[7]

But he wrote this article more than 30 years ago. Have things changed since then? Not in our most recent survey, where most millionaires (nearly 78%) have 1% or less of their wealth in tangible collectibles. And not much has changed according to the recent IRS estate tax data.[8] Overall, among those millionaires with wealth of $2 million or more, only 1.3% of their wealth is held in tangible works of art. Even this small percentage may be overstated given that some very pricey art may likely be bogus.

Art is just one more asset category to which a large number of millionaires we surveyed have said, "Don't own. Never owned." The same is true for a variety of other assets discussed in detail in *Stop Acting Rich*. Only a minority of millionaires has ever owned a vacation home, boat, plane, wine collection, prestigious make of motor vehicle, or expensive suit.

Characteristics of Successful Investors

Consider the following description of individual investors:

> *The investors who inhabit the real world and those who populate academic models are distant cousins. In theory, investors hold well diversified portfolios and trade infrequently so as to minimize taxes and other investment costs. In practice, investors behave differently. They trade frequently and have perverse stock selection ability, incurring unnecessary investment costs and return losses. They tend to sell their winners and hold their losers, generating*

unnecessary tax liabilities. Many hold poorly diversified portfolios, result-ing in unnecessarily high levels of diversifiable risk, and many are unduly influenced by media and past experience. Individual investors who ignore the prescriptive advice to buy and hold low-fee, well-diversified portfolios, generally do so to their detriment.[9]

Action bias, or the propensity to take action as opposed to taking no action, can lead investors of any level of experience to take action when no action is required. These extreme investing "doers" end up buying and selling at the wrong time because they have a propensity toward taking action. The other side, of course, includes those who are averse to taking any action, taking their time instead to create investment strategies that may be obsolete before they are even ever implemented.

What makes a *successful* investor? One who is able to invest when the mar-ket is down and be comfortable with investments that have higher associated risks with them? Like the behaviors that distinguish high-potential household CFOs from those who are less able to build wealth, there are a few characteris-tics and behaviors that separate successful investors from others regardless of the economic times or governmental factors. We know that courage and a willing-ness to take risks are highly related to net worth.[10] Millionaires throughout the past decades have shared that courage allowed them to weather storms not only in their own careers or businesses, but also in their investments. The *courage* to invest takes some level of confidence to make an investment-related decision as well as the personality to want to engage in investing in the first place. And, we also know that financial knowledge and risk-tolerance are related.[11] Knowl-edge, in particular, can be gained through self-study and research, and as has been the case over time, prodigious accumulators of wealth tend to spend more time researching and planning their investments than their under accumulating counterparts. The data also tell us that those who are anxious and worried tend to engage in more short-term, potentially detrimental investing behaviors.[12]

In our research in creating an experience- and behavioral-based psycho-logical test of risk tolerance, we found five distinguishing components of "good investing"—*good* being defined as being generally comfortable with investing in the stock market and buying (versus selling) in a down market.[13]

Personality for Risk

Successful investors tend to be able to make investment decisions even when the exact outcome is not yet known. They tend to be comfortable making investments even without perfect certainty of what the future holds.

High-Risk Preference

Those who prefer investments with greater risk (e.g., stocks) that have a greater opportunity for return and tend to make better investment-related decisions.

Confidence in Investing

While overconfidence can trick investors into making ill-advised decisions, some level of self-confidence and self-efficacy differentiates successful from unsuccessful investors. Without an effective dose of confidence, investing-related decisions may be second-guessed and ultimately changed, often with disadvantageous financial effects.

Judgment/Knowledge Regarding Investments and Investing

As quoted by Warren Buffett, "Risk comes from not knowing what you are doing." Those who build knowledge in how investing works, the potential up and downsides of investments, and the cyclical nature of the stock market are more likely to make better investment decisions overall. We know that prodigious accumulators of wealth spend time researching investments more so than their underaccumulating counterparts, and that investing knowledge relates to better investing decisions.[14]

Composure

Composure typically refers to the ability to withstand changes (typically, downturns but also boom times) in the market. Those investors who can remain calm and courageous in the face of a market crash tend to make better decisions than their anxious counterparts.

Characteristics of Millionaire Investors

The successful investor profile above pertains to a broad sample of investors, including those in the mass affluent. And as in the case of building wealth in general, it is a combination of these characteristics and behaviors that can impact our ability to obtain success in investing. What, then, are the characteristics of *millionaire* investors? Are they similar to what we've found with broader samples of Americans? Millionaire investors tend to be a confident group. In our latest study, just over 70% of them believe that they know more about investing than others. We know that confidence in investing can be a double-edged sword, as *overconfidence* in investing can have detrimental effects on investment-related decision-making (e.g., a belief that you can time the market).[15]

In some ways, though, the investment-related decisions, and decisions about how to use resources in general, come back to the success factor of *discipline*. Nearly 60% of millionaires (or three out of five) have clear short- and long-term goals, and nearly 55% rarely get distracted when working on a project. Just over 60% say that they spend time planning for their future financial situation.

When it comes to how they invest, nearly 55% of millionaires believe that investing success is due more to their own efforts in studying and becoming educated than advice they receive from professionals. Similarly, just under one-third of millionaires reports relying on a financial professional to make investment-related decisions. We see, too, in research conducted with mass affluent investors, that those who have the best investing-related behaviors also tend to be more likely to fire an advisor or other professional they deem to be less than valuable.[16] The take-away for financial professionals targeting millionaire investors is that they should be the best of the best and clearly convey that reality to their target audience.

Millionaire investors spend time building knowledge and expertise in managing investments. They spend on average 10.5 hours per month studying and planning for future investments, and we see differences in prodigious accumulators of wealth versus under accumulators of wealth in those hours: specifically, 11.3 hours per month for prodigious accumulators compared to 8.7 hours per month for under accumulators. They spend time researching investments and where to place their money, even if that means investing their money in their own businesses. We know that their literacy in financial matters means that they are more tolerant of taking investment-related risks.[17] Future outlook and financial knowledge typically relate to taking greater financial risk[18], so the time they spend in managing and researching investments helps in decision-making.

Table 7-3. Investing Statements by Millionaires' Agreement

Statement	Percentage Strongly Agree/Agree
I know more about investing than most people.	70.4
I spend a lot of time planning my financial future.	61.8
The appreciation of my investments is more a function of self-study than professional advice.	54.8
To make investment decisions, I rely heavily on an investment advisor.	33.2

Investors who have a bias toward taking action, any action, in the face of new, seemingly relevant information, tend to perform worse over the long haul. Millionaire investors do take *some action* in managing their investments. On average, in 2016, millionaires made 17 investment-related transactions throughout the year. About one in five millionaires holds his investments for less than three years. The importance here is in whether the decision to take action was prudent and well-thought-out, or if it was rash (and the result of action bias). Appropriate financial decision-making is a complex mix of knowledge (including financial literacy), future orientation, and remaining calm in the maelstrom of environmental factors. We tend to make better decisions about our finances when we have both a long-term and future-oriented outlook, when we have the knowledge required to make appropriate financial decisions, and when we're calm. These factors have been found both in the laboratory and in the field.[19]

Table 7-4. Average Holding Periods for Investments

Typical Period for Holding Stocks/Stock Mutual Funds	Percentage of Investors		
	Millionaires	Wealth Accumulation Groups	
		PAWs	UAWs
Days–Months	6.3	6.0	9.4
1–2 years	16.3	17.9	16.1
3–5 years	30.7	30.6	30.2
6–10 years	18.6	19.4	11.4
More than 10 years	28.2	26.1	32.9

Risks Required

What other characteristic defines millionaire investors? They are willing to take risks and are future oriented. Consider the opposite: As one millionaire next door from Florida told us, "My spouse has a fear of investing. . . . only wants a low-interest savings account. My mutual fund investing has been criticized as 'reckless' for two decades now—yet it accounts for a huge portion of our wealth." Many millionaires are entrepreneurs, and entrepreneurs tend to be less risk averse.[20] Civil servants are less risky than those in the private sector. Risk avoiders have lower satisfaction, too.[21]

Regardless of mistakes made, or perceived to have been made, successful investors, and economically successful Americans, take risks in investing. Generally, high-net-worth, affluent households report engaging in different types of investing-related behaviors from their mass affluent or mass market counterparts. Affluent households report taking above-average risks in investing, understanding the nature of investing in general, and understanding the appropriate level of risk to engage in within their portfolio more frequently than do their non-affluent counterparts.[22] While this isn't necessarily causal, it does highlight the importance and perhaps the necessity of a greater level of knowledge and risk-taking that is required of affluent households. Millionaires in our current study reported taking more investment risks earlier in their careers than they currently do today, perhaps mirroring the age of our sample where the average age is 61.

Table 7-5. Investing Strategy of Millionaires by Percentage

How would you rate . . .	Risky/Very Risky	Balanced	Conservative/ Very Conservative
Your investment strategy when you began working full-time?	55.6	28.6	15.7
Your current investment strategy/portfolio?	17.5	56.0	26.5

Every dollar that you save loses some of its purchasing power every year because of inflation. Prodigious accumulators of wealth understand that money must be productively invested to avoid this loss of purchasing power from inflation and to *grow* the money to meet future needs and wants. The data here indicates that prodigious accumulators of wealth most typically take a "risky" or "very risky" approach to investing early in their careers, and then balance out that approach to a more moderate and conservative investing style as they accumulate more assets and their time horizon for needing the money shortens. One of our readers shares a story that is a tale of two savers and how they invested:

> My parents played great defense and faithfully managed and saved their hard-earned salaries over the years. But their hard-earned savings went into a coffee can each month and year (literally or figuratively). My wife's father, on the other hand, did not save quite as much each year, but he was a more savvy (or maybe lucky) investor and plowed all these saved dollars into the Fidelity Magellan Fund each year. My father-in-law came out much farther ahead than my parents who didn't achieve nearly the investment returns that he did.

Prodigious accumulators of wealth regularly help themselves on both of these fronts: They are committed to saving chunks of their earnings and successful at investing those savings in productive assets that allow for long-term growth. Imagine the power of increased annual savings of 143% (our calculated "behavior savings alpha") then compounding with an additional 3% of investing alpha for portfolio returns each year (whether through reduced investing costs, so-called Advisor's Alpha, improved investing behaviors [buy low, sell high . . . not the other way around], or all of the above). Prodigious accumulators of wealth find a way to employ most (or all) of these advantages to their long-term benefit.

Investing Mistakes: Learning on the Job

In the prediction of net worth and making sound investment decisions (e.g., buying low and selling high), confidence plays an important role, but it is often confidence with a touch of humility and realism about one's abilities and skills as they relate to investing and managing finances in general. As Warren Buffett once said, "Investors should remember that excitement and expenses are their enemies. And if they insist on trying to time their participation in equities, they should try to be fearful when others are greedy and greedy only when others are fearful." A consistent pattern of behaviors and life experiences that demonstrates a moderate level of confidence about one's ability and skills related to investing is related to net worth, regardless of one's age, income, and percentage of inherited wealth.[23]

In the investing arena, overconfidence can be detrimental. Investing over-confidence has been shown to be related to unsuccessful decisions regarding one's investments, including frequent trading, overestimates in a security's value, and poor selection of mutual funds. In fact, in one large-scale study regarding investor overconfidence, the researchers concluded, "We believe that there is a simple and powerful explanation for the high levels of counterproductive trading in financial markets: overconfidence."[24]

Since 1996, one of the trends in investing psychology is the emphasis in academia and elsewhere, including the halls of the major brokerages, on *behavioral finance*, a term describing the underlying psychological and cognitive biases that can impact the way in which individual investors make decisions about buying and selling securities, among other things. Richard Thaler, who won the 2017 Nobel Prize for his work in behavioral economics, demonstrated empirically what savvy investors knew—that biases in investing, and relying on emotions, can negatively impact one's ability to make sound financially related decisions. The practical application of behavioral finance is that if investors are aware of these biases, or if their advisor is aware, then they can prevent the individual from making disadvantageous investment-related decisions based on irrational beliefs or biases about the market.

Successful investors become more risk tolerant and have better attitudes toward financial risks because they have experiences—good and bad—with investing.[25] And, they undoubtedly have made some mistakes along the way. Typically what makes a *better* investor is dedication to learning over time.

The typical mistakes of millionaire investors, reported by more than one-half of our millionaire sample, included *market timing* mistakes, specifically selling too late or too early, or waiting on highs and lows of the market to sell or buy. Those mistakes, of course, are easy to see in hindsight. Millionaires have shared that some of their most fantastic mistakes in investing led to their current perspective and behaviors on how to make money grow. Overconfidence was often the culprit.

Other types of investing mistakes included trying to balance a portfolio between more reliable or safe investments with investments that are more exotic or speculative. Improving on these behaviors takes either self-study and discipline or the advice and counsel of advisors who are dedicated to their client's best interests (rather than their own).

Table 7-6. Reported Investing Behaviors of Millionaires[26]

Investing Behaviors	Percentage Reporting Behavior
Selling a bad stock too late	73.6
Selling a great stock too early	60.3
Waiting too long to sell stocks at a market high	58.1
Waiting too long to invest at a market low	55.3
Trying to balance a "safe" portfolio with a "speculative" portfolio	53.5
Purchasing/holding employer's stock	44.4
Worrying more about losses than gains	41.6
Investing based on a recommendation from a friend or relative	41.5
Trying to time the ups/downs of the market	37.5
Investing in stock options/highly speculative stocks	36.9
Allowing someone else to manage my finances	34.8
Selling a stock based on recent lows	34.2

Mistakes with specific investment types or in certain companies is typically in the eye of the beholder. There isn't a secret stock or set of investments that millionaires listed as the "best" or "worst." As we've been asked multiple times over the years for a "best" and "worst" list of stocks as rated or ranked by millionaire investors, we decided to ask this question in our latest survey. As most wise investors and millionaires have shared with us, indeed those best and worst stocks are in the eye of the stockholder. A discussion of individual stocks, while perhaps headline-worthy, is not worthwhile, with the exception of some themes garnered from the lists:

- Hot Internet stocks were often listed as the worst stock ever invested in.

- Headline-worthy stocks that collapsed were also listed as the worst stock ever invested in (e.g., WorldCom, Enron).

- Solid blue-chip stocks were often cited as the best (e.g., 3M, IBM).

- Employer-related stocks were a mixed bag.

- Some of the "best" investments included (some tongue-in-cheek): "My wife," "My business," and "My education."

Paying for "Advice"

Millionaires select their advisors (and technologies) wisely. While many rely on their own skills, a significant portion of millionaires continue to work with financial advisors. In 1996, there were 246,000 investment managers and stockbrokers in the United States.[27] In 2014, that number was 341,500.[28] More than 70% of millionaires in our sample reported having accounts with full-service investment companies, and just 15% reported having accounts with a trust department. But they pay little, relatively, for the service they're receiving: one-third of millionaires allocated 0% of their income to investment advice–related fees: 56% of millionaires allocated 1%.

But regardless of how many millionaires use financial institutions or advisors in some capacity, the majority does not rely on their advice. As we mentioned before, less than one-third of millionaire investors *rely* heavily on an investment advisor, and 70% say they know more about investing than most advisors. More than half of millionaires reported saying that appreciation in their investment portfolios is due more to self-study than to professional advice. This sentiment is consistent with research demonstrating that even experts don't often outperform "nonexperts" when it comes to portfolio creation and returns.[29]

At the very least, financial professionals working with millionaires should be focused on preventing the top investment-related mistakes. The Vanguard "Advisor's Alpha" studies, demonstrating the value of working with a financial professional, attribute half of the gains of working with an advisor (that is, half of the 3% increase in portfolio performance from working with an advisor) to altering or improving investor-related *behaviors*.[30]

Financial Advisory Services and Fiduciaries

Mr. Jack, a full-service, commission-based wealth manager, told me recently that he is becoming frustrated with his job. He increasingly hears that the world as he knows it, which includes commission-based selling of financial services to affluent populations, is moving toward video rental store status with the proliferation of do-it-yourself investment technology and a new emphasis on fiduciary advisors that are precluded from accepting commissions for the investment products they recommend to their clients. He's searching for ways to make money, through whatever means possible, in a new world of "robo-advisors" and reduced fees for his "investment expertise." So, he figures he will reduce his "minimums" to include emerging millionaire-next-door types, hoping they will stick with him as they build wealth over time.

Mr. Jack wants a map that will take him directly to these individuals. In this conversation, he has asked me, specifically, how I can help him find them. Surely, he thinks, because of my father's research and now mine, I can give him such a map. Yes, that map is available. Examining the behavioral patterns and financial experiences of prospective clients will help him understand if he's dealing with a potential millionaire next door.

What Mr. Jack fails to understand, though, is that even if he can find them, emerging millionaires will most likely not be interested in what he's selling. Technology has allowed them to become savvy consumers of financial services and typically demand high quality at low cost, whether they are a DIY type or looking for professional assistance. And those who desire to work with a financial professional now have a myriad of options, including a new generation of fee-only financial planners who operate under a fiduciary oath that previously had only been found in trust departments. In this environment Mr. Jack will have to put on quite a show to demonstrate his value to individuals who are self-made, emerging millionaires next door.

The trouble for Mr. Jack's business is it does not include the key value of working directly with a financial professional: guidance on behaviors related to all things financial. Mr. Jack is uninterested in any type of deep commitment to help his clients become more confident in their financial- or investment-related decisions.

But the real value to be provided by financial advisors today is in helping their clients evolve from under accumulator to prodigious accumulator status. That comes from changing financial behaviors more so than altering portfolio compositions.

So, unfortunately for Mr. Jack, whether he knows it or not, what he's really looking for is a client who *believes* he's the millionaire next door, but behaves as most pseudo-affluent do by overpaying for nearly every consumer good, equating income with wealth, and spending *in anticipation* of being rich. The clients that would fit him best are not interested in hearing anything related to behavioral change or employing any self-reflection. They want Mr. Jack to beat the market.

These are Mr. Jack's ideal clients, and they will gladly pay Mr. Jack additional fees on investment-related transactions for the privilege of working with him.

The Millionaire Next Door Finds You

Let's contrast Mr. Jack's approach to searching for prospective millionaires next door with that of Ms. Jenkins, a fee-only financial advisor who operates under a fiduciary standard. Her advice and counsel must be in her client's best interest and cannot be conflicted as a result of a potential commission for a particular product. At the end of the day, while Mr. Jack is selling products, Ms. Jenkins is demonstrating to her target market that she is focused on working with individuals to increase their chances of being successful long term. Instead of *selling* to the millionaire next door, success for her is measured by being a trusted advisor and guiding her clients toward better decisions and behaviors related to investments. She states clearly what she can or cannot do for clients, and those she can or cannot help. Her transparency helps her find and attract those people who want to do what is sometimes the hard work of becoming more aware and disciplined about wealth. She educates prospective clients and visitors through her writings on blogs and in articles, demonstrating her expertise and approach. She coaches her clients to become savvy investors. For this valued service, *millionaire-next-door types seek her out.*

Everything from her branding ("I can't help you if you want to beat the market") to the way she charges clients for her advice highlights the *behaviors* she wants her clients to adopt. Ms. Jenkins bases her success on how she can help her clients improve their wealth trajectory. By comparison, Mr. Jack views his success as the next commission check coming in from the high-load mutual fund he just sold to an unwitting target.

The financial professionals who will attract the next millionaire next door realize that it requires certain behaviors, not cars, accessories, or even job titles, to build wealth. Those who want to succeed in the long-term game of wealth-building will seek out advisors who view themselves more as coaches in the long-term game of economic success.

Selling Financial Products

In 1996, a key focus of any financial professional was that of an investment manager, like Mr. Jack, someone who could buy and sell securities on your behalf,

Building Wealth Revisited

With all of the advances in technology, the trend in the financial services industry has not been a full-scale (or even moderately large-scale) abandonment of financial professionals by the affluent or even emerging affluent. What has been interesting over time is the trend by some to indulge in consumer products but neglect advice and services on the investing and retirement planning side. This was highlighted by my father in 2014:

[F]or purposes of building wealth . . . once you are in a high-income bracket [$100,000 or more] it matters less how much more you make than what you do with what you already have.

The balance-sheet affluent by definition are in the top 25% of the net worth distribution. The balance-sheet affluent tend to put every dollar they can into investments, not into consumption. The balance-sheet affluent spend an average of 100 hours a year researching and planning their investments. Their counterparts, the "income-statement affluents" or, who are in the bottom 25% of the wealth distribution, spend about 50 hours a year in such activities. What is interesting is the significant correlation between time spent in studying/planning and net worth. *My studies show that the balance-sheet affluent have 6 to 10 times more net worth than do the income-statement affluent!*

The balance-sheet affluent also use that time more effectively by seeking professional advice in order to help them make important decisions themselves. They usually assemble a team of advisors from lawyers and accountants to brokers and bankers (trust officers) and are willing to pay handsomely for good advice.

It's a startling irony that there's an inverse relationship between the willingness to pay for luxury items and the willingness to buy investment advice. The income-statement affluents spend heavily on cars, boats, and houses and tend to skimp on investment advice. The balance-sheet affluent however skimp on the luxuries and are usually more willing to pay top dollar for good legal and financial advice.

meanwhile taking a hefty commission for doing so. Presumably the investment manager would also be suggesting rebalancing, taking advantage of tax-loss harvesting, and making other strategic decisions that benefited the client or investor. Millionaires in the 1980s and 1990s required *someone else* to trade on their behalf.

Shortly after the publication of *The Millionaire Next Door*, online trading opened up a new world of trading to investors. Everyone, for better or worse, had direct access to buy and sell on a whim. No longer did investors even have to interact with stockbrokers if they didn't want to.

But as with any job or profession, successful investment managers have certain knowledge, skills, abilities, and other competencies that allow them to be successful in this endeavor. Most often, it's a function of the time and effort put into research investments (for example, intense study of the company itself, the industry, and market). Like the investment managers of the 1990s, the typical understanding of success in "stock picking" is that only 7% can do so effectively.

What does that mean for the millionaire next door? For the self-made, self-reliant American? In 1996, the advice was to go to a trust department to help manage wealth. At the time, it was the source for individuals who would operate under a fiduciary standard (as opposed to a suitability standard, connected primarily to those who make commissions off of sales). Today, there is an entire sub-industry that adheres to a fiduciary standard of counsel in the world of financial services that is more accessible at a broader range of income and wealth levels than before. These are the individuals who will act in your best interest.

Awareness of the Financial Services Space

In 2002, researchers from American University and Washington State University concluded their research article with recommendations for individuals hoping to invest in a way that would avoid typical investing mistakes.[31] These included behaviors that were already apparent to those seeking economic independence:

- Understand biases in investing. Many of the biases and behaviors reported by millionaires fall into common investing bias categories.

- Identify investment objectives and constraints in investing: What are the goals, and how can they be reached given the risks?

- Develop quantitative decision-making guidelines . . . guidelines that avoid emotion.

- Diversify investments.
- Review investments and reallocate as needed.

Today, many of the recommendations can be achieved through technologies: in other words, setting and forgetting investments via an automated investment service (aka robo-advisors) thus taking much of the emotional aspect out of the investing process. It allows for diversification and reallocation based on investment-related goals and uses algorithms that take out the emotions from many types of decision-making.

With that, why would individual investors need advisors? We continue to see a shift from what might traditionally be thought of as "stockbrokers"—individuals selling investments—to those who engage in investment management or in financial planning specifically.

Consistent with the data and findings reported here and in my father's prior books, he suspected that financial advice would move more in the direction of *behavioral management* and away from portfolio management. Because of the "Vanguard effect," asset management is in the process of being commoditized. After all, if your portfolio can achieve returns that are better than 90% of the well-heeled, big-dollar college endowment funds at the cost of a couple of hours at your personal computer and 10 basis points a year, why pay more for less? But what our data also shows is that there are large gains to be had for the individual in the arena of behavioral management. Over the decades, we have certainly encountered a large number of individuals for whom our behavioral data produced a "well, duh" reaction (even for this group our work was valuable because they all had someone close to them who *didn't get it*, and the data served as an unbiased third party to echo their arguments in support of a frugal lifestyle). But the majority of the feedback we received from readers fell into the camp for which these behavioral insights were a true "eureka!" moment. Some of these people shared stories of being able to change their behaviors on a dime and move in the prodigious accumulator of wealth direction almost immediately. But most described the process as a difficult one that did not come naturally, and that required a lot of work to overcome years of contrary programming. Indeed, in many cases they were seeking support and guidance on this journey.

Our data indicates that financial advisors are spending more and more time discussing "nonfinancial" matters with their clients. As technical platforms (the

Should You Listen to the Financial Analyst?

Successful wealth accumulators excel at assessing the quality of financial information that they receive and therefore what they decide to rely on, and don't blindly accept the advice of someone carrying a "professional" title. My father wrote this about financial analysts in 2011:

Out of the 200 top high-income job categories, financial analysts consistently rank among the top 10 in the proportion of those who have annual realized incomes of $200,000 or more. But are they wealthy? Many of them are. The financial analysts group ranks #1 in terms of the percent of its members with $1 million net or more in investments. But be selective in listening to analysts; not all of them have a great track record. And not all are excellent at transforming income into wealth. According to my estimate, they rank 116th in this regard. It takes the equivalent of 154 high income analysts to produce 100 millionaires.

In a 2011 *USA Today* article, a study by Edward Swanson, a finance professor at Texas A&M, was cited that analyzed the recommendations of investment analysts. The study was first published in *The Accounting Review*. According to the article: ". . . you could add significant performance to your stock picks by combining information from analysts and short sellers. . . . specifically: buy stocks that have a 'sell' recommendation by analysts yet have a very low amount of shorting activity. Sell stocks that have a 'buy' recommendation by analysts yet have lots of shorting activity."[32]

What is the meaning of "lots of shorting activity"? It means simply that there are a lot of sophisticated investment dollars wagered in anticipation of the stock declining.

Clearly, this doesn't say much for analyst research (or maybe honesty and integrity). And it does give a great deal of credit to short sellers—not what they say but what they do.[33]

In fairness, some financial analysts have an excellent batting average. Many of those who do are mentioned in the *Wall Street Journal*'s annual profile of top analysts. Part of being a wise investor is to determine the reliability of the various sources of available information.

robo-advisors) continue to penetrate the market for purely technical assistance in the areas such as portfolio selection, rebalancing, and tax-loss harvesting, behavioral management and coaching may be the last and best arena for in-person financial advisors to survive and thrive.

Unfortunately, not all advisors are focused on the best interests of their clients. As Mr. Dennis P., a 60-year-old advisor working for one of the major financial services institutions in this country puts it, "I want clients who lack confidence." He operates in the full-service, full-commission, broker-dealer model of financial advice. His clients tend to be the "new" executive-type, high-income-producing, status-seeking professionals who have little time to bother with researching their investments or those that provide investment-related advice. They "enjoy" hot stock tips and game-like investment strategies. They have little time to manage their own investments, tend to be into playing the game of investing and want the latest hot stock, and enjoy the prestige of using a name-brand financial services firm. It's easy to say "I work with X [insert name of a name-brand brokerage]" and feel good around other equally time-strapped, income-statement affluent social climbers. The cost of this convenient privilege is a cool 2% of assets Mr. P manages each year for doing very little. Perhaps our Mr. Jack needs a different strategy: one targeting this group.

While executive-level leaders may be the majority of his clients, Mr. P also has in his book clients who lack self-esteem or self-efficacy when it comes to investing. This advisor prefers that his clients be totally dependent upon his counsel and expertise. Indeed, we've encountered other professional service providers (lawyers, doctors, etc.) who feel the same way; clients who think they know more than the pros can be a real headache (or so we've been told). But to the extent that a financial advisor seeks out clients who lack confidence to take advantage of them by churning account assets and selling them unnecessary expensive financial products, it is no surprise that the industry as a whole has a tremendous PR problem.

The waves of change both in regulations and popular culture about financial planners is leading to a slow adoption of the fiduciary standard: the advisor who provides recommendations solely in the best interest of her client. As discussed in *The Millionaire Next Door* related to "teaching thrift," it is now somewhat common knowledge that if an advisor is unwilling to make that commitment, to sign a fiduciary oath, then millionaire beware.

We believe and have seen in past research that being economically successful also requires picking the right team of trusted advisors. Many millionaires have shared with us that they want to be able to focus on their expertise (e.g., running their business) while letting other experts (CPAs, financial planners) focus on theirs. With that in mind, what should an aspiring millionaire next door be looking for as he evaluates hiring professional expertise to manage finances? Here are the most fundamental questions to ask:

1. What specifically am I going to pay you?
The days of paying a "stockbroker" a hefty commission for the privilege of buying a financial product that you may not have really needed (or if you did, could have been bought independently much cheaper) are over. The financial services industry and the general public at large just don't know it yet. It will take years or maybe decades for this big-money industry to die a slow death, but it is underway. So-called "fee only" financial advisors that don't take commissions (or any other form of kickback from large financial products companies) for the financial products they invest your money in have been a small but steadily growing segment of the industry for years now, and prodigious accumulators of wealth understand that this is the only way to pay for financial advisory services. The "fee" can be a percentage of "assets under management" (or "AUM" in the lingo), or a more predictable and straightforward "retainer" or "subscription" fee per month or year.

2. What value am I getting from you?
The value delivered by a financial advisor should be readily ascertainable—even if not obviously visible. For many years now, Vanguard has conducted a research study titled Advisor's Alpha that catalogs and quantifies the additional value provided by professional financial advisors. The Vanguard study calculates an incremental benefit of on average approximately 3% of additional portfolio return based on benefits from items such as portfolio rebalancing, portfolio construction, and improved investing behaviors (e.g., not buying high and selling at the bottom). But this analysis quantifies only the benefit received from professional financial advisors in relation to the money *already saved and invested*. What about *additional monies* that are saved (and ultimately invested) because of professional financial advisory services? Our market research conducted through Data-Points indicates that individuals who are able to improve their wealth-building

What Still Makes Them Different

When the good times roll on Wall Street, so, too, do they roll for the luxury retailers nearby, as you can see in this piece my father shared on his blog a few years ago:

In a 2012 broadcast of *Mad Money*, Jim Cramer did an analysis of several retailers who cater to the affluent. One of these was Tiffany's. Jim indicated that the company's stock price, of course, was highly correlated with its sales and ultimately its profits. Further, he proposed that the performance of this upscale retailer is highly correlated with the performance of financial products and services and the organizations that sell them. In English, this means that when Wall Street types get big bonuses they spend heavily on the products offered by Tiffany's.

My own data suggest that marketers of investment products and services are more likely to be of the income-statement affluent variety than of the balance-sheet type. When incomes are high among this population of consumers, you are likely to find a series of newspaper articles which detail their prolific consumption habits. Conversely, when payouts are reduced conspicuous consumption is reduced and upscale retailers worry about their future. In a *New York Times* article, Kevin Roose stated, ". . . securities firms in New York made . . . $13.5 billion in 2011 down sharply from $27.6 billion in 2010. . . . feeling the pinch of lower Wall Street pay . . . luxury goods stores . . . in New York stand to suffer."[34] What impact will this have on Tiffany's sales? You know the answer.

Ah, the income-statement affluent. When they encounter a significant upswing in income they are inclined to go into hyper-consumption mode. Contrast the Wall Street affluent with a different segment. Recently, farmers in this country encountered a major upswing in their incomes: ". . . net income for U.S. farmers was a record $98.1 billion in 2011 up 24% over the prior year." Most farmers are balance-sheet affluent types. They tend to allocate windfall profits to capital improvements and quality stocks and bonds rather than to trophies of diamonds and silver. New silos and tractors are the status symbols in farm country. As reported in the *Wall Street Journal*, there is a ". . . tight relationship between [John Deere's] stock and corn's price per bushel. . . . When farm income is high, farmers are motivated to invest in Deere's big green and yellow machines [tractors, etc.].[35]

In *Stop Acting Rich*, I profiled farmers in terms of their productivity in transforming income into wealth. They rank 8th along this dimension among the top 200 high-income occupational groups in America. What about the other group, marketers of investment services? My acid test in this context is the proportion of millionaires produced as a function of high-income generators within this segment. They rank well below farmers, in between high-income physicians and lawyers. But in terms of the proportion generating high incomes ($200,000 or more), they rank in the top 10.

behaviors stand to benefit from an increased annual savings rate that is 143% more than their low-performing peers (17% versus 7%). (And note: these benefits can be achieved through improved financial behaviors implemented either on a do-it-yourself basis or through the assistance of a professional financial advisor.) In other words, individuals who consistently exhibit successful wealth-building behaviors in areas including frugality, social indifference, responsibility, and others, save on average 143% more each year than their low-scoring peers. If a financial advisor can help you boost your annual savings rate by even half this much, she will be worth her weight in gold.

3. Are you acting in my best interest? (i.e., can I trust you?)

This should really be the first question in any professional services relationship, and financial advisors are no different. We are always looking to assess this issue in the people we do business with and seek counsel from, and in the arena of managing our money it is critically important. For decades now, "financial advisors" operating under the "stockbroker" model of selling products for commission have made this question a difficult one to answer. But the fee-only financial advisors referenced above of today are typically operating under a "fiduciary standard"—the same way that attorneys have operated under state bar rules—that demands and requires that they act in the best interest of their clients at all times. (This is one of those areas where a new rule is unveiled and it's hard to imagine that it hasn't *always* been the rule.)

Advising on More Than Finances

Our financial responsibilities and behaviors are intertwined with the rest of our lives. That's partially why those in the financial service industry who are focusing on a holistic approach to working with individuals are finding success. We bring to the financial management job, as we discussed earlier, all the other characteristics, experiences, challenges, family relationships that permeate the rest of our lives. What does this mean for the financial services industry? The expertise needed is a true blend of financial planning, psychology, counseling, and life planning.

Family, health, and marital issues, as well as grief and religion, are just a few of the nonfinancial topics that financial advisors work through with their clients. A few years ago, a large-scale study of advisors yielded a wealth of information on the evolving role of financial advisors as coaches.[36] The research, which included approximately 1,400 advisors associated with either the Financial Planning Association or the Certified Financial Planner Board of Standards, highlighted the topics, challenges, and critical incidents faced by advisors related to nonfinancial issues. Nearly 90% of advisors reported engaging in nonfinancial coaching or counseling, and 25% of the advisors' contact with clients consisted of nonfinancial issues. Three-quarters of those surveyed estimated that time has increased in the past five years. Some of the nonfinancial issues discussed included:

- Personal life goals (64%)
- Physical health (52%)
- Career-related issues (50%)

Death of family members or friends, conflicts or disagreements with children, and marital problems were also listed as top areas discussed. In terms of amount of time spent, advisors reported that personal life goals, a client's career or job, and physical health took up the most time.

The evolution of financial advisory services, from transaction-focused to relationship-focused[37], from sales-based advisement to holistic practice, is also challenging the distinctions between financial coaches, counselors, and advisors often used by academics and practitioners today. These blurred lines give advisors who are focused on the well-being of their clients the opportunity to build expertise in this area, and also communicate that offering to potential clients.

The study's authors concluded:

Divorce, family strife, suicide, drugs, mental health, religion and spirituality, illness, and death—this reads like a list of issues that would and should be managed by a member of the clergy, social worker, psychologist, or physician. Our research reveals that financial planners often face these issues. Knowledge about investments and insurance will not solve these problems. Possessing advanced degrees in accounting, taxation, finance, or investments will serve planners well, but will not be sufficient. To the extent that financial planning is designed to help a client meet personal life goals, coaching and life planning skills will become requisite skills for financial planners.[38]

These kinds of topics are almost too much for Mr. Jack or Mr. P. But as we're now seeing more and more, ignoring the interwoven nature of financial management and life management is going out of style. Ms. Jenkins's approach may prove to win out in the long term.

Investing in Knowledge

Less than one-third of millionaires in our latest sample rely heavily on an investment advisor. How then, are these economically successful individuals able to manage their investments? Part of building wealth is the allocation of time, a nonrenewable resource, to manage what money comes in efficiently. This time is also spent building knowledge.

Investing abilities are more reliant on nurture versus nature. The complexities and knowledge required take instruction, lessons that most of us don't receive from home. For example, in one of our studies with mass affluent investors, less than one-fifth of them reported that their parents taught them how to invest, whereas more than 55% of them said their parents taught them the importance of saving for the future.[39] As one millionaire from Alaska (a drillsite petroleum engineer) explained to us: "I wish I had learned to invest when I was young. My parents didn't really understand and I think their long-term plan was a pension and a hobby-farm small business. . . . In the early '90s, when oil prices crashed along with Alaska real estate values we lost all of our net worth. It was a tough time for us but that experience is a huge influence on our investing and financial management today. All that we have today has been grown since then."

Whereas most millionaire investors in our most recent sample agreed that they spent a considerable amount of time on their investments, we also see a consistent pattern among our accumulator of wealth groups. Specifically, PAWs consistently spend more time studying investments and planning for future investment decisions than UAWs, although the differences between these two groups have decreased since 1996. In the 1996 survey data, UAWs reported spending 55% of the time that PAWs spent each month studying and planning for future investment decisions. In the 2016 data, UAWs reported spending nearly 77% of the time that PAWs put in. The reason for this change is not clear, but we suspect that it is at least partially due to the increased availability of quality investment-related news and commentary online. In 1996, to access this type of objective information, an investor would have needed to subscribe to (often expensive) publications like private newsletters or periodicals such as *Barron's*. In 2016 those sources are still available (for a price), but there is also a universe of quality (free) sources of information in the form of websites, blogs, podcasts, etc. Investing has thus been democratized not only through the proliferation of index funds and the dramatic reduction of fees, but also through the spread of free content and information.

Time spent managing investments and planning for future investment-related decisions is positively related to net worth, regardless of (or, in statistical speak, controlling for) age and income. Is it any wonder, then, that those who are economically successful, that is, successful at transforming income into wealth, spend more time than their under accumulating peers on investing research?

Conclusion

Believe in yourself! Have faith in your abilities! Without a humble but reasonable confidence in your own powers you cannot be successful or happy.
—Norman Vincent Peale

IF THERE IS A PLAYBOOK FOR WHO WILL BECOME THE NEXT MILLIONAIRE NEXT door, it's not to be found in a specific zip code, in the driver seat of a particular automobile, or with a certain watch or type of portfolio. Instead, the formula to help find (or more importantly, to become) the next millionaire next door belongs in the patterns of wealth-related behaviors and experiences that make up our daily lives.

Unless you want to simply allow demographics to set your course, you'll have to rely on what you do day in and day out. That is why self-made millionaires are wealthy: They allocate their time, energy, and money in ways that allow them to build wealth; they are disciplined savers, spenders, and investors in a world of professional consumers; and they are aware of both their own strengths and the market, economic, and close-to-home conditions that might trip them up in the future.

Today and in the future, those who wish to build wealth without an excessively high income or substantial windfall will have to change both lifestyle and behaviors. Indeed, many of us aren't willing to do it. And because we *don't like what we need to do* some will declare that there's no way to become financially independent on your own.

Whether we're looking at consumer purchases or investing, home purchases or other financial worries, we have seen throughout the years that those who are adept at transforming income into wealth continue to be contrarians. They think and behave differently than what you might expect, and certainly differently than the norm. Those who want to excel at building wealth and becoming economically successful may have to give up on traditional versions of education, careers, and investing. Indeed, our lives and lifestyle may look very different from our parents, especially if our upbringing included heavy consumption.

Anecdotes and findings regarding prices of jeans or investing mistakes to avoid are interesting and potentially moderately helpful, but they are not enough to create a pattern of behaviors conducive to building wealth long term. As we discussed in Chapter 5, the job of managing one's financial affairs requires certain competencies, certain sets of behavioral patterns that are consistent and effective in transforming income into wealth. It's not enough, or even barely sufficient, to be frugal one day of the year or make one wise car purchase.

Instead, building wealth requires a combination of our ability and willingness to live below our means, to be confident in our financial decisions, and to ultimately take responsibility for the economic outcomes of our households. It requires us to ignore the incessant barrage of what others are doing, driving, and wearing, and be focused enough to monitor what's going on in our own financial lives. And it takes being intentional about our financial path: creating goals and plans based on how we want our lives to look and then setting a course to meet those goals. We find it interesting that a recent "economic forecast" report from Vanguard—a report designed, presumably, to help traders make short- or even medium-term trading decisions—ultimately concluded by informing the reader that the greatest impact on one's ability to build wealth over time is *saving*.

Even if we're not naturally confident in our money-related decisions or if we prefer shopping as one of our pastimes, the good news for all of us is that each of these behavioral traits, to a varying extent, is a result of a combination of nature *and* nurture. To put it another way: No matter where you are right now, you can change your financial behaviors and your lifestyle. To put it one more way:

High-potential wealth accumulators are largely made, not born.

This is the good news. Our financial behaviors can transcend any groups we may belong to, gender or otherwise. What happened in the past, although perhaps predictive to some extent of our future, isn't necessarily our future, especially if we focus and train for a better financial path. The good news is that there are resources, many of which are free and accessible—much more so than in 1996— to those who wish to grow, learn, and obtain the knowledge needed to manage their financial affairs. Used in a beneficial manner, technologies can spur us on to

Satisfaction: Enjoying the Journey to Wealth

What about those who don't have to change anything about their lifestyle because they have a substantial safety net? Those who receive ample doses of economic outpatient care, my father wrote in 2010, do not have the privilege of experiencing the pursuit of wealth, and therefore, perhaps take it all for granted:

Yes, it is challenging today to build wealth on your own. It was also challenging in 1996. But, it is possible, and it is necessary if one wants to live in Independentsville.

What about those who inherit their wealth? Perhaps they live on Easy Street. Even for those who inherit their wealth there are considerable individual differences in what they ultimately do or make of that wealth. These "inheritor achievers" versus "inheritor underachievers" may be in your own family or neighborhood.

How do I categorize millionaires who inherited all or most of their wealth? I do not consider them to be fortunate. Actually, I think of them as being deprived. They were deprived of the great pride and satisfaction derived from building one's own fortune. Countless millionaires have told me that it is the journey to wealth which is much more satisfying than the destination. When they look back over their history of building wealth, they recall constantly setting economic goals and the great satisfaction gained from achieving them. Yes, in the context of economic achievement, it is the trip, the journey to Independentsville about which they most often boast.

One should never envy those who inherited their destination. Most trips to financial independence begin with the first dollar saved. Next time you see an acorn lying about take it home and put it on your desk. It will be there to remind you that even the most gigantic oak tree, like fortunes, began with a simple acorn.

If you have read *The Millionaire Next Door*, you may recall the excerpts of an interview I conducted with Dr. Dave North.[1] Dave was just elected to the millionaire-next-door hall of fame on his first nomination. He maintained that it was his journey to financial independence (his net worth was more than $7 million) that was much more satisfying and gave him much more pride than the condition of his current balance sheet. During my interview with Dave he explained how he enhanced his self-esteem and satisfaction during his early years of building wealth:

"Even when I was 11 years old, I saved my first $50 from working in a grocery store. It's just like today . . . only today the number of zeros change. . . . More zeros, but it's the same rule, same discipline. When I was going to school, my wife taught. We had a small income. . . . Even then we always had a rule . . . to save—even then we saved. You can't invest without something . . . The first thing is to save. You must take advantage of investment opportunities. . . . You should have something to take advantage of excellent opportunities. . . . It's part of my background."

You don't have to be a highly compensated professional or executive like Dave to become financially independent. Four out of five millionaires in America are self-made. Fully 42% of the 944 millionaires profiled in *Stop Acting Rich* had a net worth of *zero* or less when they first began working full-time. Learn to derive happiness from the journey to wealth, not the appearance of wealth. Experience the constant joy of being in control of your life and not allowing consumption to control you.

change for the better. How we behave with respect to our finances can change at any time, regardless of who is president of the United States or where our family came from.

So where is the millionaire next door today? In all his various forms, the millionaire next door will continue to exist and thrive as long as this country continues to afford its unique freedoms and rewards for enterprise, discipline, and hard work. Below is a summary of what will continue to be required by those who seek financial success:

- Ignoring the myths of wealth, including the confusion between income and net worth, and the barriers for creating self-made wealth.

- Recognizing the influences others may have on financial attitudes and behaviors, and learning from those who are equally committed to financial success over and above appearing to be rich.

- Making consistently good consumer decisions, starting with neighborhood, understanding its potential effect on reaching financial goals.

- Assessing strengths and weaknesses related to finances to improve where possible in areas such as frugality, owning responsibility for financial outcomes, and confidence to make decisions based on knowledge.

- Deciding early on a philosophy for work and careers and not assuming that the traditional view of work, one that seems to dictate an 8 a.m. to 6 p.m. existence from ages 25 to 67, is the only path.

- Recognizing that successful investing behaviors can be learned and improved and that the fruits of effectively investing what is saved over time provide security for the more important aspects of one's life.

Perhaps in 20 years' time, researchers will find a secret formula or pill that will reliably and effortlessly transform earned income into wealth. When it has been found, we'll stop talking about behaviors and discipline, frugality, resource allocation, and perseverance. Until then, those who wish to pursue a path of economic success have at their fingertips a map for the challenging and rewarding journey ahead.

Appendix A: Studies

Targeting by Neighborhood and Business Ownership Status

The millionaire study used in the majority of the tables and discussions in this book was conducted between April 2015 and January 2016. To identify this affluent sample, we used a commercially available residential and business-related database source. Specifically, we used a company that employed similar methodology to what was used to identify millionaire households in the past research studies (e.g., those in *The Millionaire Next Door* and *The Millionaire Mind*). That is, the identification of high-income and/or high-net-worth households relied on geocoding. We selected an Experian mosaic group, American Royalty, which represents approximately 0.73% of the population in the United States.[1] This group represents the wealthiest households in America as defined by Experian, and is based on geocoding of zip codes and addresses. Then, we used the Statistics of Income 2012 data[2] from the IRS to rank all states by their estate tax returns. We undersampled households in the top seven states in terms of total amount of returns (20% of sample; states included were California, Florida, Illinois, New Jersey, New York, Pennsylvania, and Texas), and oversampled the remainder of the states (80% of the sample). We oversampled from states that had a smaller number of millionaires to ensure a broader cross section of Americans were included in the sample.

In addition to residential households, we included a subset of small business owners in the sample, utilizing the same company, utilizing the business owner options, and included job titles such as president, owner, chief executive officer, and founder.

In total, we selected 9,947 heads of households as well as 1,516 small business owners to include in the study.

We created a survey instrument that included questions about lifestyle, demographics, behaviors, and habits. Many of the same questions that were used in previous surveys (those that went into *The Millionaire Next Door* and *The Millionaire Mind*, for example) were included, along with new sections related to purchasing real estate and investing-related behaviors. A paper and online version of the survey instruments were created. The A. L. Burruss Institute of Public

Service and Research at Kennesaw State University administered the survey (including mailing and collection) and entered data for the paper-based surveys. Multiple waves of data collection were conducted:

Wave 1: 5,000 heads of households were contacted via mail and asked to complete the survey in exchange for $1, and received a reminder to complete the survey approximately three to four weeks after the survey instrument was mailed. This wave resulted in 461 respondents for a response rate of 9.2%.

Wave 2: This wave of data collection included two samples of 500 heads of households that were either (a) mailed an introduction letter followed by a paper survey, or (b) mailed an introduction letter followed by a postcard asking them to complete an online survey, each with an incentive of $2. The response rates were 18.2% for paper version, 11.4% for web-based version. For this wave, 148 out of 1,000 heads of households contacted participated in the study.

Wave 3: The survey instrument was divided into two conditions to shorten its length, and participants in this wave were randomly assigned to either form A or B. This wave of data collection included 3,947 heads of households and 1,516 small business owners who were sent an introductory letter followed by a postcard inviting them to complete an online survey in exchange for $2. The response rates for this wave of data collection were 7.32% and 6.6% for heads of households (n = 289) and small business owners (n = 100), respectively.

A total of 998 responses were received in time to be included in our analyses. Overall, the response rate was 9%. Of the responses received, 164 were incomplete, leaving 834 responses. Out of the 834 responses, 669 were millionaires or decamillionaires.

Additional Studies

Just as in *The Millionaire Next Door* and other related works, additional samples and studies were included in this book in some cases. One of the main sources of additional data is described here. Using the same survey instrument as in the affluent sample mentioned above, we surveyed 528 individuals using a crowd-sourcing service (Amazon's Mechanical Turk). Respondents were paid $2 in exchange for participation. To be eligible for participation, individuals had to have an annual pretax income of at least $25,000, had to be responsible or jointly so for financial management in their households, and had to be at least 25 years of age. This resulted in a mostly mass affluent sample, with an average age of

37.9, who were mostly male (53.5%), and had an estimated median income of $87,101.21. Nearly half of the sample (47.7%) had net worth below $200,000, while 44.2% of the sample had a net worth between $200,000 and $999,999.

Behaviors and Experiences Studies

The study of the predictive nature of past experiences and behaviors was examined using multiple studies between 2012 and 2017. These studies examined the usefulness of biodata-based measures of wealth accumulation with two different samples: Affluent Market Institute Research Panel members and two crowd sourced samples of mostly mass affluent Americans. Details of this research may be found in the Building Wealth Technical Report and the Financial Behaviors and Wealth Potential White Paper from DataPoints[3], as well as journal articles and presentations.[4]

Appendix B: Rankings of Sole Proprietorships by Percentage Profitable (1998 & 2015)[1]

Industry	1998		2015	
	% profitable	Number of returns	% profitable	Number of returns
Plastic and rubber products			98	3,188
Offices of physicians, mental health specialists	93	21,698	91	37,200
Investment bankers and securities dealers	49	2,246	90	12,810
Offices of dentists	94	91,998	89	77,693
Offices of podiatrists	75	6,296	88	7,905
Social assistance	83	75,876	87	834,770
Securities brokers	67	20,839	86	10,176
Offices of chiropractors	84	31,285	86	33,912
Other ambulatory health care services (including ambulance services, blood and organ banks)	–	–	86	35,594
Waste management and remediation services	69	15,741	85	24,059
Hospitals	–	–	85	9,787
Construction of buildings	–	–	84	622,635
Specialty trade contractors	87	1,789,725	84	2,035,724
Construction	86	2,243,044	84	2,696,797
Health care and social assistance	86	1,506,387	84	2,181,372
Drafting, building inspections, and geophysical surveying	91	50,347	83	44,376
Nursing and residential care facilities	72	48,026	83	81,300
Automotive body shops	79	80,665	83	70,691

Industry	1998		2015	
	% profitable	Number of returns	% profitable	Number of returns
Legal services	83	318,005	83	345,480
Administrative and support and waste management services	–	–	82	2,471,954
Administrative and support services	83	1,235,496	82	2,447,895
Offices of physicians (except mental health specialists)	87	170,538	82	179,425
Scientific research and development services	53	12,566	82	40,461
Warehousing and storage facilities	74	3,826	82	8,290
Truck transportation	–	–	82	643,728
Ambulatory health care services	87	760,492	81	1,255,515
Outpatient care centers and other miscellaneous health practitioners	–	–	81	259,314
Other transit and ground transportation	–	–	80	655,423
Personal and laundry services	81	1,208,071	80	2,493,940
Offices of mental health practitioners and social therapists	92	150,205	80	197,753
Transportation and warehousing	80	790,262	80	1,619,557
Other accounting services	83	345,408	80	356,199
Other services	81	1,857,237	79	3,512,160
Home health care services	83	93,523	79	386,214
Offices of certified public accountants	93	48,585	79	46,475
Unclassified establishments	82	348,125	78	589,940
Fabricated metal products	75	29,319	78	36,733
Testing laboratories	–	–	78	6,564

Industry	1998		2015	
	% profitable	Number of returns	% profitable	Number of returns
Commodity contracts brokers and dealers	65	7,621	78	3,031
Educational services	79	292,813	77	855,798
Offices of optometrists	98	12,810	77	22,796
Miscellaneous repairs	85	342,797	77	398,593
Couriers and messengers	76	182,092	77	189,460
Furniture and related products	58	31,772	76	23,881
Architectural services	87	70,786	76	102,545
Air and rail transportation	61	13,722	76	16,929
Advertising and related services	81	86,337	75	144,018
Market research and public opinion polling	49	28,111	75	53,368
Museums, historical sites, and similar institutions	–	–	75	8,028
Architectural, engineering, and related services	84	226,852	75	249,754
Auto repair and maintenance	78	306,369	75	360,747
All nonfarm industries	75	17,408,809	74	25,226,245
Electrical equipment, appliances, and components	71	7,936	74	8,239
Professional, scientific, and technical services	78	2,431,374	74	3,486,604
Medical and diagnostic laboratories	83	19,427	74	17,709
Religious, grantmaking, civic, professional, and similar organizations	–	–	74	258,879
Automotive mechanical and electrical repair and maintenance	77	138,276	74	197,540
Other miscellaneous services	75	454,840	73	775,788
Other professional, scientific, and technical services	76	1,145,409	73	1,932,153
Wood products	44	37,081	73	31,955

Industry	1998		2015	
	% profitable	Number of returns	% profitable	Number of returns
Management, scientific, and technical consulting services	77	563,555	73	918,517
Leather and allied products			72	6,038
Computer systems design services	74	205,552	72	286,069
Support activities for mining	70	12,818	71	19,300
Offices of real estate agents, brokers, property managers, and appraisers	–	–	71	858,484
Miscellaneous manufacturing	–		71	66,390
Data processing, Internet publishing and broadcasting, and web search portals	–		71	100,357
Engineering services	74	86,090	71	85,798
Support activities for transportation (including motor vehicle towing)	–		71	90,138
Insurance agencies and brokerages	77	294,680	70	311,554
Chemical manufacturing	–		70	15,976
Insurance agents, brokers, and related activities	76	387,774	70	422,069
Other auto repair and maintenance (including oil change, lubrication, and car washes)	–		70	92,517
Support activities for agriculture and forestry	62	121,885	70	106,930
Other insurance related activities and other financial vehicles	73	93,095	70	110,515
Real estate	77	796,471	69	1,167,939
Petroleum and coal products	–		69	1,030
Real estate and rental and leasing	–		69	1,214,655
Finance and insurance	73	598,939	68	636,234
Computer and electronic products	70	12,937	68	16,891

Industry	1998		2015	
	% profitable	Number of returns	% profitable	Number of returns
Forestry and logging (including forest nurseries, timber tracts)	–	–	67	52,006
Manufacturing	67	361,254	67	380,959
Motion picture and sound recording	59	54,643	67	112,826
Restaurants (full & limited service) and drinking places	–	–	66	427,770
Automotive equipment rental and leasing	80	17,803	66	15,330
Motor vehicle and parts dealers	69	131,095	66	132,250
Other activities related to real estate	79	102,301	66	257,276
Water transportation	98	2,720	66	6,033
Information	65	212,455	66	337,957
Durable goods, including machinery, wood, metals, etc.	74	186,195	66	189,507
Performing arts, spectator sports, and related industries	60	820,312	66	1,346,487
Printing and related support activities	77	36,768	66	31,950
Utilities	44	7,147	65	20,235
Arts, entertainment, and recreation	61	986,769	65	1,499,737
Specialized design services	60	141,563	65	270,473
Credit intermediation and related activities	76	63,151	65	39,213
Securities, commodity contractts, and other financial investments	64	148,034	65	174,952
Accommodation, food services, and drinking places	64	302,777	65	486,163
Food and beverage stores	81	127,853	65	92,538
Mining	50	119,376	64	134,638
Amusement, gambling, and recreation industries	67	165,341	64	145,222
Heavy and civil engineering construction	–	–	64	38,439

Industry	1998		2015	
	% profitable	Number of returns	% profitable	Number of returns
Oil and gas extraction	61	23,213	63	109,099
Apparel	73	27,061	63	22,701
General merchandise stores	70	48,598	63	28,966
Publishing industries (except Internet)	73	376,581	62	77,200
Wholesale trade (merchant wholesalers)	64	115,889	61	371,148
Other financial investment activities (investment advice)	100	8,092	61	147,617
Transportation equipment	85	32,967	61	11,931
Machinery	–	–	61	24,012
Other mining	64	288,922	61	6,239
Agriculture, forestry, hunting, and fishing	60	269,704
Food manufacturing			60	54,971
Building material and garden equipment and supplies dealers	73	51,639	59	26,585
Electronic stores and household appliance stores	82	39,038	59	13,704
Surveying and mapping (except geophysical) services	100	15,598	59	10,471
Nondurable goods, including food, fiber, chemicals, etc.	71	190,386	58	142,190
Nonmetallic mineral products	88	8,078	58	9,178
Broadcasting (except Internet) and telecommunications and Internet service providers	–	–	58	47,574
Fishing, hunting, and trapping	–	–	58	66,144
Miscellaneous store retailers	48	453,894	57	618,370
Clothing and accessories stores	70	120,917	57	164,182
Travel accommodation (including hotels, motels, and bed and breakfast inns)	–	–	56	38,853

Industry	1998		2015	
	% profitable	Number of returns	% profitable	Number of returns
Retail trade	55	2,349,535	55	2,460,635
Gasoline stations	71	37,767	55	16,546
Sporting goods, hobby, book, and music stores	61	140,232	54	104,898
Rental and leasing services	58	75,143	54	45,550
Scenic and sightseeing transportation	40	4,491	54	9,556
Wholesale electronic markets and agents and brokers	–	–	53	39,451
Accommodation	63	56,380	53	58,393
Health and personal care stores	44	143,921	53	136,758
Furniture and home furnishing stores	78	58,877	52	25,876
Nonstore retailers	47	1,017,241	52	1,099,962
Lessors of real estate (including mini-warehouses and self storage)	–	–	51	52,178
Commercial and industrial machinery and equipment rental and leasing	–	–	50	15,176
RV (recreational vehicle) parks and recreational camps	72	14,107	49	9,999
Rooming and boarding houses	56	11,862	47	9,542
General rental centers and other consumer goods rental	52	13,620	45	11,906
Consumer electronics and appliances rental	–	–	38	2,671
Textile and textile product mills	94	5,668	35	13,115
Animal production (including breeding of cats and dogs)	25	26,188	34	44,625
Primary metal industries	–	–	27	2,781
Securities and commodity exchanges	–	1,439	11	1,317

Appendix C: Selected Job Titles of Moonlighting Mass Affluent Prodigious Accumulators of Wealth

Academic Advisor
Advertising Copywriter
Analyst
Assistant
Attorney
Auditor
Automation Engineer
Bookkeeper
Business Analyst
Business Owner
Business Owner-Operator
Business Owner/Agricultural Manager
Business Owner/Contractor
Business Program Director
Clergy
Consultant
Court Administrator
Data Entry
Daycare Provider
Digital Marketing Manager
Educational Advisor
Educator
Engineer
Entrepreneur
Farmer
Financial Analyst
Financial Manager
Food Scientist
Forklift Driver
Freelancer
Health Care Professional
High School History Teacher
Homemaker
Insurance Rep
Investor
IT
IT Manager
Landlord
Lecturer
Legal Writer
Lunch Supervisor

Maintenance Manager
Manager
Manager and Business Partner
Middle Manager
Nurse
Office Manager
Operations Manager
Paralegal
Personnel Clerk
Pharmacy Technician
Photographer
Physicist
Programmer
QA Director
Quality Manager
Realtor
Recreation Leader
Recruiter
Research Program Manager
Retail Manager
Retired
Sales and Business Development
Sales Manager
Scientist
Self-Employed—Freelance
Senior Health Care Consultant - IT
Small Business Owner
Software Engineer
Statistical Research Consultant
Stay-at-Home Parent
Student
Supervisor
System Administrator
Teacher
Team Lead
TV News Writer
Unemployed
Vegetation Management
Web Administrator
Web Developer
Writer

Notes

Preface
1 Stanley and Danko, 1996, 3.
2 Federal Reserve, 2015.
3 American Psychological Association, 2015.
4 Fallaw, 2017.

Chapter 1
1 Mr. Money Moustache, 2013.
2 Rockstarfinance.com, 2018.
3 Stanley and Danko, 2010.
4 World Economic Forum report, 2017.
5 Spectrem Group, 2018.
6 United States Census Bureau, 2017.
7 Congress of the United States Congressional Budget Office, 2016.
8 Federal Reserve, 2017a.
9 Semega, Fontenot, and Kollar, 2017.
10 Federal Reserve, 2017a.
11 Genworth, 2016.
12 United States Census Bureau, 2017.
13 Bureau of Labor Statistics, 2017.
14 Kruger, Grable, and Fallaw, 2017; Fallaw, Kruger, and Grable, 2018.
15 Gatewood & Feild, 1998.
16 Kruger, Grable, and Fallaw, 2017; Fallaw, Kruger, and Grable, 2018.
17 Fallaw, 2017.
18 Cassuto, 2013.
19 Associated Press-NORC Center for Public Affairs Research, 2017.
20 Federal Reserve, 2015.
21 Internal Revenue Service Statistics of Income, 2015.
22 Crowdsourced samples came from research conducted by both the Affluent Market Institute and DataPoints between 2013 and 2017.
23 Pew Research Center, 2017.
24 Shoen, 2015.

Chapter 2
1 Bureau of Labor Statistics, 2016a.
2 Numbers related to income and net worth in this section are from 2013.
3 Tax Foundation, 2012.
4 Johnson, Raub, and Newcomb, unknown.
5 Muller, 2011.
6 Stanley, 2012.
7 Stanley and Danko, 1996.

8 Berkowitz, 2013.
9 Sahadi, 2011.
10 Berkowitz, 2011.
11 Kroll, 2012.
12 Fallaw, 2017.
13 Taylor, Klontz, and Lawson, 2017.
14 Trevelyan et al., 2016.
15 Stanley, 2009.
16 Horwitz, 2011.
17 Kroll, 2012.
18 Paletta, 2014.
19 Leonhardt, 2014.
20 Sorkin, 2011.
21 Corrado, 2011.
22 Pew Research Center, 2014.
23 Stanley, 2009. Note in 2016, 80% of millionaires rated hard work as important or very important to their success.

Chapter 3

1 Global Financial Literacy Excellence Center, 2018.
2 Stokes, Mumford, and Owens, 1989; Snell, Stokes, Sands, and McBride, 1994.
3 Solheim, Zuiker, and Levchenko, 2011.
4 Letkiewicz and Fox, 2014.
5 Ibid.
6 Gatenby, 2000.
7 National Bureau of Economic Research, 2012.
8 Zagorsky, 2005.
9 Stanley, 2000; Yarrow, 2015.
10 Dokko, Li, and Hayes, 2015.
11 Easton, 2012.
12 Stanley, 2000.
13 Internal Revenue Service, 2012.
14 Norton, 2014; Anderson, Kraus, Glainsky, and Keltner, 2012.
15 Mangleburg, Doney, and Bristol, 2004.
16 Lee, 2012.
17 Fallaw, 2017.
18 Bentley, 2010.
19 Stanley, 2009, 21.
20 Bureau of Labor Statistics, 2016e.
21 Stanley, 2013.
22 Stanley and Danko, 1996, 75.
23 Stewart, 2016; Asano, 2017.
24 See, for example, Wang, Yu, and Wei, 2012.
25 Margalit, 2016.

26 Godin, 2008.
27 Byron, 2010.
28 Ibid.
29 Inmar, 2014.
30 Cavale, 2018.

Chapter 4

1 Stanley and Danko, 1996, 27.
2 Fallaw, 2017; Fallaw, Kruger, and Grable, 2018.
3 Weinberg, Reagan, and Yankow, 2004.
4 Stanley, 2009, 43.
5 Zhang, Howell, and Howell, 2014.
6 Williams, 2014.
7 Federal Reserve Bulletin, 2017b.
8 Bankrate.com, 2012a.
9 Bankrate.com, 2012b.
10 Bernardo, 2017.
11 Stanley and Danko, 1996, 68.
12 Note: The dollar amounts for 1996 were converted into 2016 dollars using the Bureau of Labor Statistics' CPI Inflation Calculator.
13 Statistic Brain, 2017.
14 Cotton Incorporated, 2013.
15 ShopSmart, 2010; Tuttle, 2011.
16 American Apparel and Footwear Association, 2016.
17 Mesnik, 2017.
18 Stanley, 2000, 289.
19 Snyder, 2011.
20 Sawyers, 2013.
21 Stanley, 2009, 14.
22 Internal Revenue Service, 2017.
23 Stanley and Danko, 1996, 37.

Chapter 5

1 Bureau of Labor Statistics, 2016c.
2 Fallaw, 2016; Fallaw, 2017; Fallaw, Kruger, and Grable, 2018; Grable, Kruger, and Fallaw, 2017; Kruger, Grable, and Fallaw, 2017.
3 Fallaw, Kruger, and Grable, 2018.
4 Schmidt and Hunter, 1998.
5 Letkiewicz and Fox, 2014.
 Fallaw, 2017.
6 Ibid.
7 Chernow, 2018.
8 Bolduc, 2012.

9 Fallaw, 2017.
10 Stanley, 2009, 54 (paraphrased).
11 National Center for O*NET Development, 2016.
12 Lehrer, 2011.
13 Zagorsky, 2007.
14 McGrath, 2015.
15 Lusardi and Mitchell, 2011.
16 Ibid.
17 Letkiewicz and Fox, 2014.
18 Rich, 2012.
19 *Atlanta Journal-Constitution*, March 4, 2012.
20 Stanley, 2009, 97.
21 Ibid, 296.
22 Ibid.
23 Stanley, 2000, 107.
24 *Atlanta Journal-Constitution*, March 18, 2012.
25 Judge and Hurst, 2007.
26 Fidelity Investments, 2016.
27 Federal Reserve, 2017b.
28 National Center for Education Statistics, 2018.
29 Hanks, 2015.
30 Schmidt and Hunter, 1998.
31 Stanley, 2000, 83.
32 Cassuto, 2013.
33 Stanley, 2000, 85.
34 O'Connor, 2012.
35 Stanley, 1998.
36 Stanley, 2004.
37 Stanley, 2000, 98.
38 Bureau of Labor Statistics, 2016h. (All data except social media usage)
39 Asano, 2017.
40 University College of London, 2009; Farrell, 2015.
41 Farrell, 2015.
42 Fallaw, 2017.

Chapter 6

1 Neuharth, 2013.
2 Bureau of Labor Statistics, 2016g.
3 Levanon, Kan, and Li, 2016.
4 Pew Research Center, 2013.
5 Society for Human Resource Management, 2015.
6 Gallup, 2017.
7 CareerBuilder, 2017.
8 Martin, 2014.

9 Stanley, 2000, 393.
10 Stanley, 2005, 8.
11 *Atlanta Journal-Constitution*, 2014.
12 Stanley and Danko, 1996, 241.
13 Semega, Fontenot, and Kollar, 2017.
14 Bureau of Labor Statistics, 2016b.
15 Stanley, 2014; Stanley, 2011.
16 Stanley and Danko, 1996, 256.
17 Phillips, 2013.
18 Speights, 2017.
19 Hagerty, 2014.
20 Stanley, 2000, 120–21.
21 Geldhof and Lerner, 2015.
22 Richards and Fox, 2010.
23 Ibid, 103.
24 Ibid, 173.

Chapter 7
1 Su, 2016.
2 Financial Industry Regulatory Authority, 2017. Note that this figure is different than that of the Bureau of Labor Statitics (2016).
3 Grable, Lytton, O'Neill, Joo, and Klock, 2006.
4 Buffett, 2017.
5 Lynch, 2012, 86, 140, 185, 190, 191, 227–28, 305.
6 Carlson, 2017.
7 Stanley and Moschis, 1984.
8 Internal Revenue Service, 2017.
9 Barber and Odean, 2011, 36–37.
10 Finke and Huston, 2003.
11 Grable, 2000; Grable and Joo, 2004; Wang, 2009.
12 Mayfield, Perdue, and Wooten, 2008.
13 Fallaw, 2018a.
14 Ibid.
15 Barber and Odean, 2001.
16 Fallaw, 2018a.
17 Sages and Grable, 2010.
18 Grable, 2000.
19 Howlett, Kees, and Kemp, 2008.
20 Hartog, Ferrer-i-Carbonell, and Jonker, 2002.
21 Sages and Grable, 2010.
22 Kruger, Grable, and Fallaw, 2017.
23 Fallaw, 2018a.
24 Barber and Odean, 2001.
25 Corter and Chen, 2006.

26 The complete list of investing behaviors is available from DataPoints.
27 Bureau of Labor Statistics, 1996.
28 Bureau of Labor Statistics, 2016f. Note that this number differs from Financial
Industry Regulatory Authority (2017) estimate of the number of registered representa-
tives, or stockbrokers, in the US.
29 Bodnaruk and Simonov, 2015.
30 Vanguard, 2016.
31 Baker and Nofsinger, 2002.
32 Waggoner, 2011.
33 Ibid.
34 Roose, 2012.
35 Jakab, 2012.
36 Dubofsky and Sussman, 2009.
37 Fallaw, 2016.
38 Dubofsky and Sussman, 2009, 57.
39 Fallaw, 2018b.

Conclusion
1 Stanley and Danko, 1996, 72–93.

Appendix A
1 Experian, 2014.
2 Internal Revenue Service, 2012.
3 Fallaw, 2016; Fallaw, 2017; Fallaw, 2018a.
4 Grable, Kruger, and Fallaw, 2017; Kruger, Grable, and Fallaw, 2017; Fallaw, Kruger,
and Grable, 2018.

Appendix B
1 Internal Revenue Service, 1998; Internal Revenue Service, 2015. Note rankings are for
proprietorships with more than 1,000 returns. Due to changes in categorizations of proprietorships between 1998 and 2015, some direct comparisons cannot be made.

References

American Apparel and Footwear Association. (2016). "ApparelStats and ShoeStats 2016 At-a-Glance." https://www.aafaglobal.org/AAFA/ApparelStats_and_ShoeStats_at -a-glance.aspx.

American Psychological Association. (2015). "Money Stress Weighs on Americans' Health." http://www.apa.org/monitor/2015/04/money-stress.aspx.

Anderson, C., Kraus, M. W., Galinsky, A. D., and Keltner, D. (2012). "The Local-Ladder Effect: Social Status and Subjective Well-Being." *Psychological Science* 23(7), 764–71.

Associated Press-NORC Center for Public Affairs Research. (2017). "Phasing into Retirement: Older Americans' Experiences with Work and Retirement Planning." http://www.apnorc.org.

Asano, E. (2017). "How Much Time Do People Spend on Social Media? [Infographic]. *Social Media Today*. https://www.socialmediatoday.com.

Baker, H. K., and Nofsinger, J. R. (2002). "Psychological Biases of Investors." *Financial Services Review* 11(2), 97.

Bankrate. (2012a). "How Much House Can I Afford?" https://www.bankrate.com/ calculators/mortgages/new-house-calculator.aspx.

Bankrate. (2012b). "Home Values: Prices Rise, Fall Equally." https://www.bankrate.com/ finance/real-estate/home-values-prices-rise-fall-equally.aspx.

Barber, B. M., and Odean, T. (2001). "Boys Will Be Boys: Gender, Overconfidence, and Common Stock Investment." *Quarterly Journal of Economics*, 261–92.

Barber, B. M. and Odean, T. (2011). "The Behavior of Individual Investors." http:// dx.doi.org/10.2139/ssrn.1872211.

Bentley, T. (2010, October 16). "A Chart Topping Cave Dweller." *Wall Street Journal*. https://www.wsj.com/articles/SB1000142405274870384380457553451306394317 0.

Berkowitz, B. (2011, October 12). "Buffett Tells Congressman He Paid $6.9 mln taxes." Reuters. https://www.reuters.com/article/buffett/buffett-tells-congressman-he -paid-6-9-mln-taxes-idUSN1E79B1AV20111012.

Berkowitz, J. (2013, April 23). "Checkpoint Carlo: How Tax Cops Killed Italy's Super-car Market." Car & Driver. https://www.caranddriver.com/news/checkpoint-carlo -how-tax-cops-killed-italys-supercar-market.

Bernardo, R. (2017, March 13). "2017's Happiest Places to Live." Wallethub. https:// wallethub.com/edu/happiest-places-to-live/32619/.

Bodnaruk, A., and Simonov, A. (2015). "Do Financial Experts Make Better Investment Decisions? *Journal of Financial Intermediation* 24(4), 514–36.

Bolduc, B. (2012, February 11). "Leadership Secrets of George Washington." *Wall Street Journal*. https://www.wsj.com/articles/SB1000142405297020436940457721101055 07347208.

Buffett, W. (2017, February 25). Berkshire Hathaway Letter to Shareholders 2016. www.berkshirehathaway.com/letters/2016ltr.pdf.

References

Bureau of Labor Statistics. (1996). *Occupational Outlook Handbook, 1996–1997*. https://www.bls.gov/news.release/history/ecopro_031596.txt.

Bureau of Labor Statistics. (2016a). "College Tuition and Fees Increase 63 Percent Since January 2006." -2006.htm.

Bureau of Labor Statistics. (2016b). "Employed Persons by Disability Status, Industry, Class of Worker, and Sex, 2016 Annual Averages." https://www.bls.gov/news.release/disabl.t04.htm.

Bureau of Labor Statistics. (2016c). "Entrepreneurship and the U.S. Economy." https://www.bls.gov/bdm/entrepreneurship/entrepreneurship.htm.

Bureau of Labor Statistics. (2016d). *Occupational Outlook Handbook: Personal Financial Advisors*. http://www.bls.gov/ooh/business-and-financial/personal-financial-advisors.htm.

Bureau of Labor Statistics. (2016e). *Occupational Outlook Handbook: Physicians and Surgeons*. https://www.bls.gov/ooh/healthcare/physicians-and-surgeons.htm.

Bureau of Labor Statistics. (2016f). *Occupational Outlook Handbook: Securities, Commodities, and Financial Services Sales Agents*. https://www.bls.gov/ooh/sales/securities-commodities-and-financial-services-sales-agents.htm.

Bureau of Labor Statistics. (2016g). "Self-Employment in the United States." https://www.bls.gov/spotlight/2016/self-employment-in-the-united-states/pdf/self-employment-in-the-united-states.pdf.

Bureau of Labor Statistics. (2016h). "Time Spent in Detailed Primary Activities and Percent of the Civilian Population Engaging in Each Activity, Averages per Day by Sex, 2016 Annual Averages." https://www.bls.gov/tus/a1_2016.pdf.

Bureau of Labor Statistics. (2017). CPI Inflation Calculator. Retrieved from https://www.bls.gov/data/inflation_calculator.htm.

Byron, E. (2010). "Wash Away Bad Hair Days." *Wall Street Journal*. https://www.wsj.com/articles/SB10001424052748704911704575327141935381092.

CareerBuilder. (2017). Living Paycheck to Paycheck is a Way of Life for Majority of U.S. Workers, According to New CareerBuilder Survey [press release]. http://press.careerbuilder.com/2017-08-24-Living-Paycheck-to-Paycheck-is-a-Way-of-Life-for-Majority-of-U-S-Workers-According-to-New-CareerBuilder-Survey.

Carlson, B. (2017). "How the Bogle Model Beats the Yale Model" [blog entry]. http://awealthofcommonsense.com/2017/02/how-the-bogle-model-beats-the-yale-model/.

Cassuto, L. (2013, July 1). "Ph.D. Attrition: How Much Is Too Much?" *Chronicle of Higher Education*. https://www.chronicle.com/article/PhD-Attrition-How-Much-Is/140045.

Cavale, S. (2018, March 1). "P&G Says Cut Digital Ad Spend by $200 million in 2017." Reuters. https://www.reuters.com/article/us-procter-gamble-advertising/pg-says-cut-digital-ad-spend-by-200-million-in-2017-idUSKCN1GD654.

Chernow, R. (2010). *Washington: A Life*. Boston, MA: Penguin Press.

Congress of the United States Congressional Budget Office (2016). *Trends in Family Wealth: 1998–2013*. https://www.cbo.gov/sites/default/files/114th-congress-2015-2016/reports/51846-familywealth.pdf.

References

Consumer Reports (2017). "Consumer Reports' Car Reliability FAQ." https://www
.consumerreports.org/car-reliability-owner-satisfaction/consumer-reports-car
-reliability-faq/.

Corrado, C. (2011, November 20). "The Wealth Race." *American Thinker.* https://www
.americanthinker.com/articles/2011/11/the_wealth_race.html.

Corter, J. E., and Chen, Y. J. (2006). "Do Investment Risk Tolerance Attitudes Predict
Portfolio Risk?" *Journal of Business and Psychology,* 20(3), 369–82.

Cotton Incorporated. (2013). "Driving Demand for Denim Jeans." http://lifestyle
monitor.cottoninc.com/driving-demand-for-denim-jeans/.

Credit Suisse Research. (2016). *The Global Wealth Report 2016.* http://publications
.credit-suisse.com/tasks/render/file/index.cfm?fileid=AD783798-ED07-E8C2
-4405996B5B02A32E.

Dokko, J., Li, G., and Hayes, J. (2015). "Credit Scores and Committed Relationships."
Retrieved March 1, 2018 from www.kiplinger.com/article/credit/T017-C023-S002
-what-your-credit-score-says-about-your-love-life.html.

Dubofsky, D., and Sussman, L. (2009). "The Changing Role of the Financial Planner
Part 1: From Financial Analytics to Coaching and Life Planning." *Journal of
Financial Planning,* August 2009, 48–57.

Easton, N. (2012). "Don't Blame the 1% for America's Pay Gap." *Fortune.* http://fortune
.com/2012/04/24/dont-blame-the-1-for-americas-pay-gap/.

Experian. (2014). *Experian Mosaic Guide* [PDF document]. Costa Mesa, CA: Experian.

Fallaw, S. S. (2016). *Financial Behaviors and Wealth Potential* [white paper]. DataPoints.
https://www.datapoints.com/research/.

Fallaw, S. S. (2017). *The Building Wealth Technical Report.* DataPoints. https://www.data
points.com/.

Fallaw, S. S. (2018a). *The Investor Profile Technical Report.* DataPoints. https://www.data
points.com/.

Fallaw, S. S. (2018b). *Understanding Great Investors: The Competencies of Investing Success.*
[white paper]. DataPoints. https://www.datapoints.com/research/.

Fallaw, S. S., Kruger, M., and Grable, J. (2018). *The Household CFO: Using Job Analysis to
Define Tasks Related to Personal Financial Management.* 2018 Academic Research
Colloquium for Financial Planning and Related Disciplines. https://ssrn.com/
abstract=3040904.

Farrell, M. (2015). "New Year, Same You." *Psychology Today.* https://www.psychology
today.com/blog/frontpage-forensics/201501/new-year-same-you.

Federal Reserve. (2015). *Report on the Economic Well-Being of U.S. Households in 2015.*
https://www.federalreserve.gov/2015-report-economic-well-being-us-households
-201605.pdf.

Federal Reserve. (2017a). "Changes in U.S. Family Finances from 2013 to 2016: Evidence from the Survey of Consumer Finances." *Federal Reserve Bulletin* 103(3),
1–42. https://www.federalreserve.gov/publications/files/scf17.pdf.

Federal Reserve. (2017b). *Report on the Economic Well-Being of U.S. Households in 2016.*
https://www.federalreserve.gov/publications/files/2016-report-economic-well
-being-us-households-201705.pdf.

References

Fidelity Investments. (2016). *10th Annual College Savings Indicator: Executive Summary of Key Findings.* https://www.fidelity.com/bin-public/060_www_fidelity_com/ documents/press-release/csi-exec-natl.pdf.

Financial Industry Regulatory Authority. (2017). Key Statistics for 2017. Retrieved from http://www.finra.org/newsroom/statistics.

Finke, M. S., and Huston, S. J. (2003). "The Brighter Side of Financial Risk: Financial Risk Tolerance and Wealth." *Journal of Family and Economic Issues* 24(3), 233–56.

Gallup. (2017). *State of the American Workplace Report.* Retrieved from http://news.gallup.com/reports/199961/7.aspx.

Gatenby, R. (2000). Married only on the weekends? A study of the amount of time spent together by spouses [research paper]. Office for National Statistics. Retrieved from https://www.ons.gov.uk/ons/rel/lifestyles/time-use/2000-edition/married-only-at-the-weekends--a-study-of-the-amount-of-time-spent-together-by-spouses.pdf.

Gatewood, R. D., & Feild, H. S. (1998). *Human Resource Selection* (4th edition). Fort Worth, TX: The Dryden Press.

Geldhof, J., and Lerner, R. M. (2015, May 26). "How to Recognize a Budding Entrepreneur." *Wall Street Journal.* https://www.wsj.com/articles/how-to-recognize-a-budding-entrepreneur-1432318006.

Genworth. (2016). *Annual Cost of Care Study: Costs Continue to Rise, Particularly for Services in Home.* Retrieved March 1, 2018 from http://investor.genworth.com/ investors/news-releases/archive/archive/2016/Genworth-2016-Annual-Cost-of-Care-Study-Costs-Continue-to-Rise-Particularly-for-Services-in-Home/default .aspx.

Global Financial Literacy Excellence Center. (2018). *The TIAA Institute-GFLEC Personal Finance Index.* http://gflec.org/initiatives/personal-finance-index/.

Godin, S. (2008, January 31). "Permission Marketing" [blog entry]. https://seths.blog/ 2008/01/permission-mark/.

Grable, J. E. (2000). "Financial Risk Tolerance and Additional Factors That Affect Risk Taking in Everyday Money Matters." *Journal of Business and Psychology*, 14(4), 625–31.

Grable, J. E., & Joo, S. H. "Environmental and biophysical factors associated with financial risk tolerance." *Financial Counseling and Planning.* 15(1), 1–6.

Grable, J. E., Kruger, M., & Fallaw, S. S. (2017). "An Assessment of Wealth Accumulation Tasks and Behaviors." *Journal of Financial Service Professionals*, 71(1), 55–70.

Grable, J. E., Lytton, R. H., O'Neill, B., Joo, S. H., and Klock, D. (2006). "Risk Tolerance, Projection Bias, Vividness, and Equity Prices." *Journal of Investing*, 15(2), 68–74.

Hagerty, J. R. (2014, January 25). Entrepreneur Let No Impediment Stop Him. *Wall Street Journal.* Retrieved March 2, 2018 from https://www.wsj.com/articles/ entrepreneur-let-no-impediment-stop-him-1389835205.

Hanks, T. (2015, January 14). "Tom Hanks on His Two Years at Chabot College." *New York Times.* https://www.nytimes.com/2015/01/14/opinion/tom-hanks-on-his-two-years-at-chabot-college.html?_r=0&mtrref=undefined&gwh=3CEBA5FE3A28B 253BDDD61A2BF967E2E&gwt=pay&assetType=opinion.

References

Hartog, J., Ferrer-i-Carbonell, A., and Jonker, J. (2002). "Linking Measured Risk Aversion to Individual Characteristics." *Kyklos* 55 (1), 3–26.

Horwitz, S. G. (2011, January 26). "Data Overlook Upward Mobility." *Atlanta Journal-Constitution*. https://www.ajc.com/news/opinion/data-overlook-upward-mobility/2R5x19rNC2jfAnkd0ppPQI/.

Howlett, E., Kees, J., & Kemp, E. (2008). "The Role of Self-Regulation, Future Orientation, and Financial Knowledge in Long-Term Financial Decisions." *Journal of Consumer Affairs* 42, 223–42.

Inmar. (2014). *2014 Coupon Trends: 2013 Year-End Report*. http://go.inmar.com/rs/inmar/images/Inmar_2014_Coupon_Trends_Report.pdf.

Internal Revenue Service. (1998). Table 3—1998, Nonfarm Sole Proprietorships: Business Receipts, Selected Deductions, Payroll, and Net Income, by Industrial Groups Classified with the North American Industry Classification System. https://www.irs.gov/statistics/soi-tax-stats-nonfarm-sole-proprietorship-statistics.

Internal Revenue Service. (2012). *SOI Tax Stats—Individual Income Tax Returns—2012*. https://www.irs.gov/statistics/soi-tax-stats-individual-income-tax-returns.

Internal Revenue Service. (2015). Table 1. Nonfarm Sole Proprietorships: Business Receipts, Selected Deductions, Payroll, and Net Income, by Industrial Sectors, Tax Year 2015. https://www.irs.gov/statistics/soi-tax-stats-nonfarm-sole-proprietorship-statistics.

Internal Revenue Service. (2017). *SOI Tax Stats—Individual Income Tax Returns—2016*. https://www.irs.gov/statistics/soi-tax-stats-individual-income-tax-returns.

Internal Revenue Service. (2018). *SOI Tax Stats—Estate Tax Filing Year Tables*. https://www.irs.gov/statistics/soi-tax-stats-estate-tax-filing-year-tables.

Jakab, S. (2012, February 15). "It Is Time to Reap What Deere Has Sown." *Wall Street Journal*. https://www.wsj.com/articles/SB1000142405297020406270457722362416400 9432.

Johnson, B., Raub, B., and Newcomb, J. (unknown). A New Look at the Income-Wealth Connection for America's Wealthiest Decedents. Internal Revenue Service, Statistics of Income. https://www.irs.gov/pub/irs-soi/13rpwealthdedents.pdf.

Judge, T. A., and Hurst, C. (2007). "Capitalizing on One's Advantages: Role of Core Self-Evaluations." *Journal of Applied Psychology* 92 (5), 1212.

Kahlenberg, R. D. (2012). "Should Colleges Consider Legacies in the Admissions Process?" *Wall Street Journal*. https://www.wsj.com/articles/SB100014240529702046536045772492301 64868846.

Kroll, L. (2012, September 12). "The Forbes 400: The Richest People in America." *Forbes*. https://www.forbes.com/sites/luisakroll/2012/09/19/the-forbes-400-the-richest-people-in-america/.

Kruger, M., Grable, J. E., and Fallaw, S. S. (2017). "An Evaluation of the Risk-Taking Characteristics of Affluent Households." *Journal of Financial Planning* 30(7), 38–47.

Lehrer, J. (2011, April 2). "Measurements That Mislead." *Wall Street Journal*. https://www.wsj.com/articles/SB10001424052748704471904576230931647955902.

Lee, S. H. (2012). "When Are Frugal Consumers Not Frugal? It Depends on Who They Are With." *Advances in Consumer Research* 40, 584.

References

Leonhardt, D. (2014, January 23). "Upward Mobility Has Not Declined, Study Says." *New York Times*. https://www.nytimes.com/2014/01/23/business/upward-mobility -has-not-declined-study-says.html?_r=0&mtrref=undefined.

Letkiewicz, J. C., and Fox, J. J. (2014). "Conscientiousness, Financial Literacy, and Asset Accumulation in Young Adults." *Journal of Consumer Affairs* 48(2), 274–300.

Levanon, G., Kan, M., and Li, A. (2016, July 19). "Job Satisfaction Continues to Rise." *Conference Board* blog. https://www.conference-board.org/blog/postdetail .cfm?post=5231.

Lusardi, A., and Mitchell, O. S. (2011). "Financial Literacy around the World: An Overview." *Journal of Pension Economics and Finance* 10(4), 497–508.

Lynch, P. (2012). *Beating the Street*. New York: Simon and Schuster.

Mangleburg, T. F., Doney, P. M., and Bristol, T. (2004). "Shopping with Friends, and Teen's Susceptibility to Peer Influence." *Journal of Retailing* 80 (2), 101–16.

Margalit, L. (2016). "What Screen Time Can Really Do to Kids' Brains." *Psychology Today*. https://www.psychologytoday.com/blog/behind-online-behavior/201604/ what-screen-time-can-really-do-kids-brains.

Martin, D. (2014). "Paula Kent Meehan, Co-Founder of a Hair Giant, Dies at 82." *New York Times*. https://www.nytimes.com/2014/06/26/business/paula-kent-meehan -hair-care-entrepreneur-dies-at-82.html.

Mayfield, C., Perdue, G., and Wooten, K. (2008). "Investment Management and Personality Type." *Financial Services Review* 17, 219–36.

McGrath, M. (2015, November 18). "A Global Financial Literacy Test Finds That Just 57% of Adults in U.S. Are Financially Literate." *Forbes*. https://www.forbes .com/sites/maggiemcgrath/2015/11/18/in-a-global-test-of-financial-literacy -the-u-s/#62cf5a0c58f0.

Mesnik, H. (2017, April 10). "Fast Fashion: with the Rise of Disposable Fashion Trends, Americans Are Purchasing and Throwing Out Clothing Faster Than Ever." *State Press*. www.statepress.com/article/2017/04/spmagazine-sustainability -recycling-fashion-in-arizona.

Mr. Money Moustache. (2013, February 23). "Getting Rich: from Zero to Hero in One Blog Post" [blog post]. https://www.mrmoneymustache.com/2013/02/22/ getting-rich-from-zero-to-hero-in-one-blog-post/.

Muller, J. (2011, December 30). "What the Rich People Really Drive." *Forbes*. https:// www.forbes.com/sites/joannmuller/2011/12/30/what-the-rich-people-really -drive/#7a34b9e54e04.

National Bureau of Economic Research. (2012). *Were They Prepared for Retirement? Financial Status at Advanced Ages in the HRS and Ahead Cohorts*. NBER Working Paper No. 17842. www.nber.org/papers/w17824.pdf.

National Center for Education Statistics. (2018). Table 303.70. Total undergraduate fall enrollment in degree-granting postsecondary institutions, by attendance status, sex of student, and control and level of institution: Selected years, 1970 through 2026. https://nces.ed.gov/programs/digest/d16/tables/dt16_303.70.asp.

National Center for O*NET Development. (2016). *Summary Support for Ship Engineers* (53-5031.00). https://www.onetonline.org/link/summary/53-5031.00.

Neuharth, A. (2013, March 28). "Neuharth: Best Way to Get Rich Is the Stock Market." *USA Today*. https://www.usatoday.com/story/opinion/2013/03/28/neuharth-best-way-to-get-rich-is-the-stock-market/2029129/.

Norton, M. I. (2013). "All Ranks Are Local: Why Humans Are Both (Painfully) Aware and (Surprisingly) Unaware of Their Lot in Life." *Psychological Inquiry* 24(2), 124–25.

O'Connor, C. (2012, March 7). "Undercover Billionaire: Sara Blakely Joins the Rich List Thanks to Spanx." *Forbes*. https://www.forbes.com/sites/clareoconnor/2012/03/07/undercover-billionaire-sara-blakely-joins-the-rich-list-thanks-to-spanx/#8dfe410d736f.

Paletta, D. (2014). "New Data Muddle Debate on Economic Mobility." *Wall Street Journal*. https://www.wsj.com/articles/new-data-muddle-debate-on-economic-mobility-1390453098.

Pew Research Center. (2013). "The Demographics of Job Satisfaction." www.pewsocialtrends.org/2013/12/11/on-pay-gap-millennial-women-near-parity-for-now/sdt-gender-and-work-12-2013-4-06/.

Pew Research Center. (2014). "Most See Inequality Growing, but Partisans Differ over Solutions." http://assets.pewresearch.org/wp-content/uploads/sites/5/legacy-pdf/1-23-14%20Poverty_Inequality%20Release.pdf.

Pew Research Center. (2017). "Key Trends in Social and Digital News Media." www.pewresearch.org/fact-tank/2017/10/04/key-trends-in-social-and-digital-news-media/.

Phillips, M. M. (2013, April 13). "This Ain't No Bull: Nary a Cowboy Can Ride 'Em These Days." *Wall Street Journal*. https://www.wsj.com/articles/SB10001424127887323916304578400503374361938.

Rich, M. (2012, January 31). "In Atlanta, Housing Woes Reflect Nation's Pain." *New York Times*. http://www.nytimes.com/2012/02/01/business/economy/in-atlanta-housing-woes-reflect-nations-economic-pain.html?ref=motokorich.

Richards, K., and Fox, J. (2010). *Life*. London: Little, Brown and Company.

Rockstarfinance.com (2018). *Rockstar Directory: A Directory of Personal Finance Blogs (and Resources)*. https://directory.rockstarfinance.com/personal-finance-blogs/category/general-finance.

Roose, K. (2012, February 29). "Bonuses Dip on Wall St., but Far Less Than Earnings." *New York Times*. https://dealbook.nytimes.com/2012/02/29/as-bank-profits-plunge-wall-street-bonuses-fall-modestly/.

Sages, R. A., and Grable, J. E. (2010). "Financial Numeracy, Net Worth, and Financial Management Skills: Client Characteristics on Financial Risk Tolerance." *Journal of Financial Service Professionals* 64(6), 57–65.

Sahadi, J. (2011, October 12). "Buffett Made $62,855,038 Last Year." CNN Money. http://money.cnn.com/2011/10/12/news/economy/buffett_taxes_2010/index.htm.

Sawyers, A. (2013, September 23). "Leases Buoy Market, Add Factory Risk." *Automotive News*. www.autonews.com/article/20130923/RETAIL/309239957/leases-buoy-market-add-factory-risk.

Schmidt, F. L., and Hunter, J. E. (1998). "The Validity and Utility of Selection Methods in Personnel Psychology: Practical and Theoretical Implications of 85 Years of Research." *Psychological Bulletin* 124(2), 262–74.

Semega, J. L., Fontenot, K. R., and Kollar, M. A. (2017). Income and Poverty in the United States: 2016. United States Census Bureau. https://www.census.gov/library/publications/2017/demo/p60-259.html.

Shoen, J. W. (2015). "Why Does a College Degree Cost So Much?" CNBC. https://www.cnbc.com/2015/06/16/why-college-costs-are-so-high-and-rising.html.

ShopSmart. (2010). Jeaneology: ShopSmart Poll Finds Women Own 7 Pairs of Jeans, Only Wear 4 [press release]. https://www.prnewswire.com/news-releases/jeaneology-shopsmart-poll-finds-women-own-7-pairs-of-jeans-only-wear-4-98274009.html.

Snell, A. F., Stokes, G. S., Sands, M. M., and McBride, J. R. (1994). "Adolescent Life Experiences as Predictors of Occupational Attainment." *Journal of Applied Psychology*, 79(1), 131.

Snyder, J. (2011, January 10). "Retail Joins Fleet in Driving Growth." *Automotive News*. www.autonews.com/article/20110110/RETAIL01/301109953/retail-joins-fleet-in-driving-growth.

Society for Human Resource Management. (2015). *2015 Employee Job Satisfaction and Engagement: Optimizing Organizational Culture for Success*. https://www.shrm.org/hr-today/trends-and-forecasting/research-and-surveys/pages/job-satisfaction-and-engagement-report-optimizing-organizational-culture-for-success.aspx.

Solheim, C. A., Zuiker, V. S., and Levchenko, P. (2011). "Financial Socialization Family Pathways: Reflections from College Students' Narratives." *Family Science Review* 16(2).

Sorkin, A. R. (2011, August 29). "The Mystery of Steve Jobs's Public Giving." *New York Times*. https://dealbook.nytimes.com/2011/08/29/the-mystery-of-steve-jobss-public-giving/?mtrref=undefined.

Spectrem Group. (2018). New Spectrem Group Market Insights Report Reveals Significant Growth in U.S. Household Wealth in 2017 [press release]. Retrieved from https://spectrem.com/Content/press-release-new-spectrem-group-market-insights-report-reveals-significant-growth-in-US-household-wealth-in-2017.aspx.

Speights, K. (2017, May 21). "Success Rate: What Percentage of Businesses Fail in Their First Year?" *USA Today*. Retrieved March 2, 2018 from https://www.usatoday.com/story/money/business/small-business-central/2017/05/21/what-percentage-of-businesses-fail-in-their-first-year/101260716/.

Stanley, T. J. (1989). *Marketing to the Affluent*. Irwin Professional Publishing.

Stanley, T. J. (1991). *Selling to the Affluent: The Professional's Guide to Closing the Sales That Count*. Irwin Professional Publishing.

Stanley, T. J. (1993). *Networking with the Affluent and Their Advisors*. Irwin Professional Publishing.

Stanley, T. J. (2000). *The Millionaire Mind*. Kansas City, MO: Andrews McMeel Publishing.

References

Stanley, T. J. (2005). *Millionaire Women Next Door: The Many Journeys of Successful American Businesswomen.* Kansas City, MO: Andrews McMeel Publishing.

Stanley, T. J. (2009). *Stop Acting Rich: . . . and Start Living Like a Real Millionaire.* Hoboken, NJ: John Wiley & Sons.

Stanley, T. J. (2011, July 26). "One Man's Junk, Another Man's Treasure" [blog post]. www.thomasjstanley.com/2011/07/one-mans-junk-another-mans-treasure/.

Stanley, T. J. (2012, January 31). "Drive Rich or Be Rich" [blog post]. http://www .thomasjstanley.com/2012/01/drive-rich-or-be-rich/.

Stanley, T. J. (2013, November 30). "Wealth? No, Not Yet!" [blog post]. www.thomas jstanley.com/2013/11/wealth-no-not-yet/.

Stanley, T. J. (2014, March 25). "Does Your Chosen Vocation Have Great Market Opportunities?" [blog post]. www.thomasjstanley.com/2014/03/does-your-chosen -vocation-have-great-market-opportunities/.

Stanley, T. J., and Danko, W. D. (1996). *The Millionaire Next Door.* Atlanta, GA: Longstreet Press.

Stanley, T. J., and Moschis, G. P. (1984). "America's Affluent." *American Demographics* 6 (3), 28–33.

Statistic Brain. (2017). Denim Jeans Industry Statistics. https://www.statisticbrain.com/ denim-jeans-industry-statistics/.

Stewart, J. B. (2016). "Facebook Has 50 Minutes of Your Time Each Day. It Wants More." *New York Times.* https://www.nytimes.com/2016/05/06/business/facebook -bends-the-rules-of-audience-engagement-to-its-advantage.html.

Stokes, G. S., Mumford, M. D., and Owens, W. A. (1989). "Life History Prototypes in the Study of Human Individuality. *Journal of Personality* 57(2), 509–45.

Su, J. B. (2016, September 28). "The Global Fintech Landscape Reaches Over 1,000 Companies, $105B in Funding, $867B in Value: Report." *Forbes.* https://www .forbes.com/sites/jeanbaptiste/2016/09/28/the-global-fintech-landscape-reaches -over-1000-companies-105b-in-funding-867b-in-value-report/#66689d1326f3.

Tax Foundation. (2012). Fiscal Fact No. 317: *Who Are America's Millionaires?* https:// taxfoundation.org/who-are-americas-millionaires/.

Taylor, C. D., Klontz, B., and Lawson, D. (2017). "Money Disorders and Locus of Control: Implications for Assessment and Treatment." *Journal of Financial Therapy* 8(8), 124–37.

Trevelyan, E., Gambino, C., Gryn, T., Larsen, L., Acosta, Y., Grieco, E., Harris, D., and Walters, N. (2016, November). *Characteristics of the U.S. Population by Generational Status: 2013.* United States Census Bureau. https://www.census.gov/content/dam/ Census/library/publications/2016/demo/P23-214.pdf.

Tuttle, B. (2011). A Weak Argument: Why Some Jeans Cost $300. *Time.* http://business .time.com/2011/07/08/a-weak-argument-why-some-jeans-cost-300/.

United States Census Bureau. (2016). *State and County Quickfacts.* http://quickfacts .census.gov/qfd/states/00000.html.

United States Census Bureau. (2017). *Wealth and Ownership Data Tables - 2013.* https:// www.census.gov/topics/income-poverty/wealth/data/tables.all.html.

References

University College London. (2009). "How Long Does It Take to Form a Habit?" www
.ucl.ac.uk/news/news-articles/0908/09080401.

Vanguard. (2016). "Vanguard's Advisor Alpha." https://www.vanguard.com/pdf/ISGAA
.pdf.

Waggoner, J. (2011). "Pit Stock Analysts vs. Short Sellers for Rich Clues." *USA Today*.
https://usatoday30.usatoday.com/money/perfi/columnist/waggon/2011-02-18
-investing18_st_N.htm.

Wang, A. (2009). "Interplay of investors' financial knowledge and risk taking." *The
Journal of Behavioral Finance*, 10(4), 204–213.

Wang, X., Yu, C., and Wei, Y. (2012). "Social Media Peer Communication and Impacts
on Purchase Intentions: A Consumer Socialization Framework." *Journal of Interactive Marketing* 26(4), 198–208.

Weinberg, B., Reagan, P. B., Yankow, J. (2004). "Does Neighborhood Affect Hours
Worked? Evidence from Longitudinal Data." *Journal of Labor Economics* 22(4),
891–924.

Williams, G. (2014, April 30). "The Hidden Costs of Moving." *US News & World
Report*. https://money.usnews.com/money/personal-finance/articles/2014/04/30/
the-hidden-costs-of-moving.

World Economic Forum (2017). *We'll Live To 100—How Can We Afford It*. http://
www3.weforum.org/docs/WEF_White_Paper_We_Will_Live_to_100.pdf.

Yarrow, A. L. (2015). "Falling Marriage Rates Reveal Economic Fault Lines." *New York
Times*. https://www.nytimes.com/2015/02/08/fashion/weddings/falling-marriage
-rates-reveal-economic-fault-lines.html?mcubz=0.

Zagorsky, J. L. (2005). "Marriage and Divorce's Impact on Wealth." *Journal of Sociology*
41(4), 406–24.

Zagorsky, J. L. (2007). "Do You Have to Be Smart to Be Rich? The Impact of IQ on
Wealth, Income and Financial Distress." *Intelligence* 35(5), 489–501.

Zhang, J., Howell, R. T., and Howell, C. J. (2014). "Living in Wealthy Neighborhoods
Increases Material Desires and Maladaptive Consumption." *Journal of Consumer
Culture* 16(1), 297–316.